Studies of the Policy Process

A case analysis

MICHAEL MARINETTO

PRENTICE HALL EUROPE

LONDON ● NEW YORK ● TORONTO ● SYDNEY ● TOKYO ● SINGAPORE

MADRID ● MEXICO CITY ● MUNICH ● PARIS

First published 1999 by
Prentice Hall Europe
Campus 400, Maylands Avenue
Hemel Hempstead
Hertfordshire, HP2 7EZ
A division of
Simon & Schuster International Group

Typeset in 9½/12pt Meridian
by Fakenham Photosetting Limited, Fakenham, Norfolk

Printed and bound in Great Britain by TJ International, Padstow, Cornwall

Library of Congress Cataloging-in-Publication Data

Marinetto, Michael.
    Studies of the policy process: a case analysis/Michael Marinetto.
        p. cm.
    Includes bibliographical references and index.
    ISBN 0-13-916255-0 (alk. paper)
    1. Policy sciences. 2. Policy sciences – Case studies. I. Title.
H97.M37 1998
320'. 6–dc21

                                                                98–7605
                                                                CIP

British Library Cataloguing in Publication Data

A catalogue record for this book is available from the British Library

ISBN 0-13-916255-0

1 2 3 4 5 03 02 01 00 99

17-99

Studies of
the Policy Process

This book is dedicated to Debbie with much
love and affection

Contents

Preface and acknowledgements

The origin of this book dates back to work that I conducted as a research assistant in the School of Policy Studies, Politics and Social Research at the University of North London.

The purpose of the book is to provide a general text for both undergraduate and postgraduate study on the expanding area of policy analysis. It is not a text which focuses on conceptual models and arguments about how policy is made and delivered. Rather it uses detailed case studies of the policy process to examine how theoretical models and concepts stand up in practice. What this text also does is to address the whole issue of policy from a sociologically informed point of view. Sociology, contrary to commonsense thinking, provides conceptual clarity, and it contributes an eclectic theoretical approach which is ideally suited to elucidating the complex range of forces that shape policy.

A number of people made very helpful contributions during various stages of this book's gestation. First, I am indebted to Aidan Rose who supervised this whole project and acted as a close adviser throughout the research and writing of this text, painstakingly reading through a number of drafts. His comments on earlier drafts proved central to the text's content and style.

The head of Policy Studies, Politics and Social Research, Dave Phillips, and Dean of the Faculty of Environmental and Social Studies, Jennifer Somerville, both provided invaluable support, especially as they were partly responsible for employing me in the first place. I am particularly grateful to Dr Somerville and Roger Hallam, Deputy Dean, who agreed to provide already stretched Faculty resources for my Dutch fieldwork trips. I would also like to extend my sincere thanks to the staff in PPSR – whom I count not only as colleagues but also as friends – for providing such a supportive and intellectually stimulating milieu for carrying out this work. I am grateful in particular to Peter Hodgkinson, Mohammad Nafissi, Marcy O'Reilly, Dorothy Sefton Green, Angela Sinclair, Martin Todd, Brian Tutt and Nicholas Watts for their support. I am also grateful to

Judy Hague and Miles 'Milo' Tollan, both formerly of the Ukraine project at UNL, for their help, as early versions of some of these case studies were fed into teaching sessions with postgraduate internship students from the Academy of Public Administration in Kiev. I am also thankful to all those undergraduate students at UNL who had a number of these studies inflicted on them in teaching sessions. Their cooperation and responses have been very helpful. Also, the librarians at Ladbroke House have provided a first-rate service, for which I am grateful.

All those involved in the project at Harvester Wheatsheaf have been very understanding and have provided invaluable advice and support. In particular I am thinking of Christina Wipf, former acquisitions editor for sociology at Harvester, who started the ball rolling in the first place but gained a promotion before she could witness the completion of this project. Latterly, Derek Moseley and Janet Young from Harvester have provided thoughtful assistance through the final phase of the project. The anonymous referees at various stages of the process made invaluable comments and recommendations which I have tried to integrate into the text. I am very grateful to all of them for putting their scholarly insights at this book's disposal.

Moreover, I am indebted to all the people whom I interviewed for the case studies in this text. They must remain anonymous, but I am thinking particularly of those individuals I met from Bath and North East Somerset Council, NIAD, METROPOLINK, the Dutch Department of Health, the University of Amsterdam, and those linked to the Chelsea and Westminster Hospital. I am also indebted to Sue Lawrence and Anthony Sobers from the School of Social Work at UNL for their support during one of my Dutch fieldwork trips, and to Maggie Mapley for all her help with finances and adminstration.

My final word of thanks goes to my wife Debbie, to whom this book is dedicated with much love and affection, for her loving and unselfish encouragement. All mistakes are my own. Credit for any achievements are shared with the above.

Michael Marinetto
April 1998

Aims and overview of the text: a guide for users

General aims of the case analysis

Policy studies as an academic teaching discipline is without doubt a growth industry in higher education. A conspicuous expansion has taken place in the number of undergraduate and postgraduate courses dedicated to studying this field. Policy units feature in social science courses, and there are even whole or combined policy degrees offered by some institutions. Indeed, the emphasis placed by the Dearing inquiry on the 'vocational experience' is likely to increase the relevance of disciplines like policy analysis which have applied concerns.

Despite such interest, the corresponding expansion in general teaching texts has proven to be limited. Many of these texts, although worthy scholarly renditions, are better suited to those specializing in policy studies. They generally prove less useful for the diverse range of students taking up policy courses on modular teaching programmes.

This book offers a general examination of policy that will appeal to students from a variety of disciplinary backgrounds. Unlike established policy texts it is not pitched at a purely conceptual level. Although theoretical issues form a significant part of this analysis, an attempt is made to involve users directly and practically in studying the dynamics of the policy process. A two-pronged strategy has been followed to achieve these objectives.

First, this book draws upon sociological insights and those policy perspectives that offer socially informed analysis. Sociology is an eclectic field of investigation suitable for policy analysis, which by its nature is multidisciplinary. Hence, the text will be pertinent to students from different subject backgrounds. Secondly, the mainstay of this text (Part II) is based around a number of detailed case studies. These cover a range of policy issues and institutional locations. Case analysis was chosen for very specific purposes. This methodological approach generates detailed and qualitative empirical material from a limited number of actual policy events or issues. Such data provide the means for a realistic, practical examination of the extent to which theory and practice relate to actual policy contexts. The actual subjects covered in the five case studies include the following: health service reorganization; hospital closure in a district health authority; service privatization in local government; developments in urban policy; and changes in drug control policy.

These subject areas were chosen to some degree because they form part of recent policy initiatives and developments. The literature on such issues tends to be confined to academic journals. Thus the case studies in this text will help bring a number of specialist interests under the broad analytical umbrella that is policy analysis. The range of areas covered in the cases provides a degree of flexibility. Users can draw upon the text for very specific purposes of learning about particular policy issues like reorganizing the health system in London or privatization in a unitary local authority. The text may also be used to gain a general understanding of how the policy process works across a range of different policy settings. Indeed, case studies of issues such as drug policy or health care are used primarily in this book to illustrate and explore the dynamic forces that drive the policy process. In particular, these detailed studies provide examples from real policy situations of what is an underlying concern of this text – the links between actors and structural factors.

Using this book as a 'learning device'

Such observations point to the fact that this book as well as being a general text on policy has specific pedagogic aims. Central to all this is that the text provides users with support devices for self-managed learning. These learning devices and materials accompany each case study chapter in Part II of the text, and are located at the end of each of the six chapters included in this section. The support materials are composed of three central elements.

First, a detailed chronological survey of the policy area examined in the preceding chapter. For example, Chapter 5 has a broad chronology covering the development of urban policy from the 1960s through to the 1990s. These chronologies provide distilled summaries of the events surrounding the policy areas in question, illustrating the way policy issues emerge and progress over time. Such chronological devices have the benefit of reinforcing the details encountered in the case analysis. Thus users will be able to identify in summary form key developments and events. Secondly, the learning materials include points for review and further consideration. These are each linked to particular sections and passages found within the cases. Such follow-up questions are designed to enable users to assess their understanding and to reflect critically on the issues raised in the chapters. Some of the questions may also assist seminar discussions. In particular, they may prove especially useful in structuring debate for when small subgroups are formed within seminars. Finally, included with the materials are guides to further reading. These sections reinforce the fact that reading widely around a subject is vital for gaining a proper and fully formed understanding of the issues.

Organization of the book

The rationale of this text, the reasons for adopting a case approach and how the studies can form part of an active learning tool have all been discussed. The aim now is to explain how the book is organized from Chapter 1 through to Chapter 10.

Part I provides a general overview of key theoretical positions in policy analysis. Although by no means an exhaustive theoretical analysis, these three chapters focus on major theoretical contributions to the policy field, and provide necessary background material for the studies outlined above. Chapter 1 is a short introduction to policy analysis and the different approaches which have emerged in this field. It is concluded that the study of the policy process is the most relevant area of investigation for analytical observers. The policy process is largely concerned with the way policy emerges and advances over time. Central in all this is the role of dynamic internal forces and structural factors. The next two chapters in this section are more substantive. Each is organized according to the relative weight attached by theories to either the role of agency or the role of structure as factors in the policy process.

Chapter 2 provides an overview of theoretical perspectives and studies that have focused on the role of agency in the policy process. Agency is defined here as the capability of individuals to make a difference and to achieve results in the policy process. Early theoretical contributions in policy analysis focused in the main on the nature of decision-making. Two distinct positions on decision analysis are examined: the rational and the incremental models. For some researchers, analysis of decision-making extends only a normative view of agency. Here actors carry out pre-existing social roles and expectations, with varying degrees of constraint. A contrasting view of agency is postulated by action-orientated theory. As will be summarized, this perspective emphasizes the experiences and views of those agents responsible for delivering governmental legislation or policy programmes. Here, organizational behaviour can be understood only in terms of the meanings attached to situations by purposeful actors.

Models which stress the part played by agency tend to ignore the importance of structural factors. Hence, Chapter 3 discusses the influence of structural forces on the policy process. Structure refers to the objective setting or context in which policy is made and delivered. In other words, structural forces are the pre-existing social, political and economic arrangements in which policy-makers operate. The policy process is not an autonomous phenomenon; it is inextricably bound with these arrangements. As such, these structures can influence and constrain the development of policy. This summation is divided into two main sections. The onus is mainly on functionalist and Marxist theories. However, certain theories have looked at structural arrangements within government institutions. These perspectives point to the interrelations between institutions.

Following this theoretical overview, the book turns to the policy case studies. The chapters in Part II are based on case studies of the policy process within various settings. The objective is to understand the nature of the policy process – the influence of ideas, the interaction between structures and agency, and conflicts between interest groups. First, Chapter 4 provides an overview of the case study approach as a methodology for engaging in policy analysis. In many respects, this chapter offers a justification for employing the case study method. There is an additional objective: to provide actual recommendations about the construction of a case study and the procedures of data collection. It is maintained that mainly qualitative methods of research, open to a variety of techniques, is best suited for analyzing the policy process. The chapter concludes by providing an overview of the way in which the central case studies are organized and relate to each other.

These case studies, as explained in greater detail in Chapter 4, are separated into two main sections. The studies in the first section are organized in terms of the fact that they reflect different levels of analysis. Thus Chapter 5 provides, in the main, a content analysis of urban policy and its progress since the postwar period. In this opening study, the development of urban policy is examined according to those three levels of analysis which are central to the policy process: first, the role of individual political agents, especially the influence of ideological priorities; second, the institutional context, focusing on the delivery structure of urban policy; and third, the world outside urban policy institutions, especially the impact of uneven economic development.

The following case study in Chapter 6 is preoccupied with the level of agency and decision-making. This chapter is concerned with the role of individual purposive actors in the policy process. The question it seeks to explore is this: what are the general characteristics concerning the operations of agents in policy contexts? A case study of compulsory competitive tendering in local government is used to explore this issue. Compulsory competitive tendering requires local authorities to compare the costs of certain in-house services with those of private contractors. Legislation throughout the 1980s and 1990s extended this financial discipline to various local government services. The rationale underlining this case study is to focus on the development of contract relations within one particular authority, the new unitary authority of Bath and North East Somerset. It is shown that the new contract legislation requires local officers to operate in a highly rationalistic manner. The aim of the study is to explore whether this legislation has transformed the behaviour of policy agents in local government.

Chapter 7 focuses on the intermediate level of analysis – the relationship between central political institutions and local or peripheral institutions. This chapter uses the National Health Service to understand the interrelationship between central government and 'local' policy actors. The analysis is based on a case study of a specific locale within the whole system, the former Riverside District Health Authority in central London. The study focuses on a major restructuring programme within the Riverside Health Authority. It is shown that the central executive, rather than controlling crucial policy areas, is reliant on local policy actors to shape programmes. In addition, the case study highlights the authority of select interest groups and the complex interdependencies that exist within local institutional structures.

The case studies in the second section of Part II look at different stages or phases of the policy process. Chapter 8 is based on a case study of the Tomlinson-led reorganization of London's health service in the early 1990s. The study initially focuses on the emergence and formulation of policy and its subsequent implementation. The formation of this policy was linked to certain organizational factors. This subsequently leads to an examination of implementation, which, as the study shows, is not a straightforward process. Several theories explaining the implementation phase are considered and these are assessed using material on the Tomlinson reorganization.

In Chapter 9, the case study examines what is normally considered to be the final stage of the policy life cycle – the evaluation of policy. The aim of this chapter is to examine what is involved, and what criteria can be used, to evaluate policy. This task can be undertaken by internal government agencies and external research bodies. Typically, the evaluation of policy both in the United States and in Britain has proven to be highly instrumental. The policy process is a very complex phenomenon. Such a fact should be reflected in the way it is actually evaluated and assessed. As in the other chapters in this text, the analysis does not remain at a purely conceptual or abstract level. A detailed study of a specific policy issue is used to illustrate and debate many of the concerns that have already been spelt out. This particular chapter focuses on Dutch drug control policy. The main objective is to explore different approaches to evaluation, the intention being to find which analytical practices are suited to evaluating the impact and success of a policy. The concluding chapter, Chapter 10, reviews the main arguments covered during the course of the book. It suggests possible directions in which a sociology of the policy process might further develop.

part I

Policy
perspectives

Chapter 1

Introduction: approaches to policy analysis

1.1 Defining key concepts

This text offers a case analysis of public policy. The subject matter of this book is defined here as the courses of action undertaken by public agencies and institutions under the authority of government. Superficially, government action could be viewed in terms of formal outputs: namely, official regulations and legislation. Although these are significant, policy encompasses a broader, more diffuse set of interventions. In fact, it is possible for policy to involve forms of non-intervention. Heclo (1972: 85) notes: 'A policy, like a decision, can consist of what is not being done – for example, the inaction which prevents "costs" already affecting some groups from being removed.'

In a telling observation, Jenkins (1993: 34) notes that policy involves a set of interrelated decisions taken by political actors, focusing on a set of objectives. As a consequence, policy does not emerge from a single source. A network of organizations, officials and politicians contribute to the whole process. Decisions in this policy-making network normally emerge over a period of time, usually after numerous modifications. These policy decisions can be driven and be subject to a whole range of factors. As Ham and Hill (1984: 12) note, it 'is dynamic rather than static and that we need to be aware of shifting definitions of issues'.

Why should the dynamics of government action be of interest to both practitioners and academics? It is clear that analytical interest in policy can be explained, in part, by the expansion of public institutions. One of the most salient features of contemporary British society has been the growth, in size and function, of government. From the late nineteenth century and throughout the twentieth century, government in Britain, as in much of the Western world, underwent considerable expansion. Government spending provides a revealing index of this development: between 1850 and 1900, public expenditure in Britain doubled (Ashford, 1981: 262). From

1963 to 1993, government spending as a percentage of gross domestic product (GDP) grew by 5 per cent, from 39 per cent to 44 per cent (Dilnot, 1995: 6). Such growth can be attributed to the way governments became increasingly engaged, throughout the twentieth century, in society and the economy. Such intervention proceeded in an incremental fashion during the interwar years through such schemes as social insurance provision. After the Second World War, state intervention, fuelled by American support, grew to unprecedented levels with the formation of the welfare state and the implementation of nationalization programmes.

The expansion of government in the late nineteenth century coincided with the emergence of the social sciences. A number of practitioners from these fledgling disciplines became actively interested in the intricacies and nature of government action. Weber, one of the founding gurus of sociology, concentrated his early work on the effects of Germany's free trade policy. Marx, on the other hand, conducted a wide range of policy-based analyses, including studies of labour law and foreign interventions (see Hughes *et al.*, 1995). There was also the prevailing view – a strong vestige of Enlightenment thinking – that the social sciences could be of practical service to governments. Keynes during the 1930s used economic analysis to inform governments on the effects of high wages. Beveridge, on the other hand, examined unemployment policies.

Academic interest in policy up to and beyond the Second World War was dispersed across a range of disciplines – economics, sociology, political science and so on. The semblance of a unified approach to the study of policy emerged in American academic institutions. This process began tentatively during the interwar period but assumed greater momentum in the postwar years. Academic input from writers such as Lasswell, Easton, Lindblom and Simon proved instrumental in the development of the policy sciences or a policy approach. In Britain, disciplinary collaboration in developing a certain degree of analytical closure around the study of policy came at a later date. From the mid-1970s onwards, publications dealing explicitly with policy were in circulation. In the same period, policy-orientated teaching and research institutes, such as the School for Advanced Urban Studies at the University of Bristol and the Institute of Local Government Studies, were formed.

Of equal significance in the formation of policy analysis as a body of knowledge and research was the establishment of independent research units and think-tanks on policy. There is in Britain a long distinguished history of external research centres that endeavoured to change the intellectual climate in government and beyond, dating back to the Fabian Society of 1884. It was in the postwar years, though, that these intellectual forums for policy discussion and advice mushroomed. Their number included the Institute of Economic Affairs (established in 1955), the Centre for Policy Studies (1974) and the Adam Smith Institute (1976), all of which were aligned to the political right. Policy analysis on the left was carried forward by the Policy Studies Institute (formed in 1976), the Institute for Public Policy Research (1988) and, latterly, DEMOS, formed in 1993. This think-tank enlightenment in the policy arena has not been confined to Britain. These bodies in the United States are highly developed, with the seminal Brookings Institution founded in 1927, and the influential RAND Corporation, formed in 1948, leading the way.

The interest surrounding government action and the formalization of research around this issue has produced different orientations in the policy approach. The concern now is to distinguish between the various types of policy analysis.

1.2   The field of policy analysis

Analyzing policy is about understanding what governments do and the factors that shape such actions. It also means assessing the repercussions or the effects of government intervention (Dye, 1976: 1). Because policy is not a straightforward activity, as alluded to earlier, studies of government intervention can address their subject matter from a variety of positions. However, the policy industry, as it were, can be systematized and organized into distinct categories of activity. The enduring distinction is that, as expressed by Lasswell (1970: 3), between 'knowledge of the policy process; knowledge in the process', or analysis *for* and analysis *of* policy. The distinction made by Lasswell is quite straightforward. On the one hand, analysis of policy refers to those analytical studies which attempt to understand policy from an academic perspective. On the other, analysis for policy refers to the production of practical knowledge to be applied in actual policy contexts and situations. It could be said that independent think-tanks deal in part but not exclusively in this type of analysis.

These two fields of policy analysis are by no means mutually exclusive. Contact between the academic and applied spheres 'has increased and takes a variety of forms' (Aucoin, 1979: 1). Lasswell (1970: 13), though, expresses a note of caution by observing that academics involved in government are 'half man, half brain'. Nevertheless, university academics have engaged directly in practical policy matters. The growing contribution of academics to economic policy are a prime example of this interface between the academic and the applied field (Colvin, 1985). There are instances where politicians and officials have brought in external academic researchers to assess government programmes. The Department of Environment used analytical expertise to evaluate the operation of privatization measures in local government (see Walsh, 1991) and the effectiveness of urban policy (Robson *et al.*, 1994). The Widdicombe Committee, established by the Conservative government to research the political structures and activities in local government, employed top academic names in this field to conduct the research. The final report provided one of the most extensive and influential studies into the politics of local government (Widdicombe, 1986). Indeed, the report became the basis of an academic text written by the researchers involved in the committee (Gyford *et al.*, 1989).

Although academically orientated and applied forms of policy analysis can be linked, the two are quite different entities. Gordon *et al.* (1993) argue that this distinction between analytical and applied approaches can be further refined. The authors outline a range of distinct analytical emphases along a continuum which is applied at one end and analytical at the other. On the applied side of this continuum, Gordon *et al.* identify policy advocacy and information for policy. The first category of policy advocacy encompasses forms of policy analysis where recommendations are made or officials are instructed to pursue a favoured course of action. Thus research carried out by policy advocates will be shaped to promote a set of desired outcomes. Information for policy, on the other hand, is less narrowly prescriptive. Nevertheless, the objective here 'is to provide policy-makers with information and perhaps advice' (Gordon *et al.*, 1993: 6). Hence this activity may involve the provision of useful data, informing the development of policy. At the same time, it could focus on specific variables and consequently offer more definite advice.

At the other end of this continuum (policy for analysis), Gordon *et al.* include the analysis of policy content and the analysis of policy determination. The analysis of policy content involves mainly descriptive accounts of the origins and mechanisms of specific policy areas. Typical of this form of policy analysis are the studies carried out of housing, education, health and welfare programmes. Studies of policy determination, or studies of the policy process, focus on the range of factors that shape the development of a policy issue. More of this point later. Gordon *et al.*'s final analytical category – policy monitoring and evaluation – spans both sides of the policy for and policy of continuum. This type of policy analysis assumes the guise of evaluating the effectiveness of specific aspects of government intervention. The importance of such monitoring is that it can influence future policy activity, allowing decision-makers to fashion more effective programmes of intervention.

This summary shows that public policy can potentially encompass a broad field of analysis. Taking the lead from Ham and Hill's (1984) comprehensive textbook, this text focuses on a specific, though significant, aspect of the field identified by Gordon *et al.* – the policy process. Some areas of this text will actually involve aspects of content analysis. On the whole, however, much of the work here attempts to focus on the policy process.

The policy process is concerned with how government programmes emerge and progress through different stages of development. The central concern here is to understand the various forces and influences that shape policy. Conventional or classical thought about the way governments operate has maintained that policy is the product of rational action. Decisions are set by purposive actors. They operate by considering various policy alternatives and opt for the strategy that will most effectively achieve their objectives. According to the rational model, policy typically emanates from senior officials and ministers. Once a policy is set in motion by these central figures, it is seen to follow a linear course of development from implementation to completion.

This is very much an ideal version of how governments work. Policy is more complex and problematic than depicted by the rational model. Governments are not autonomous or independent entities. What governments do is closely intertwined with the political, social and economic context in which they operate. Neither are governments unified organizational entities. They are replete with competing interest groups that bring within the body politic differ-ent values and ideologies. The rational model is so concerned with efficiency in decision-making that the influence of these social and political forces are ignored. Policies influenced by social factors are explained away as oversights by legislators; or they are portrayed as deficiencies within the decision-making process. In reality, the policy process cannot be disassociated from broader social and political con-siderations.

The relationship between society and the policy process is not viewed as problematic, an unwelcome factor whose influence should be minimized. Rather, it forms the central analytical focus of this proposed text. The argument here is that this analytical emphasis is best pursued by adopting a sociological perspective. Below a detailed account of this sociologically informed approach is outlined.

1.3   A sociology of the policy process

As Ham and Hill (1993: 11) note, it is useful in studying the policy process to draw upon a whole range of social science disciplines. The range of disciplines that have been used in policy analysis include political science, economics, sociology, history, public administra-tion, and even geography. Wildavsky (1979: 15) observes: 'Policy analysis is an applied sub-field whose content cannot be determined by disciplinary boundaries but by whatever appears appropriate to the circumstances of the time and the nature of the problem.'

Bobrow and Dryzek (1987: 7) profile the main disciplinary frameworks that have prevailed in contemporary policy analysis. They note that these 'do not exhaust the range of conceivable approaches, but together they cover most kinds of policy analysis currently undertaken'.

Five main disciplinary approaches are singled out. First, welfare economics is orientated towards quantitative methods such as cost-benefit analysis. This disciplinary 'sub-field', according to Bobrow and Dryzek, has the greatest number of practitioners. Second, the public choice strand focuses in the main on decision-making and it covers such disciplines as microeconomics, politics and public administration. Third, social structure is predominantly a sociologi-cal form of analysis. Fourth, the information processing framework draws upon a highly diverse range of disciplines, including variants of psychology, organization studies, and information science. The objective of practitioners within this framework is to scrutinize the way decisions and choices are made in organizations. Key exponents in this framework include the likes of Lasswell, Simon and Lindblom, who made seminal contributions to the development of policy analysis. Finally, political philosophy utilizes moral and ethical analysis to examine the policy process (Bobrow and Dryzek, 1987: 6–7).

The present study falls within Bobrow and Dryzek's social structure frame of reference. This means that the approach adopted here is informed by sociological research and theorizing. The reasoning behind the choice of a sociological framework is twofold. First, sociology as a discipline is characterized by a divergent panoply of competing theories and conceptions. It is a discipline which overall lacks a proper orthodoxy. For a subject like public policy, which cannot be easily confined to strict disciplinary boundaries, an openness to different analytical approaches is a definite advantage. Second, a sociological conception has certain applicable utility, but not to the extent that it provides a set of ready-made solutions to social problems. The usefulness of sociology 'consists much more in the gradual diffusion of understanding about how society works, its integration, strains and conflicts' (Bulmer, 1990: 137). Bulmer observes that sociological research in such areas as eduction, labour markets and mental illness has enlightened policy-makers. The question now is to ascertain how a sociology of the policy process can be developed.

It has already been noted that the social structural approach is highly eclectic in terms of an openness to different sociological theories. Much sociological thinking can be distinguished in terms of the relative weight that is attached to either agency or structure. Views are divided in social thought over how the main object of analysis in sociology – society – should be conceived. These debates revolve around the dualism between agency and structure. Society is either viewed as an emergent force with structural properties that constrain individual action, or is seen as the aggregate of dynamic interpersonal relations between individuals.

Similar theoretical divisions are evident in the analytical literature on policy. Gordon *et al.* (1993) point out that theories of the policy process can be influenced and shaped by two distinct sets of factors:

> Attempts to analyse the policy process are inescapably based upon explicit or implicit models of the policy system. In some cases the model is seen as being 'driven' by environmental forces ... in yet others by the internal perceptions of the external environment. (ibid. 6)

They also point to the fact that there are those approaches which emphasize external or emergent structures, such as features of the economy and society, which drive the policy process. For instance, the model of structural functionalism which was cultivated by sociologists has its policy equivalent in the form of Easton's (1979) systems theory. Easton's view is that policy is shaped by real objective forces external to the political system. On the other hand, there are those approaches which focus on active decision-makers and policy agents as the central variables determining the development of policy. Lipsky (1980), for example, examined the creative resources used by officials on the ground when implementing policy decisions originating from the centre.

The following two chapters in Part I provide a general discussion of the theoretical approaches and models that have surfaced in policy analysis. Such theoretical coverage provides the necessary insight required for understanding and examining the case material, which focuses on the problematic nature of policy in action. In these chapters, the approaches are distinguished according to whether their appreciation of the policy process can be viewed in emergent or active terms. The theories that appear under each of these general analytical categories are by no means homogenous, as the emphasis on either structure or agency tends to differ from one theoretical model to the next. Nevertheless, the common denominator comes down to their emphasis along the structural–agency axis.

While the models covered in these chapters can be distinguished in such terms, the concern expressed in this text is that a sociology of the policy process should not seek to prioritize either agency or structure at the expense of the other. Instead, the policy process is shaped through an interrelationship between structure and agency. Though it is crucial to emphasize links between these two domains, each has distinct properties that cannot be reduced to simpler more basic processes. The idea is that a sociological framework provides a multidimensional view of the factors which drive the policy process.

The point being made is this: policy is the product of individual action and decision-making in government, of conflict between various interest groups within and without the state, and of constrictions placed by wider structural forces. As Ham and Hill (1993: 188) note:

> The study of the policy process is the study of conflicts between interests ... the study of individuals and groups securing positions within the autonomous state and then being able to make choices in both the making and implementation of policy and the study of action constrained by strong, but not unalterable, structural forces.

There have emerged within the policy field and cognate areas research work that is relevant to this type of sociological thinking. One of the most notable contributions emanates from the policy action perspective popularized by Barrett and Fudge. Moreover, there is the work of Ham and Hill, which has combined political science and sociology in the study of Policy. From the sociological research tradition of organizations, the most significant set of studies for a policy perspective are those that have emerged from the Corporate Strategy Research Group at Warwick University. Such work as will be shown will inform the analysis in this book.

2

Agency and the policy process

2.1 Introduction

The chapters in this section consider the theoretical activity generated by policy analysis. Such coverage will help underline many of the debates and approaches found in the policy field. Theoretical positions of the sort covered here explain features about policy which are highly complex and not readily observable. They also focus on matters which, from the point of view of the theoretician, are crucial in the understanding of public policy.

The theoretical survey in this chapter begins with those theories that have stressed the centrality of purposeful actors in policy-making. The specific aim is to examine models focusing on the role of agency in the policy process. Their object and level of analysis is the microworld inhabited by the human subject. The purposeful individual is viewed to be engaged in activities that decisively contribute to the policy process.

In the social sciences, agency has definite analytical connotations and meanings. This becomes apparent from this comment by Giddens (1984: 9): 'Agency refers not to the intentions people have in doing things but to their capability of doing those things in the first place (which is why agency implies power . . .). Agency concerns events of which an individual is the perpetrator.' Giddens' formulation attaches importance to the power possessed by human agents and their ability to achieve certain effects. A similar conception of agency is advocated by Dietz and Burns (1992: 194):

> Agency requires that actions be *effective* in changing material or cultural conditions, that they be *intentional*, sufficiently *unconstrained* . . . and that the actor possesses the ability to observe the consequences of an action and to be *reflexive* in evaluating them. (original emphasis)

The onus in this definition is on the agent's ability to effectively transform the course of events through the intentional and active pursuit of particular objectives.

Attempting to understand the relationship between agency and policy is not a straightforward matter. The impact of individuals in policy-making can encompass a multitude of possibilities. Nonetheless, theories in this category have tended to focus on specific components within the realm of agency. Two general components are singled out for particular scrutiny. One notable tradition revolved around decision-making. The main preoccupation concerned the mechanics of decision-making among agents responsible for policy. Other policy theorists looked to broaden their thinking beyond the decision process. The main analytical component of such work is the interactive behaviour between policy actors. Below we begin to flesh out details of how agency with regard to these key features has been theorized within the literature.

2.2   Agency and decision-making

There are theoreticians for whom the phenomenon of agency can be broken down into distinct elements. Herbert Simon (1976) argues that this is a good analytical practice. A concept like role or social action is too broad or, to use Simon's words, is 'too gross a unit'. The unit of decision is a smaller unit of analysis, according to Simon, but it can encompass a whole variety of features: 'many premises are involved in any specific decision or action' (ibid. xxxvii).

This tradition of research into decision-making has not ignored wider structural questions completely. For example, Simon acknowledges that organizations can be studied in terms of more global factors and that structural features can give administrative behaviour special character (ibid. xxxv). But for Simon and other theoreticians concerned with the process of decisions, the role of agency, or the unit of decision-making, takes analytical priority. This is because organizational features are seen as the products of decision-making.

Writers focusing on the nature of decision-making have made a vital and formative contribution to policy literature. This theoretical orientation was evident in much early, predominantly American, academic research into policy. As is usual in the academic free market of ideas, competing positions emerged and tussled for acceptance. There were three principle combatants. First, there were those perspectives stressing the predominantly rational nature of decision-making in modern organizational settings. Second, alternative perspectives were put forward that were critical. These maintained that decision-makers characteristically took cautious, measured steps in reaching judgements about policy. Third, other theoreticians saw relevant points of interest in each perspective and attempted to synthesize features of both perspectives. Each will be examined in turn.

2.2.1 The rational actor as decision-maker

Interest in rationality has long been apparent in social and economic thought. The classical economists and utilitarian thinkers of the Enlightenment theorized about the underlying rationality of human behaviour. For the likes of Jeremy Bentham and Adam Smith, human beings behaved in a way which was always commensurate with the essentially selfish motive of personal self-interest. This required a highly calculative and rational form of decision-making, especially evident in the economic sphere. According to this view, individuals will pursue that course of action, having considered alternative options, which allows them to fulfil their interests and main objectives.

One of the formative contributors to the study of policy, Herbert Simon, was similarly concerned with rational behaviour. His main concern was to unravel the rational nature of decision-making in modern organizations. However, his conception of administrative rationality was distinct from the view of economic man held by classical economists:

> Concentration on the rational aspects of human behavior should not be construed as an assertion that human beings are always or generally rational. That misconception, which permeated utilitarian political theory and a large part of classical economic theory, has been decisively refuted by modern developments in psychology and sociology. (Simon, 1976: 61–2)

The modern developments in psychology and sociology that Simon is specifically referring to are the writings of Harold Lasswell. Using Freud and Marx, Lasswell drew attention not to rationality but to the psychopathology of decision-making and political action in the pursuit of power.

In the light of these developments, Simon attempted to introduce a new agenda to classical discussions of rationality. This was set out most influentially in his classic text, *Administrative Behavior*. In this text, he pursued an examination of rationality linked more to actual circumstances than to ideal theoretical terms (Parsons, 1995: 275). The notion of 'administrative man' personifies a limited form of rational behaviour. It contrasts with the idealized rational figure of 'economic man' held by classical economists. According to Simon, the ability of administrative man to act in a fully rational manner is circumscribed and limited by a number of factors.

Rationality, according to Simon, is limited by the unconscious skills, habits and reflexes, such as manual dexterity. An individual's personal values and objectives may diverge from an organization's goals and thus limit capacity for rational decision-making. An individual's ability to act in a fully calculated manner will be confounded by the extent of his or her knowledge (Simon, 1976: 241). Simon also points to psychological features of decision-making that undermine rationality. To act rationally requires complete knowledge of the consequences that will follow from alternative choices. This is impossible on several counts: such knowledge is always fragmentary and in actual behavioural situations only a limited range of choices come to mind (ibid. 81).

In addition to the restrictions posed by human and psychological capacities, there are the limitations generated by the organizational context in which decisions are made. Simon acknowledges 'that there *are* practical limits to human rationality, and that these limits are not static, but depend upon the organizational environment in which the individual's decision takes place' (ibid. 240–1; original emphasis). This was a point further explored by Simon in a later work, *Models of Man* (1957). In an exploration of employment relations, Simon reiterated the importance of non-rational elements. For instance, Simon argues that historical forces, which become increasingly significant as an institution develops over time, can circumscribe the extent to which rational forms of behaviour are possible. This leads to a more realistic assessment of employment relations than those made by traditional economic theories of the firm (Simon, 1957: 192). Elsewhere he considers the broad environment in which decisions are made and the limits this places upon the capacities of individuals. Hence, 'organisms adapt well enough to "satisfice"; they do not, in general, "optimize" ' (ibid. 261).

Greater emphasis was given to such issues by Simon in later editions of *Administrative Behavior* and in subsequent texts. Simon makes the point that rational action within organizations is not an impossibility. The type of decision-making that prevails in organizational contexts is not comprehensive rationality but a form of bounded rationality: 'Administrative theory is peculiarly the theory of intended and bounded rationality – of the behaviour of human beings who *satisfice* because they have not the wits to *maximize*' (Simon, 1976: p. xxviii; original emphasis). The concept of bounded rationality is used to detail how decision-making actually proceeds within government organizations. Simon's argument is that problems associated with policy are highly intricate. Hence, there are only a limited range of issues which can be properly addressed at any time. As such, policy-makers will attempt to select a course of action which, to use Simon's terminology, will produce a 'satisficing' of policy aims – it is less a matter of maximizing ends than a perfunctory fulfilment of values or purposes.

There is a clear sense of realism about the possibility of rational action. At the same time, Simon was a staunch advocate for improving the level of rationality within organizations. This argument was made because of what such changes can bring in terms of augmenting effective decision-making and strategic choices for organizations. Throughout his *oeuvre* there is a distinct willingness to furnish practical advice on the sort of arrangements that could improve rational decision-making. One possibility is organizational design: 'A way to begin that is frequently fruitful, however, is to investigate the information flows that are essential for accomplishing the organization's objectives' (Simon, 1976: 335).

Simon also placed great store on modern techniques and technologies: management techniques, operations research and systems analysis were seen to maximize the possibilities for rationality in organizations. In *The New Science of Management Decision*, Simon (1977: 31–2) explores the potential of computers and various forms of automation to aid decision-making and management. Simon found that computer and heuristic programming have been shown to assist cognitive processes. He goes on to note, 'there are reasons to hope that the potential of the information-processing approach is not limited to cognition but may extend to the affective aspects of behaviour as well' (ibid. 35). Moreover, recent trends in public sector reforms, especially in Britain, have shown that the pursuit of organizational rationality continued beyond Simon's published output. Successive governments in the 1980s introduced various reforms which attempted to inject greater rationality into the public sector, particularly where financial activities were concerned. Greater coverage shall be given to such issues in Chapter 6, which examines more closely the role of agency in the policy process.

Not all theorists and schools in the policy field have valorized rationality to the same extent. The confidence shown by Simon towards a science of management, promoting rational action in organizations, was by no means shared across the analytical board in policy and organizational studies.

2.2.2   Incremental steps of the agent

Charles Lindblom mounted a sustained and influential critique of the rational conception of decision-making. Although a critic of rational theorists like Simon, Lindblom did share the latter's views on comprehensive forms of rationality (Parsons, 1995: 284). He maintained that comprehensive rationality is unattainable, and, in fact, a detrimental aspiration in normal conditions. 'Nothing would be more paralyzing to an administrator than to take seriously the prescription of the rational comprehensive model that he make no decision until he canvas all possible alternative ways of reaching well formulated goals' (Lindblom, 1964: 157). To begin with, decision-makers have to deal with issues of a complex nature. Moreover, rationality is circumscribed by the mental capacities of humans: practitioners cannot consider every possible course of action and they do not have access, or are unable to attain, all the information that may be required. In these conditions, the decision on which policy actions are based can only proceed through what Lindblom termed 'successive limited comparison'.

Lindblom begins to depart from the bounded rationality thesis on the point that the quality of rational decision-making can be improved. For Simon, providing certain conditions prevail, individuals can operate in a way approaching comprehensive rationality. Lindblom, on the other hand, maintains that there are benefits to be had from the limitations placed on decision-making by human information capacities and the complexity of decision issues. Such limitations provide a method or model for decision-making. This requires decision-makers to operate gradually, moving cautiously from one stage to the next. Lindblom terms this process the method of successive limited comparisons. The method of successive limited comparisons is not only realistic but is the most effective way for proceeding in real conditions. For Lindblom, it is ideally suited for dealing with complex issues; for addressing a range of variables; and it is adaptable to the limited problem-solving capacities of individuals. Successive limited comparisons enables policy-makers to simplify the decision-making process: 'Such a limitation immediately reduces the number of alternatives to be investigated and also drastically simplifies the character of the investigation of each' (Lindblom, 1959: 84). The range of possible alternatives under consideration are limited to those which are similar to existing policies.

Lindblom's conception of agency in organizational contexts is one where individuals are seen to muddle through in the decision-making process. Lindblom (1980: 65) observed: 'No ostensible policy makers can fully formulate their policy, and few attempt it. They know they cannot write a law, for example, that covers all contingencies, all possible cases.' What he means by this is that actors are involved in a constant process of mutual adjustment. Essentially, decision-making agents in policy contexts proceed in an incremental fashion, involving errors, rather than grand design, and limited achievements, as opposed to ultimate goal-attainment.

The concept of incrementalism was further developed by Lindblom in subsequent works. It came to form a central plank in discussions about the nature of policy-making in democracies. The most notable work in this respect was co-authored with Braybrooke, *A Strategy of Decision* (Braybrooke and Lindblom, 1963). The authors note how disjointed incrementalism forms a key strategy for policy-makers in dealing with the complexities of decision-making. The strategy shares distinct similarities with the process of muddling through, which Lindblom imputes as a general feature of decision-making in organizations. A key feature of the strategy is that policy-makers focus 'on incremental alteration of existing social states' (ibid. 84). Thus, policy-makers will restrict themselves to considering those policies that offer incremental changes. Such are the limitations of human capacities that comparative analysis must be confined to those policies which offer marginal and subtle changes of the status quo. Analysis of non-incremental options often proves inappropriate: 'while one can speculate on nonincremental alternatives, an analyst is often without adequate information, theory, or

any other organized way of dealing systematically with nonincremental alternatives' (ibid. 89). Disjointed incrementalism does not
just limit the range of policies to be considered. It also sets definite
restrictions on examining the various consequences related to different policy options. This renders policy-making more manageable,
simplifying the process of analysis (ibid. 91).

Hence, the critical idea of disjointed incrementalism is that
policy is based on comparisons between alternative policy options.
Those agents adopting this approach do not presume to have ready-
made solutions to policy issues. The objective is to change conditions
gradually, to ameliorate rather than solve problems. This may
require policy-makers to adjust their objectives in accordance with
the means available to them. According to Braybrooke and
Lindblom, disjointed incrementalism is a prevalent strategy among
policy analysts in the United States. In this setting, policy agents
operate by series of approximations (ibid. 111–43).

Incrementalism was further modified by Lindblom in *The
Intelligence of Democracy* (1965) to understand the collective operations of policy-makers. Here Lindblom concentrates on political
leaders and their decisions. Centrally coordinated action among the
political and policy elite is less a matter of grand, centralized design
and more a product of what Lindblom (1965: 9) terms partisan
mutual adjustment: 'There are no coordinators in partisan mutual
adjustment; such coordination as is achieved is a by-product of ordi-
nary decisions, that is, of decisions not specifically intended to
coordinate.' Central to partisan mutual adjustment is the process of
bargaining and negotiation over crucial issues before reaching
decisions. As a consequence, final collective decisions over policies
are a matter of compromise, of mutual adjustment to different policy
positions. With partisan mutual adjustment, participants attempt to
overcome conflicts of values. They do this through finding points of
agreement with adversaries and by endeavouring to build alliances:
'their search for allies motivates them to explore very widely for
points of agreement rather than limit themselves to finding agreement with those with whom they are in conflict' (ibid. 212).

It is befitting for a model which stressed the importance of practical experience in policy decisions that it has enjoyed wide-ranging
empirical support. Research on policy-making has underlined the
paucity of comprehensive rationality in real policy situations (see
Heclo and Wildavsky, 1981; Allison, 1971; Elmore, 1978: 191–9). In

contrast, the concepts developed by Lindblom to depict policy action – incrementalism, successive limited comparisons, and disjointed incrementalism – hold greater descriptive validity, being evident in actual institutional settings. The model has its advocates amongst those who have studied private sector organizations. Quinn (1980) found that strategy development in major corporations like General Motors, Xerox and IBM demonstrated incremental characteristics:

> Knowledgeable top executives consciously design logical incrementalism into their decision process. They also wisely use formal management practices to ensure continuity, balance and cohesion of action taken in this incremental mode. (Quinn, 1980: 203)

The public sector has also seen the prevalence of incremental forms of decision-making. Studies of the health service have shown that the process of organizational change has progressed gradually, with few radical adjustments having to be made (see Strong and Robinson (1990) for an account of the new management reforms in the NHS). This has even been evident when managers have implemented major institutional reforms.

2.2.3   A 'third way' for decision-making

Even with such empirical support, incrementalism has its detractors. Incremental patterns are given such analytical priority that other forms of decision-making are given little or no consideration. A stark choice is offered: that between the unattainable grand policy design of comprehensive rationality or the seemingly more realistic but highly conservative model of decision-making offered by Lindblom. There are few possibilities for a middle way, for a realistic course of decision-making, offering the prospect for headway and advancement.

One analyst who addressed these concerns was Yehezkel Dror. Conceptualizing policy exclusively in terms of two polar opposites – 'rational comprehensive' and 'successive limited comparison' – is misleading, argues Dror. It is acknowledged that Lindblom's work constitutes a valuable and realistic contribution. However, the emphasis on incrementalism simply encourages poor practice and maintains rather than transforms the existing order (Dror, 1964: 156). For Dror, alternative policy models can be devised. These models can reflect actual circumstances, but they can aspire to improve policy and the conditions that policies endeavour to address.

Dror accepts that policy-making in modern societies has a tendency to follow incremental patterns. These practices, though, often lead to inertia. At the same time, policy-making practices may be improved by adopting what Dror terms the normative-optimum model of decision-making. The optimum model encourages greater rationality-content by embracing practices involving clearer explication of goals, extensive analysis for new alternatives and the formulation of decision-making criteria. In addition, extrarational processes contribute to optimal policy-making in complex issues. By extrarational processes, Dror refers to intuitive judgement, holistic appreciation derived from extensive involvement in a situation, and innovative approaches to developing new alternatives. These processes are integral to decision-making. They compensate for the fact that complete rationality is unattainable, and they can potentially make a positive contribution to policy (Dror, 1964: 155).

The American sociologist Etzioni, like Dror, attempted to bring decision-making analysis onto the middle ground. The main paradigms in decision-making analysis are seen by Etzioni to have major shortcomings. Rational models are rejected because they are seen as unrealistic and undesirable guides for decision-making. Incrementalism offers a less demanding approach to decision-making, but the model promotes a view of decision-making as chronically debilitated by environmental circumstances. There are two main difficulties with such a view. First, the incrementalist idea that policies are more the product of partisan mutual adjustment than the expression of collective needs of society means the underprivileged are overlooked. Second, incrementalism neglects the possibility of basic innovations and fundamental change in society being purposefully guided by policy-makers. Instead, incrementalism 'focuses on the short run and seeks no more than limited variations from past policies' (Etzioni, 1967: 387).

To overcome this deficiency, Etzioni offers a third approach to decision-making. Despite the criticisms levelled, it combines positive elements from rationality and incrementalism. This new approach is termed the mixed scanning model of decision-making. The model is based on the use of two different approaches for gathering information to be used in policy decisions. It 'combines a detailed ("rationalistic") examination of some sectors – which, unlike the exhaustive examination of the entire area is feasible – with a "trun-cated" review of other sectors' (Etzioni, 1967: 389). The former method approximates to a modified form of rationalism, and the latter to incrementalism. Such is the uncertain and complex nature of the policy environment that policy-makers should not prioritize one form of decision-making over another. A mixed scanning model enables policy agents to consider a broad range of policy options. These reviews can lead to major policy decisions, with long-term repercussions. At the same time, mixed scanning is sufficiently flexi-ble to allow incremental decisions to impinge throughout the development or emergence of major policy changes. Decision-makers can draw upon both instruments as and when required. Hence, from an incremental, short-term perspective a particular course of action may prove to be detrimental. However, from a longitudinal perspec-tive it may fulfil required objectives (ibid. 389). For instance, governments are known to implement deflationary measures, which often lead to higher levels of unemployment. The long-term aim, though, is to deliver conditions for economic stability. For Etzioni, the rationale of mixed scanning is not only about combining different levels or paradigms. It also provides criteria in situations for deciding whether to emphasize one form of decision-making over another.

The inclusive nature of this model cancels the shortcomings of different patterns of decision-making. The incremental element in the model injects a degree of reality into situations, limiting the range of information to be considered prior to making fundamental decisions. On the other hand, contextually informed rationalism overcomes the conservative bias of the other approach by consider-ing long-term policy alternatives (ibid. 390).

The accommodation reached in the mixed scanning model seems attractive in the abstract. The difficulty arises that in reality often it is difficult to distinguish between incremental and funda-mental decisions. Ham and Hill (1993: 91) note that Etzioni offers no real criteria by which to differentiate between these two forms. Part of this may have something to do with the fact that Etzioni places too great a stress on fundamental policy decisions. Grand schemes of conscious design are not always evident in policy circles, with action proceeding as the result of less evident, sometimes irrational factors.

Even with these points of criticism, there does seem wide rang-ing support for the mixed scanning model. Critics see this as a model that can be used in actual policy contexts where major decisions are being deliberated. Moreover, it should not be overlooked that Etzioni, and similar writings, did influence Lindblom's later work. The shifts that were evident from the late 1970s onwards suggest that he was responding to more inclusive conceptions of decision-making, such as those offered by Dror and Etzioni. One major shift in emphasis was Lindblom's attitude towards the distribution of power. Incrementalism was criticized for its pluralistic acceptance of popular partisan involvement in policy decisions. Lindblom, over time, modified this conception of democratic society (Lindblom, 1980: 44). In *Politics and Markets* (1977), a notable break with previous works, he discusses the privileged position of business in industrial democracies. This, according to Lindblom, has necessitated the restructuring of market interactions. These interactions now require strategic policy-making through the input of planners (Lindblom, 1977: 345–6).

In *Democracy and the Market System* (1988) Lindblom, in another break with past orthodoxies, looked at modern social problems and the implications for policy-making. For Lindblom, there are social issues such as environmental decay, urban regeneration, and underdevelopment which require periods of major, radical change, such is the unequal distribution of power in society that needs to be addressed. At the same time, Lindblom concedes that the large steps needed to resolve these issues face severe constraints. In the medium term, incremental policies still offer the best chance of introducing necessary changes (Lindblom, 1988: 249).

The models examined in the above sections hold quite different observations and prescriptions concerning the decision-making process. However, the one common feature running through these models is the conceptualization of agency predominantly in terms of decision-making. It is the actions of individuals at the level of decision-making where agency is seen to have a prime influence on policy. This overlooks and neglects the possibility of policy agents engaging in and shaping policy beyond those settings where decisions are made. In the next section, attention turns from agency as a matter of input to the fact that agents can shape policy during the output, action phase – that is, during the implementation phase.

2.3   Action theory and policy implementation

A distinct view of agency to that propounded by decision-making theory emerged out of studies examining the implementation of policy. Such work grew in prominence during the early 1970s as a response to the perceived neglect of this subject in policy research. The closer scrutiny afforded to implementation revealed that the process of enacting a policy was problematic. Policy-makers faced numerous difficulties and barriers in trying to implement their policy programmes. Explanations were given as to why this was so. One influential stream of thought argued, from a rational perspective, that those involved in policy implementation were given far too much discretion. To achieve a more effective form of implementation, the division between policy-making and implementation had to be more rigidly maintained. Rational theorists also argued that policy-makers would need to be more closely involved in, and have greater control over, the process of implementation. (Discussion of this top-down model will be given further detailed coverage in Chapter 7.)

These observations and prescriptions were rejected outright by those advocating what became known as a bottom-up model of implementation. For this model, traditional rational approaches tend to ignore the role and perspective of actors operating at various levels of the policy chain. Such theorists noted that the influence of policy agents on the ground is not problematic at all. Their contribution to policy as it becomes operationalized is an integral and necessary part of the whole process. For the present analysis, the objective is to focus on the qualitative, bottom-up model of policy implementation rather than its rational counterpart. The reason for this analytical focus is that the bottom-up perspective offers a distinct counterpoint to that provided by decision-making analysis.

The bottom-up perspective has some affinity with the social action or interactionist approach that emerged in American sociology during the 1960s. According to symbolic interactionism, individuals consciously manage interpersonal relations and the presentation of their own identity in social situations. Erving Goffman wrote extensively about such matters. In his classic contribution to the whole field, *The Presentation of Self in Everyday Life* (1971), Goffman observes that individuals perform 'scripted performances'. This is done in order to convey a certain image to other actors.

Institutional settings have been a particularly rich resource for exploring these ideas. In *Asylums* (1968) Goffman investigated the structure of the self by inmates of 'total institutions', in this case, mental hospitals. Glaser and Strauss's (1966) study of dying patients in hospitals demonstrated that social life in hospitals is in a continual state of flux. Staff and patients are engaged in recurrent modes of interaction. These effect the conditions of hospital organization and the procedures used by carers in dealing with patients. The researchers found that these situations were crucially shaped by the awareness of the patient's fate (Glaser and Strauss, 1966: 274). As Rock notes, organizations are not objective structures, although they may be perceived as such, but emerge out of interactions between participants: 'Institutions, social systems, corporations and organizations are symbolic typifications which order and amass subordinate representations ... emerging out of sociation but taking on the character of the forms of more-than-life' (Rock, 1979: 131).

Such research established a significant benchmark for studying the way actors affect the implementation of policy in organizational settings. Those researchers that focused on the role of policy implementers on the ground do share certain similarities with Lindblom's decision-making analysis examined earlier. Like the incremental model, action theorists are highly critical of rational decision-making. Moreover, there is some agreement over the significance of negotiation between relevant participants in policy contexts.

Despite these similarities, there are several points of contrast between Lindblom's incrementalism and work focusing on the influence of agents when enacting policy. First, much of the analysis goes beyond decision-making to consider the implementation of policy. This has much to do with the fact that the influence of agents in policy-making is an ongoing process. Second, the perceptions and meanings of policy actors are central to considerations of agency from this point of view. Agency in organizational contexts can be understood only according to the meanings that participants bring to those situations that confront them. Agents in this respect are seen as purposeful and intentional beings. They use the social and contextual resources at their disposal to manage and control the situations that confront them (Degeling and Colebatch, 1984: 322–3). Third, from this perspective, responsibility for making policy is not simply the provenance of decision-makers, portrayed as those occupying the higher positions in the hierarchical chain of command within an organization. Policy can be reshaped and even transformed by those engaged in the process of implementation.

2.4　Street-level policy agents

Such views concerning the nature of agency were given ready expression by the American political scientist Michael Lipsky. His work focused on front-line officials who deal with the public, or what are termed 'street-level' bureaucrats. These are typically teachers, police officers, social workers, judges, public lawyers, health officials and other public officials who act as 'gate keepers' to government services (Lipsky, 1980: 3). This research significantly made a formative contribution to implementation studies. More than this, it provided a subject-centred, qualitative appreciation of agency in the policy process. Accordingly, human interaction and the subjective life of individuals are integral to understanding agency.

For Lipsky, street bureaucrats do not act as neutral, disinterested policy agents; rather, policy is delivered in a manner that is immediate and personal. Decisions are typically made at the point of interaction between bureaucrats and members of the public. Crucially, it is in this setting of face-to-face interaction that policy is given shape and determined by street-level bureaucrats. For instance, they have an important influence over the allocation of benefits to people. These decisions, taken aggregately, have repercussions for the level of material distribution in society. Their decisions, in another respect, can impact upon life chances. This is most evident in the way the actions of street-level bureaucrats can affect the self-evaluation of individuals. If a member of the public is treated like a juvenile by an official, this might potentially lead to a self-fulfilment of the label that has been ascribed (Lipsky, 1980: 66–8). Indeed, the power of an imposed self-image on behaviour has been revealed in research into educational failure, as alluded to by Lipsky in the above reference.

From this assessment it is clear that street-level bureaucrats do not simply deliver policy – they also *make* policy. These officials may operate on the ground, but in dealing with the public they are in a position to redefine and actually construct policy. Lipsky explains the influence wielded by these officials in terms of their position in the public sector organization: 'The policy-making roles of street-level bureaucrats are built upon two interrelated facets of their positions: relatively high degrees of discretion and relative autonomy from organizational authority' (ibid. 13). Lipsky does not deny that officials on the ground are constrained by rules and norms. Such policy actors are confronted by regulations and directives imposed from above, or by codes of professional conduct. Yet, professional status and the nature of their work means that street bureaucrats exercise considerable discretion. Housing officers, according to Lipsky, will have a significant influence over their clients' access to social benefits. For Lipsky, such discretion can never be severely reduced or totally abrogated because of the type of work that street bureaucrats perform. The responsibilities taken on by the administrative professional are such that they cannot be wholly restricted by hierarchical authority. As Lipsky notes:

> The essence of street-level bureaucracies is that they require people to make decisions about other people. Street-level bureaucrats have discretion because the nature of service provision calls for human judgement that cannot be programmed and for which machines cannot substitute. (ibid. 161)

Because they enjoy a certain level of discretion and autonomy, street bureaucrats are expected to be more than faceless gatekeepers, passive and indifferent to individual concerns. Professional training and codes of conduct demand that bureaucrats should fulfil an advocacy role. In this respect, they are expected 'to use their knowledge, skill, and position to secure for clients the best treatment or position consistent with the constraints of the service' (ibid. 72). These codes of professional conduct have little basis in actual reality: advocacy is at odds with how individual clients are processed and controlled by the bureaucracies that are supposed to provide assistance. To fulfil an advocacy function, bureaucrats have to devote sufficient free attention to their clients. Large case loads and mass processing of clients limits the time that members of the public spend with professional workers. Bureaucrats also face resource constraints. While their advocacy role demands the use of discretion to gain certain benefits for their clients, they are also required by the organizations that employ them to control the level of resource distribution.

Advocacy is at the same time incompatible with the fact that professional officials have to exercise a degree of control over clients. Part of the function of being a professional within a bureaucratic situation is to assess the credibility, and make judgements about the needs, of individual members of the public. This gives the bureaucrat a certain degree of authority over clients which they have to exploit in order to perform their duties. Such control is also used by officials to cope with the pressures of client demands, the limited resources, the alienation – features which are commonly manifest in public sector organizations. Lipsky found that these front-line bureaucrats handled clients in a routine manner, enhancing their position while at the same time undermining the status of their clients. One instance of this is the way bureaucrats conceptualize their clients in terms of societal stereotypes. These in turn may be reinforced by the structure of the work environment (Lipsky, 1980: 155–6).

What we have in Lipsky's work is a conception of government action which places agents at the centre of the policy process. Front-line professionals responsible for implementing policy are seen by Lipsky to have a prime role in the development of policy: 'I argue that the decisions of street-level bureaucrats, the routines they establish, and the devices they invent to cope with uncertainties and work pressures, effectively *become* the public policies they carry out' (ibid. p. xii; original emphasis).

Lipsky's work has been replicated in organizational settings and has found support from empirical research. This is significant for a writer who stressed the importance of falsifying ideas. Weatherley's study of the Massachusetts Comprehensive Special Education Law of 1972 is a prominent example. The new legislation attempted to create opportunities for children with special needs – particularly handicapped children – to obtain regular schooling with non-disabled children, even for a part of the school day. As part of the legislation, special classes were to be located in standard educational facilities (Weatherley, 1979: 113–14). The study showed that, although the policy was formed by the central governing authorities, the real policy-making took place at the local level. The difficulty was that the law did not provide extra resources for mainstreaming. Teachers and administrators as a result adopted practices that allowed them to cope and manage the extra workload required by the legislation. In particular, rationing techniques were unofficially employed to limit the number of referrals. One method included the dissuasion of parents to request a specialist assessment by head principals. In other cases, teacher-initiated referrals were not even processed by specialists or school principals.

Similar rationing techniques were evident when schools made available special facilities. Weatherley found evidence that in order to create extra resource rooms at minimal cost, school administrators used untrained teachers. This, in effect, subverted the requirements of the original legislation, leading to 'the arbitrary sorting and dumping of children troublesome to regular class teachers' (Weatherley, 1979: 115). There were more subtle forms of dumping taking place. There was a systematic transfer of responsibility for non-mainstream teaching to specialist or resource teachers. Thus these children, rather than being integrated into mainstream schooling and receiving specialist attention, were being treated as pariahs – the obverse of what the policy originally intended. This piece of educational legislation was thus not operationalized in the way originally envisaged.

Lipsky and Weatherley's research was conducted on bureaucratic officials in the United States. Research conducted in the early 1980s revealed similar forms of behaviour among British street-level bureaucrats. Satyamurti's (1981) study of social workers is a notable example. Social workers, as is typical of street-level bureaucrats, are faced with conflicting demands. First, they are expected to show concerns about the client's often deprived situation, while being careful to control public resources. Second, social workers also face many unpredictable demands – not only from clients, but also other agencies. Finally, there is the experience of not being able to help clients.

Satyamurti found that social workers in response adopted organizational, conceptual and pragmatic methods for mitigating the effects of these pressures. For instance, discussions between colleagues tended to prioritize the social workers' emotional state. Exploration of a client's feelings was treated as over involvement and therefore to be avoided. When confronted by clients that were traumatized by a crisis, social workers would manage the problem by treating it is as a routine situation (Satyamurti, 1981: 158). Another function requiring astute management by social workers was the task of mediating with other public agencies on behalf of clients. Problems were caused when clients refused to comply with organizational regulations, such as attendance at meetings or the payment of bills. Social workers would have to give the impression of working with clients to avoid conflict and disagreement with these agencies. In other situations, social workers would distance themselves from their clients when rules had been broken. Like the bureaucrats in Lipsky's study, social workers use the autonomy at their disposal to control potentially difficult circumstances in their working lives. This is especially true in the provision of financial help. Satyamurti found social workers using this element of discretion to maintain control over their clients (ibid. 167–8).

Lipsky's writings, and those of subsequent analysts who followed the bottom-up tradition, offered a revealing and significant view of agency. For a start, they show that rational forms of behaviour cannot be properly replicated in live policy situations and settings. Policy-making is a complex process and requires more subtle and sophisticated forms of behaviour than would be accommodated within a rational framework. Moreover, Lipsky's analysis, in contrast to Simon and Lindblom's models, acknowledges that policy agents continue to shape and make policy beyond the decision-making phase.

There are, nevertheless, points in this theoretical perspective that require critical scrutiny. A similar shortcoming to that of Lindblom's early work is evident: there is little consideration of the way structural features shape policy. Lipsky and other bottom-up theorists were correct in stressing the discretion and influence exerted by officials in face-to-face situations. Influence over the policy process, though, should not be wholly viewed as a product of personal encounters. There is no real consideration of how the asymmetrical distribution of power and economic resources can impinge on the behaviour of front-line officials. The view of agency emerging from Lipsky is one that bears only tenuous links to structural aspects of organizational and social life.

There are elements of Lipsky's (1980) *Street-Level Bureaucracy* where he seems to acknowledge the role of structural features on front-line bureaucrats. Reference is made to alienation among professional bureaucrats, resulting from the lack of control over work and the social prospects of clients. There are also pressures of resources which limit the choices and decisions that can be made by street-level bureaucrats. It would be feasible to link this alienated experience, as Marx does, to the unequal distribution of power in society between those who work and those who own. However, as Ham and Hill (1993: 142) note, 'Lipsky does not really try to link his analysis to a macro-sociological perspective'. Although reference is made to the feelings of alienation, this is predominantly seen as a procedural feature of the work experience encountered by street-level bureaucrats. It is also something which can be managed on a localized basis by front-line officials assuming control of their dealings with the public.

Such points have not gone unnoticed in the policy literature.

Subsequent advocates of the bottom-up approach have attempted to rectify the neglect of structural issues. A notable effort is the policy-action model offered by Barrett and Fudge (1981a). An attempt is made to incorporate a conception of agency in the implementation process with notions of power. Policy for these authors is essentially an outcome of the interaction between those attempting to enact policy and those who may be effected by the policy. For Barrett and Fudge, interaction does not take place in a social vacuum; the issue of power is implicated in all this. The distribution of power within and between organizations, and in society generally, is integral to achieving policy goals (1981b: 250).

2.5   Conclusion

Barrett and Fudge's observations point to an alternative theoretical tradition in the policy sciences. All the models examined in the present chapter, though different in their subject matter and focus, have given analytical priority to the micro level of analysis: the purposeful individual; the decision-making process; the nature of interaction between policy agents. Although some of the theoreticians did attempt to address issues of power and inequality, most of the coverage focused on the role of agency in the policy process. The argument in this text is that an exclusive preoccupation with these can lead to a distorted view of the way governments operate. There are traditions and theoretical schools that have conceptualized policy and the role of political institutions in terms of a macro level of analysis. To gain a more balanced perspective, closer attention must be given to such theories and models of policy-making, which have placed more explicit stress on structural factors. The theories in the following chapter give greater priority to issues of power and objective features of society; policy, from their perspective, is fundamentally shaped by such factors.

3

The macro level of the policy process

3.1 Introduction

Early contributions to policy analysis were on the whole pre-occupied with policy as the outcome of purposeful individuals. However, objective conditions, whether in the form of economic and social forces, or even institutional structures, can impose constraints on individual agents. This was not lost on those engaged in policy analysis. Lindblom, for instance, in his later work demonstrated a greater sensitivity to the issue of power and its distribution in society. But in the main, these features were not accorded a great deal of prominence by Lindblom. Indeed, the same could be said about most of the formative contributors to the field of policy analysis (Ham and Hill, 1984: 17).

There were some exceptions to this rule, as will be shown below. However, by the late 1970s and early 1980s, structural issues were attaining greater credence in the policy literature. Practitioners appropriated work which prioritized, and gave greater weight to, macro features of the policy process. They emphasized that level of reality where large-scale factors, like institutional networks and the collective operation of social groups, are seen to shape the policy process. Such analysis also began to consider the influence of structural features. Social organization, asymmetries of power, patterns of social activity and cultural traditions, economic relations – these are among some of the structural factors which have exercised much greater importance in policy theory.

Much of this influential work was not of one hue. The macro tradition in policy analysis is characterized by different models. Each offers a distinct analysis of those factors that drive and influence the policy process; although the common denominator between these different positions is that macro features or the wider social setting are given analytical primacy. Below we analyze two approaches that have made a prominent contribution to our understanding of the way external forces shape the policy process. These are the functionalist-orientated systems analysis and the conflict model of policy advocated by Marxists.

3.2   External forces and policy outputs

3.2.1   A systems analysis

The formative contributions to policy studies of Lindblom and Simon were pitched at a micro level of analysis, focusing on the mechanics of decision-making. At the same time, there were those who were concerned with decision-making as part of an extensive system of relationships and institutional connections. One of the original proponents of this view was David Easton. Easton adapted the functionalist sociology of Talcott Parsons to develop a model of the political system. Parsons' sociology was in ascendency in the 1950s when Easton began his output. Significantly, Easton used these ideas to make an influential contribution to the formation of an academic identity for policy analysis.

Parsons' functionalist sociology is based on the idea that society is organized in terms of interrelating functional subsystems (Scott, 1995: 59). This idea is elaborated in a model of the 'social system', which is organized in terms of physiological, personality, social and cultural levels. Parsons uses a biological analogy, drawing attention to the way these four levels interrelate to produce an orderly social system. Like a living organism, the social system has specific needs which have to be met in order to fulfil its main function – that of integrating society (Parsons, 1951: 28). The creation of a stable social order is dependent on each level of the social system meeting what Parsons terms 'functional prerequisites'. For instance, there are the functional prerequisites of adaptation and goal attainment. The latter is dealt with through economic exchange and the other is fulfilled by the coordinating activities of the political system. It is by meeting these needs that the social system remains a functioning and integrated entity (Layder, 1994: 18–19).

Easton's work on the political system has distinct parallels with Parsons' ideas about the nature of society as an entity comprised of different functional levels. Specifically, Easton adopts a systems analysis of political life. The political system contains what Easton terms 'life processes', which are essentially those functional elements that contribute to the maintenance of political life. The system does not operate in a vacuum nor is it altogether independent of other processes. Like a biological entity, the political system must interact with and respond to the broader environment in which it is situated: 'We may begin by viewing political life as a system of behavior imbedded in an environment to the influences of which the political system itself is exposed and in turn reacts' (Easton, 1979: 17–18).

For Easton, political life is perceived as a complex set of processes. These involve inputs from the environment, in the form of supports and demands, which are then converted by the political system into outputs – these are effectively policies or major implementing decisions. Environmental demands refer to the activities of individuals, pressure groups and the media which endeavour to influence government. In later works, Easton acknowledges that demands emerge from the inputs of other political systems. For example, a lobby company can work on behalf of a foreign government to shape a piece of domestic legislation. Moreover, demands may derive from within a political system: 'frequently what people demand may derive from wants, opinions, preferences or interest bred within the political system itself' (Easton, 1979: 54). In terms of supports, these constitute collective behaviour such as voting, payment of taxes and subservience to the law. It is not necessary for such supportive behaviour to be consciously intentional. Easton points to the instance of an individual who may be hostile to the government while at the same time paying his or her taxes, 'to that degree extending support to the system, however low the amount' (ibid. 159).

The external elements of supports and demands feed into the political system. Specifically, they are fed into the black box of decision-making which produces outputs. It is through these outputs – basic responses to environmental factors – that the political system maintains stability and attempts to influence future inputs (Ham and Hill, 1993: 14).

Easton's model, taking its cue from Parsons' functional sociology, went on to influence subsequent systems approaches to the polity. As Hofferbert (1974: 142–3) notes, the systems model has been employed in comparative analyses and in work on local government. Of particular note is Almond and Powell's comparative analysis of political systems. The authors echo Easton's ideas by observing that the political system is characterized by 'some inter-dependence of parts and some kind of boundary between it and its environment' (Almond and Powell, 1978: 5). They distinguish between two types of environment that interact with the political system – the domestic and international. Political systems function as the means whereby societies are able to pursue collective objectives within the domestic and international environment. They implement a wide range of policies in these environments, from defence to redistribution of resources. The authors point out that all political systems typically function by extracting various resources from society (ibid. 289–90).

At the same time, as Almond and Powell note, political systems are effected by the environments in which they are located. The environment shapes the political system through a transaction process involving inputs, conversions and outputs. Inputs, as in Easton's work, are viewed in terms of demands and supports. A political system will typically face demands to distribute goods and services, for regulatory intervention, for social stability, for greater democratic participation (Almond and Powell, 1978: 10). The supports come in the guise of public endorsement for those pursuing a course of policy action or those intending to implement a policy. There are also subject supports in terms of financial and service provision in response to legislation. This may include taxes and general obedience to law. These external inputs are converted by the political system through the policy-making process. There are various outputs from the policy process: extraction, regulation, distribution of resources and symbolic outputs, such as statements and policy intentions ('Our inclination is to cut taxes') (ibid. 286–9).

Although very close to Easton's writings, Almond and Powell place great importance on structure and culture in policy-making. Structure simply refers to regular forms of behaviour and activities that compose a system, while culture is concerned with the attributes and characteristics of a population. There is also within their theoretical framework an acknowledgement that the political system can just as much influence as be influenced by the external environment. Even so, the main concern in the analysis is to consider environmental features and their implications for public policy (ibid. 8–9). Essentially, the role of the political system in the functionalist perspective of Almond and Powell is to achieve stability with the external environment.

The political system approach views policy as the outcome, primarily, of macro processes. Although Easton does refer to the black box of decision-making in the political system, priority is given to policy that is primarily the outcome of external forces. The same formulas appear in Almond and Powell, although the relationship between the political system and the outer environment is more mutually dependent. Nevertheless, the emphasis is on achieving stability or attaining equilibrium between a political system and its wider environment.

In the next section, the analysis considers the contribution made to policy analysis by Marxist theory. This perspective contrasts markedly with systems analysis which emphasizes the need for a political system to achieve integration and stability. As will be demonstrated, the Marxist model does share certain important similarities with systems analysis of policy. This is particularly so in terms of the way that external forces are seen to mould the political system with regard to the relationship between the political system and wider social forces. As in functionalist theory, the latter is seen to have a determining influence over the former, moulding and shaping policy outputs for a specific set of ends.

3.2.2   A Marxist perspective

The impression given by the functionalist theory of policy is that the government does not favour any particular group in society; its role is a neutral one. The main function of the political system is to achieve social homeostasis. This it does, according to the work of Easton, by mediating and dealing with inputs from the external world. This view gained popular credence during the 1950s and 1960s, particularly in American social scientific circles. But over time, severe questions were asked of functionalist analysis. Out of this, a quite distinct view of the political system's role and function in wider society was advocated by Marxist theoreticians.

Among Marx's extensive *oeuvre*, space is given to the analysis of politics and political institutions. Marx's historical tracts on Poland produced for the German Workers Association and the political pamphlet, *The Eighteenth Brumaire of Louis Bonaparte*, focus on the political dimension, with little mention of economic influences. Marx portrayed an image of the state in these texts as an essentially conservative force in society. From his study of the Bonapartist regime Marx concluded that governments in capitalist society are dependent upon those who own the means of production. As such, the state uses both repressive and ideological measures to sustain the existing arrangements of capitalist domination in society. However, Marx also indicated in the *Eighteenth Brumaire* that it is not inevitable for governments to act as the guardians of the status quo. The state in certain situations can spearhead social change (Held, 1989: 35).

Subsequent writers in the twentieth century adopted Marx's ideas to produce a more explicit and detailed examination of the state. These writers countered the functionalist view of the political system as an essentially disinterested force in society. Instead, the institutions of government were seen as related to the distinctive features of capitalism and class relations (see Burden and Campbell, 1985). In capitalist society, economic power is unequally weighted in favour of the owners of the means of production. Government action and institutionalized politics become *functionally subservient* to the interests of the dominant economic class: government intervention and policy initiatives are determined by the prerequisite of maintaining the unequal distribution of economic resources.

Miliband's *The State in Capitalist Society* (1973) provides a classic Marxist critique of the political process in Western democracies. Miliband notes that when politicians are elected to government their main preoccupation is to maintain the capitalist system. They eschew the possibility of transforming fundamentally the existing social and economic relations in society. The most they will undertake is a little fine-tuning here and there, providing it does not disrupt the balance of power and the unequal accumulation of wealth. Thus Miliband (1973: 237–8) reaches the following conclusion: 'the state in these class societies is primarily and inevitably the guardian and protector of the economic interests which are dominant in them. Its "real" purpose and mission is to ensure their continued predominance, not to prevent it.' This 'mission' is one shared and propounded by the political agents and civil servants in government, although the impression given is otherwise.

The political agents of democracies – political parties and politicians – are crucial to the democratic process of representing the popular will of the electorate. The political parties achieve this by asserting distinct philosophies, policies and views on a range of subjects. This presents the electorate with distinct choices and, as such, according to Miliband, they as voters are able to dictate the future trajectory of society. In reality, this is an illusion. Differences between the parties in advanced capitalism are generally superficial. Among political office holders, there is distinct agreement over the foundations of society: that is, the prevailing economic system based on private ownership. Even left-wing parties, which by implication are hostile to capitalism, on gaining power have not changed the foundations of privilege and the unequal distribution of wealth. They become 'bourgeois politicians', serving the interests of capital. This happens because attaining office in government is dependent on moderation; and once in office, bureaucratic and economic forces restrict the ability of politicians to introduce progressive reforms. Miliband (1973: 92) notes that governments found 'in the difficult conditions they inevitably faced a ready and convenient excuse for the conciliation of the very economic and social forces they were pledged to oppose'.

For Miliband, the servants of the state also perform a crucial role in determining the government's relationship to society. Far from acting as neutral arbiters and advisers, senior civil servants involved with the executive are the unconscious or conscious allies of existing economic and social elites. A number of factors according to Miliband account for this. One obvious reason is that top civil servants are recruited from the upper reaches of society, through the privileged selection route of a private and Oxbridge education. For Marxist writers like Coates, this is self-evident: between 1945 and 1963, 84 per cent of all permanent secretaries had attended Oxbridge, and 74 per cent attended public school. The respective figures for administrative trainees were 51 per cent and 56 per cent in 1975 (Coates, 1984: 236). Recruitment and promotion within the civil service ensures that officials are ideologically vetted. Those espousing the correct political doctrine progress. What reinforces the positive espousal of capitalism in the civil service is the propinquity of civil servants to the business world. As Scott (1979: 153) observes, the business and civil service elite tended to be educated in the same top level establishments. State intervention in the economy similarly contributes to close relations between civil servants and capitalists (see Grant, 1993).

Governing politicians and the bureaucratic elite are in Miliband's thesis infused with capitalist values. Hence, in a mature capitalist society like Britain, government policy will both reflect and sustain the unequal balance of economic power that prevails in society. For example, state policies in areas such as labour law, main-tenance of minimum conditions in factories, the provision of redundancy payments, and the funding of retraining, help to manage industrial conflict. This, at the same time, assimilates certain costs in the reproduction of labour power.

Marxist analysis of the political process has added significant insights to our understanding of policy-making. Miliband's work highlights the fact that political systems do not operate autonomously. Features integral to capitalist society – domination, the unequal distri-bution of power and class interests – effect what governments do. As a welcome antidote to systems analysis, there is a recognition that pol-itical systems do not represent its citizenry equally; rather, they help maintain and protect powerful interest groups in society.

But in tying governments so closely to the interests of capital, Miliband's analysis begins to encounter difficulties. Underlying Miliband's interpretation of politics and policy-making in capitalist societies is this assumption: that government policy is subservient to, and dominated by, the need to legitimate and maintain the capitalist economy. The result is a rather simplistic, instrumental view of the state and its role in society. In this sense, the relationship between the state and capitalist society echoes the functionalist view of policy as the outcome of governments responding to external inputs.

In both theoretical models, the onus is on policy and govern-ment action being moulded largely by external forces. With Miliband, it is the capitalist economic system which determines what the state does; the values, interests and operations of government are intertwined with capitalism and subservient to the needs of this system. In Easton's work, it is external demands and supports that determine policy outputs from government. Reference is made to the black box of decision-making. Yet the nature of political pro-cesses within the black box – the dynamics of decision-making, interrelations between institutions and the actions of policy agents – is given scant attention. In much the same way, the instrumental Marxist position, as expressed by Miliband, prioritizes external forces over politics. Government institutions and the machinations of poli-tics are of secondary importance – an epiphenomenon of broader socio-economic structures. Dunleavy and O'Leary (1987: 238) note:

> Instrumentalists have never paid great attention to the detailed institutional organization of the liberal democratic state. Most

instrumentalists agree with Marx that parliamentary processes are meaningless charades, significant only as a means of maintaining the key ideological illusion that there is effective popular control of state policy-making.

As Dunleavy and O'Leary demonstrate, there are varieties of Marxism when it comes to theorizing the modern state. Hence, Miliband's instrumental model has its detractors within the Marxist camp. One major contribution in this respect is Poulantzas', *Political Power and Social Classes* (1973). In this work, Poulantzas is critical of simplistic and vulgarized theories which conceptualize the state as a tool or instrument of the dominant class. The importance of political processes and institutions are not underestimated by Poulantzas, as he avoids the dissolution of the political into wider economic arrangements. The state, for Poulantzas, is in a position of relative autonomy in relation to the capitalist economy. This entails 'the state's relation to the field of the class struggle, in particular its relative autonomy vis-à-vis the classes and fractions of the power bloc, and by extension vis-à-vis its allies or supports' (Poulantzas, 1973: 256). The state in capitalist societies contains different interests and different autonomous levels. In this position, the state's function, *inter alia*, is to manage conflicting factions, to be seen as a neutral force, arbitrating between different interest groups.

Poulantzas constitutes an important development in Marxist theory of the state. Government is not a mere adjunct of the economy, or something which can be reduced to the requirements of capitalist production. In Poulantzas' work, the institutions of government are able to effect and influence the operations of the ruling power bloc in society. Nevertheless, the autonomy of the political institutions is relative. This means that in the last instance the requirements of the capitalist economy will prevail in the workings of the state. Hence, with Poulantzas acknowledgement is made regarding the significance of politics, but ultimately the political system is subservient to external economic forces. This in effect produces a more sophisticated conception of politics and society when compared to the mechanical views of instrumental Marxists and systems theory. In the end, this means it is difficult to gain a full understanding of policy-making using Poulantzas' framework.

This is not to deny the significance of structural factors in the policy process, whether the capitalist economy or demands and supports from the external environment. Undoubtedly, there is an objective dimension to policy-making. A range of institutional, social and historical relationships provide an exiting context under which policy is formed. These exiting arrangements in turn can influence the actions taken and even restrict the choices made by governments (see Layder, 1994: 5). However, this is different from arguing that governments are a functional arm of the ruling class. Or that they are directly subservient to the external environment, as functionalist theorists seem to imply. It is still possible for governments to act as agents of social change, detached from the strictures of capitalist relations. The policies of government, in other words, do not always actively reinforce the capitalist economy. But this does not mean that government can transform things at will; for capitalist relations and other socioeconomic forces can limit the scope of government action. As Burch and Wood (1983: 226) argue, a balance has to be attained between the constraints on government against its capacity to bring about fundamental social change: 'In practice government is neither the prisoner of social and economic forces, nor the sole determinant of the extent and shape of these forces.'

It follows on from this that governments do not just enjoy a relative autonomy from wider society. The traditions, history and mechanisms of government are independent of capitalist relations. This means that while wider society provides objective conditions in which policy institutions have to operate, it is also possible for policy institutions to impact upon society. In terms of policy analysis, this means more specific attention should be given to the institutions and intermediate structures within the political system. There is in the social sciences a theoretical tradition that has emphasized the significance of policy-making institutions and the intermediate structures that exist within these settings. It is to such work that we turn in the next section.

3.3   The intermediate structures of political institutions

A notable tradition in social and political thought argues that the state is not a mere adjunct of broader macro phenomena. Nordlinger, articulating this view, notes that public policy should be examined with reference largely to the state and its institutions. The reason for this is that the state is an independent force which is able to follow its own agenda, while at the same time influencing the course of society (Nordlinger, 1981: 1, cited in Ham and Hill, 1993: 44).

Nordlinger's views have their antecedents dating back to the early nineteenth century. Early expression of these opinions was given by Tocqueville in what he termed 'a new science of politics' (Bottomore, 1993: 3). This new science explored the basis and formation of modern society. The time at which Tocqueville was composing his treatises witnessed two major historical developments: industrialization and democratization. Both contributed to the transition from the *ancien regime* to modern society. Of these revolutionary forces, Tocqueville ascribed greater importance to political institutions in the formation of modern society. The emergence of democratic government was seen to have profound repercussions in flattening social hierarchies and inequalities. For Tocqueville, the activities of government in this respect could interfere with individual liberty. Acknowledgement was made of the industrial context in which political institutions functioned, especially in his work on the 1848 revolutions. Yet Tocqueville regarded democratic political regimes as independent forces that could shape the general circumstances of social life.

A commitment to the independent force of political systems and processes came to form an entrenched position within political theory by the end of the nineteenth century. Many writers adopted such a position in contradistinction to what they saw as Marxism's economistic excesses. Marx, although providing the framework for later interpretations of his work, was not a vulgar economic determinist. There are references made in passages of his work to the independent force of politics. A careful reading of Marx shows that his views were more subtle and complex than implied by simple interpretations of his work.

Nevertheless, there continued to be a perception that Marx's theories were essentially economic in orientation. Thus, thinkers continued to develop ideas in opposition to Marxism, asserting the primacy of political processes over those of the economy (Bottomore, 1993: 4). The elite theory of Pareto contains noteworthy statements of this theoretical intent. Pareto was for much of his life an economist, but it was in the latter part of his career that he developed an interest in sociology. It was his experience as an administrator and politician which taught him that economic theory was lacking when it came up against real experience. Pareto attempted to address the social and psychological aspects neglected by economics in his *The Mind and Society: A treatise on general sociology* (Goldthorpe, 1979: 127).

It is in the last section of the *Treatise* that Pareto turns to the question of politics and its impact on society (Goldthorpe, 1979: 131). Pareto's observations centred around his theory of the circulation of ruling elites. Rejecting the liberal ideas about historical progress, the rule by political elites was seen as universal. Pareto acknowledged that the changes in the elite structure could be brought about by various forces in society. He noted that during phases of political corruption and innovation one group manages to gain ascendancy over the prevailing group of elites. But the deposed group can never be disregarded and eventually they infiltrate the elite structure again. For Pareto, the continual shift between elites provides stability and equilibrium within society. Stability, though, is punctuated by periods of experimentation and innovation as the elite structure moves (Bottomore, 1966: 48–9).

The other main intellectual debt owed by those analysts that have asserted the primacy of politics in society is to the German sociologist Max Weber. An influential contribution came in writings about social and political groups in society. Weber generally agreed with Marx about the importance of class as a category denoting ownership or non-ownership in the economic realm. But Weber firmly diverged from Marx's view that class was the fulcrum for collective political action in society. The concept of 'status group' was utilized to demonstrate that social stratification was not just based around economic relationships (Hughes *et al.*, 1995: 109–10). The basis of group differences along the lines of status are not necessarily economic. These groups are defined according to subjective criteria – the reciprocal awareness amongst individuals that they share common interests and experiences with other group members. Here, life style, rather than positioning in the realm of production, is the criterion for membership. Weber in his early work pointed to the differences among the agrarian classes, where the high status Junker endeavoured to maintain social superiority against the emerging bourgeoisie (ibid. 111). They did this in part by distinguishing themselves socially and culturally from emerging groups, thereby emphasizing their superiority.

Such analysis was applied to the political sphere. The awareness of common beliefs and interests can result in one group aspiring to gain authority and power over other groups. The 'party' group according to Weber is central to this struggle for superiority. This can encompass associations engaged in the electoral system but also other collective entities: 'A party can base itself upon a particular social stratum, can align itself with a particular social class or ethnic group, in which case it is likely to recruit mainly ... from that group'. (Hughes *et al.*, 1995: 112).

Following this interest in the collective agents of politics, Weber also wrote extensively about the political system – a prime location where groups pursue their common interests. He underlined that the system of political authority is independent from economic forces and is able to exert a distinct influence on society (Bottomore, 1993: 54). Three different systems of authority or forms of domination were identified. First, traditional forms of power stemming from inherited positions, as typified by absolutist monarchal systems. Second, with charismatic leadership, authority is based around personal attributes. This form of domination is exemplified by religious movements, but is also evident in the political sphere especially in political parties. The third type identified by Weber is the rational–legal system, where domination is accomplished through legal sanction.

The rational–legal form of authority is characteristic of the political system in modern industrial societies. The position of political leadership in this system is based on, and justified through, democratic selection and legal sanction. Political leaders are supported by a bureaucratic organization operated by professional administrators who are chosen through a meritocratic system of selection. The bureaucratic system of administration is ideally suited for governing the type of large, concentrated population centres that are widespread in modern industrial societies. Though effective as a form of governance, the growth of bureaucracy created distinct problems. Administrators, protected from the exigencies of external society, are likely to prioritize their own administrative concerns over the objectives of politicians. This will ultimately impede the political course set for a nation by its political leaders. More significantly, the effectiveness of bureaucratic administration in the political sphere intensifies rationalization throughout society – the force of which has pessimistic consequences for individual liberty (Hughes *et al.*, 1995: 114–15).

Weber's position tended to overstate the impact of bureaucracy in creating an unbridled, liberty-sapping movement towards rationalization. Nevertheless, his work had a profound influence on modern social and political theory. Like the classical theorists discussed earlier, the importance of the social and economic context is recognized. At the same time, Weber was inclined to argue that political processes and institutions can make a distinctive contribution to society.

Subsequent authors have further elaborated and developed these classical ideas, exploring the political sphere and its place in society. Such work is relevant presently because of the perceived bearing and direction imparted by political structures on public policy. A whole number of approaches have identified various structural aspects within the political sphere that feature in policy-making. Intra- and interorganizational relations, the distribution of power among social and political factions, conventions and practices, the role of bargaining, coordination between groups: these are the sort of intermediate structural features that can effect decision-making and policy implementation. There is not space in the present chapter to provide an exhaustive analysis of this analytical terrain. In the space that is available, three of the most significant approaches – corporatist theory, elite theory and the interorganizational approach – will be scrutinized. Each focuses on a particular structural aspects of the political sphere that forms part of the intermediate conditions in which policy is made.

3.3.1   Elites and the policy process

Pluralist theory has held great sway over political literature, particularly the 'politics matters' school of thought. The central tenet of pluralism is that the ability to influence the political system is widely and equally dispersed throughout society. Individuals and social groups all have opportunities to organize action and thereby influence the political system. Dahl, one of the most influential academic voices of pluralist theory, conducted studies to show that power in the political arena is distributed across a variety of social groups; power in the political arena is not restricted to the few.

Pluralism has its critics. For some analysts, the classical works of Mosca and Pareto have formed the basis of a critical fight back against pluralist theory. What came out of this reappraisal was a conception of the political system founded and organized around a small minority grouping. For Mosca and Pareto, the elite group consists of those who hold power in the body politic. Elite rule, according to the classical view, is a universal characteristic of human society. The system of government in democracies has the distinction that the ruling elite can freely organize: such groups have to vie for power through a regulated system of competition – normally a 'popular' election (Bottomore, 1966: 112). These ideas were developed by later theorists writing under the elite mantle. Latter-day elite theorists endeavoured to refine the idea of power exercised through elites. Raymond Aron is just one such example. According to Aron, the political class which rules society is formed of different groups. It consists of members of the executive and the top administration, military leaders, and sometimes politically influential individuals from the aristocracy. At the same time, the political class also includes 'counter elites', including leaders of political parties in opposition, and representatives of social groups active in political life, including intellectuals, trade unionists, and leaders of industries.

What is significant about these observations by elite theorists is that they draw attention to the political system and its internal structures: the organizational mechanisms, the relations of power and the processes by which groups exercise power over other sections of society. Out of the elite school, there has emerged quite different emphases concerning the nature of the political system and the role of elites.

One such approach is that associated with the renowned American sociologist C. Wright Mills. *The Power Elite* (1956) by Mills outlines a critical theory of elites, combining Marx with Pareto and Mosca. An unequivocal rejection is made of democracy from the liberal point of view – one where elites are perceived to be so dispersed that they lack political and historical clout (Bottomore, 1966: 35). His analysis points to the transformation of traditional society from one where many small autonomous groups had a say over political institutions into a mass society. Here, the power elite is the main arbiter of crucial decisions and issues in the political system. Using the traditional definition of elite as those who command posts of power, Mills argues that there are three major elites in American society: the heads of corporate bodies, political leaders and military chiefs. These three principle groups form into one cohesive elite group (Mills, 1956: 296). Their shared class origins, the close personal contact between members of each group and the interchange of membership between the three elite groups have contributed to a united elite structure. Mills observes:

> The conception of the power elite and of its unity rests upon the corresponding developments and the coincidence of interests among economic, political, and military organizations. It also rests upon the similarity of origin and outlook, and the social and personal intermingling of the top circles from each of these dominant hierarchies. (ibid. 292)

The system as such is characterized by corruption due to the lack of proper accountability. What is more, the system of elite rule is an endemic feature of modern democratic societies (Bottomore, 1966: 36).

Mills offers a highly critical account of democratic politics, dominated from his point of view by a numerically small, self-perpetuating and corrupt ruling group. This is a highly pessimistic view: politics and political institutions are largely determined to feed the interests of the elite and dupe the public into acquiescing with the system. However, there are those in the elite school who have attempted to offer a more optimistic interpretation. The suggestion is that the existence of political elites is reconcilable with pluralist democracy.

This equation has been tackled from various perspectives (see Bottomore, 1966: 114–15). The seemingly irreconcilable adherence to democratic participation and the prevalence of elites was resolved by Schumpeter through recourse to economics. Elitism was legitimized on the grounds that elite groups compete in the political market. The market is made up of elite groups and political parties. The electorate are the consumers and the system of purchase is the democratic election. This system ensures popular participation and provides the means by which elites are replaced, preventing one group from dominating the political system of control: 'The principle of democracy then merely means that the reins of government should be handed to those who command more support than do any of the competing individuals or teams. And this in turn seems to assure the standing of the majority system within the logic of the democratic method' (Schumpeter, 1976: 273).

It is not only the system of competition that reconciles the existence of elites with democracy. Raymond Aron's writings point to a close affinity between elites and social classes. This leads to a pluralist elite divided between business owners, trade unions and politicians. Such divisions provide checks and balances against outright domination, as factions organize to defend their particular interests. The process of governing 'becomes a business of compromises' – those in power are well aware that there are opponents waiting and struggling to assume the reigns of control. For Aron (1950: 10–11), 'democratic societies ... are full of the noise of public strife between the owners of the means of production, trade union leaders and politicians. As all are entitled to form associations, professional and political organizations abound, each one defending its members' interests with passionate ardour.'

Elite theory has usefully singled out the political system and its structures for special analysis. Identifying the uneven distribution of power between groups and the infiltration of such groups as the military into the elite circle are significant observations. Nevertheless, there have been criticisms aimed at the likes of Mills for exaggerating the control of a homogenous political elite over the action of government and policy-making. Writings from other theorists in the elite school have addressed such concerns. Hence, policy is not just seen to be completely dominated by the political elite. The competitive system of elites underlines a significant point: that policies emerge from competition, negotiation and conflict between a divided elite.

Despite the accommodation of different emphases within elite theory, there is a deterministic logic at the heart of all elite approaches. Bottomore (1966: 19) notes: 'The fundamental argument of the elite theorists is not merely that every known society has been divided into two strata ... but that all societies *must* be so divided' (original emphasis). There are writers that have pointed to the prevalence of competition and division within the political elite acting as counterweights to domination. But even this conception of democracy is limited in scope, the reason being that contemporary elite thinkers, such as Aron and Schumpeter, argue that democracy in large, complex societies can only be of the representative and not direct kind. This conception rules out *tout court* the possibility of establishing conditions by which a larger number of citizens can take a direct part in deciding crucial matters. This issue, as will be discussed in the next section, is one to which corporatist theorists directed a great deal of attention in their writings.

3.3.2   The corporate political sector

Aspects of elite theory are evident in corporatist theory, the second politically centred model considered in this section. Corporatism emphasizes the independent status of the government machine. It broadly refers to 'a pattern of articulation between the state and functional interests in civil society which fuses representation and intervention in an independent relationship' (Cawson, 1982: 41). Much of its analysis is focused on those groups that have control of organizational and political resources (Ham and Hill, 1993: 39). However, there are marked differences with elite theory. Political power is less the preserve of an elite minority than shared among key social and economic groups – cooperation rather than outright domination characterizes the process of government. Moreover, the corporatist model stresses the independence of key social and economic groups from the state. Such groups enter a mutually dependent bargaining relationship with government, where favourable policies are traded for cooperation and expertise. These interest groups are not entirely subsumed by the state machinery but manage to retain a degree of independence (Cawson, 1982: 39). The groups can include professional associations, specialist interest groups, trade unions, representative associations of the corporate sector and so on.

Although distinguished by it emphasis on cooperation, one of the difficulties with corporatism is that it lacks a clear orthodoxy when it comes to identifying corporatist arrangements. The writings of corporatist theorists, though, do reveal certain recurring themes around the notion of collaboration by key sectional interests. Grant (1993: 28) observes that three essential concepts are covered in this theoretical school: intervention, intermediation and incorporation.

Some writers in this camp have emphasized state intervention as a key feature in corporatist arrangements and structures in government. The main area of intervention that has been identified is economic. Winkler (1976: 117) argues that the malaise in capital accumulation accounts for the more prominent economic role of the state: 'The perception of a crisis, markedly-falling aggregate economic performance, appears historically to be a precipitating cause in many major phases of state intervention in economic affairs.' The intensification of global competition, the expansion of industrial concentration, and the general decline in profitability have precipitated the need for corporatist intervention. In contrast to Marxist analysis, Winkler dismisses notions that the state is subservient to sectional class interests. Government deals independently with capital and labour as it plays a more prominent role in the economy. One example of this fair-handed treatment was the pursuit of incomes policies during the 1970s. Moreover, the private corporate sector, as a result of the long-term decline in profitability, has relied on the government for financial assistance in the form of tax breaks, subsidies, and adjustments to the money supply (ibid. 125). Cawson (1982) notes, however, that corporatism as a mode of state intervention is not confined to the economy. The much maligned form of economic corporatism of the 1970s – tripartism – is often used to illustrate the inadequacies of such relations. Yet, corporatism is shown by Cawson (1982: 41) to be firmly embedded across a wide range of policy areas, from the NHS to agriculture and farming.

One of the most prominent writers in the British corporatist tradition, Middlemas drew attention to the idea of incorporation. Here, major interest groups are brought into the system of government to share the responsibilities of exercising power. The main rationale of this inclusive approach to governing is the minimization or avoidance of conflict which causes instability. The origins of incorporation according to Middlemas can be traced back to the end of the First World War. In this period, key interest groups – namely, the trade unions and business organizations – developed close ties with government. The experience of the war and the proliferation of industrial conflict after 1918 had left the British political system, inherited from the nineteenth century, in a state of collapse. The government after the war, rather than take an authoritarian stance in relation to labour, began to incorporate the TUC and major employers' organizations into the machinery of the state. By the early 1920s, it was clear that a sufficient number of unions and business organizations saw common interest in the avoidance of conflict and the development of the mixed economy (Middlemas, 1979: 20). This process of incorporation continued through to and after the Second World War, as explored by Middlemas in subsequent texts. He notes in *Power, Competition and the State* (Middlemas, 1986) that Britain is a liberal democratic state where the corporate bias is prevalent.

Grant observes that while intervention and incorporation are central ideas in the corporate armoury, intermediation more usefully captures the nature of corporatism. The concept of intermediation does not simply denote the development of collaborative relations between the state and organized interest groups. While governments share certain aspect of power, this is a reciprocal arrangement. Interest groups are expected, in return for their incorporation into the governing process, to regulate their members, ensuring adherence to any agreements that have been hatched.

Milward and Francisco (1983), studying corporatism in America, found that intermediation of sectional interest groups takes place around specific policy areas. The fact that the United States is a federal rather than unitary system has limited corporatist manoeuvring. This has created a highly decentralized and uncoordinated system, creating a network of policy subsystems. As such, a splintered form of liberal corporatism prevails in the United States. This means that government agencies rely on the intermediation of interest groups to form policy (ibid. 273). The authors use existing research data to provide evidence for what they view as the prevalence of interest intermediation. One notable area is the growth of interest groups across a variety of sectors since the 1960s. Such proliferation took place because these groups were able to obtain funding from external agencies. Indeed, many groups were formed with government assistance after the formation of legislation. Expediency was to the fore as the government used these groups to create support and stability for new reforms:

> The important thing to note is that in sector after sector the government agencies attempt to impose order in their dealing with interests through the strategy of assisting groups or creating groups to support the programme which the government agencies fund. (ibid. 288)

The corporatist model offers an analytical model for understanding the role of government in late industrial society. The concepts that lie at the heart of corporatism reveal how aspects of the political structure effect policy. One is that policy is not the outcome of a factional group pursuing its own sectional interests. The structure of power in the corporatist state is shared among major interest groups, which become part of the governing machinery. Indeed, the government relies on interest groups to form and enact policies. This situation has come about due to the extended responsibilities of the state and the diverse constituencies implicated by government action.

As a conception of the way government works, however, several analytical shortcomings are associated with the idea of corporatism. The most significant critique is that Britain could never fully be regarded as a corporatist state, despite the attempts at tripartite economic management during the 1970s. Grant argues that part of the reason for this is that there are inherent obstacles to the development of corporatist structures. One factor that has militated against corporatism is the inability of employer associations and trade unions to systematically control their memberships (Grant, 1993: 30–1). The 'winter of discontent' at the end of the 1970s was brought about, in part, because the union leadership could not properly implement the incomes policy agreed with government. These organizations have historically preferred a *laissez-faire* approach to pay bargaining. These barriers were further compounded in the 1980s as Conservative governments dismantled many of the corporate institutions formed during the 1970s.

It is certainly true to say that macro corporatism across key policy areas has not developed systematically in Britain. This does not deny the utility of certain corporatist ideas. As corporatist theorists have noted, government relations with interest groups are pervasive. Such links do not amount to the all-encompassing style of intermediate relations envisaged by some corporatist theorists. Yet governments still have to deal, negotiate and involve interest groups in the policy process. The process of implementing policy necessitates not so much corporatism but what is called private interest government. This involves key individuals, interest associations and specially formed organizations engaged flexibly in complex policy-making networks. Grant (1993: 31) observes:

> The 1990s may see a more pragmatic style of government, in which close contacts with the employers and the unions are seen as an aid to effective policy-making and implementation, rather than a cornerstone on which an economic strategy can be built.

Corporatism has usefully drawn attention to the way policy is constructed and implemented through a variegated network of relevant policy communities. There are theorists that have further extended insights about the inclusive mechanics of government by examining the realm of interorganizational relations. Such analysis has proceeded within a more flexible theoretical framework than that provided by corporatist theory.

3.3.3   The role of interorganizational relations in policy

Government is not a monolithic entity. Those who have examined closely the mechanics of government have paid specific attention to the growing complexity of interorganizational relations within the state machine. The policy process is viewed in this context as the outcome of institutional links within a complex network, encompassing central and external organizations.

Such ideas found their initial outlet not in literature on government and public policy, but in writings on organizations. The sociology of organizations has shown that increased complexity in society has expanded interorganizational structures (Parsons, 1995: 305). Such observations have found some resonance among those writing about government organizations. This has led to approaches which examine intergovernmental relations. The onus in such studies is on the interaction and interdependency between a vast range of government units and agencies. This includes not only those organizations in the centre, but also those that can be found beyond the network of centralized, executive bodies. Aldrich (1976) in his research of Employment Service offices in New York found interorganizational links to be a critical aspect of the organizational milieu in the public sector, although transactions between organizations was shown to be problematic. Hanf (1978) acknowledges that the influence of interorganizational structures is increasingly significant for the policy process. In the same volume, Scharpf (1978: 367) argues that interorganizational policy-making is seen as 'less the outcome of purposive social action than the unintended resultant of haphazard interactions'. One solution for overcoming these problems is for greater coordination and cooperation during different phases of the policy process – something which requires much empirical analysis.

Such is the extent of the interorganizational structure in policy-making that a diverse range of theories have been developed to understand intergovernmental relations. Rhodes (1992: 320–1) identifies five main theoretical approaches: the 'new right' approach which promotes market models in government organizations; the radical approach which utilizes neo-Marxist theory to intergovernmental relations; the centre–periphery approach that examines the relationship between central government organizations and local institutions; the public administration approach that examines the decision-making processes of government and how to improve them; and the interorganizational approach that attempts to explore changing patterns of interaction between governmental institutions. (Chapter 7 in this text is particularly concerned with the questions posed by the final two approaches.)

It is not possible in the space available to do justice to all the different approaches used in the study of interorganizational relations in government. As such, attention is given to Benson's analysis on interorganizational networks, which has attempted to demonstrate how policy is formed across institutional settings. For Benson (1975: 231), this network performs two main functions. First, analysis may focus on interaction patterns concerned with the actual performance of core functions. Second, a deeper focus of analysis is that focusing on resource acquisition, where organizational participants attempt to secure an adequate supply of resources. Benson argues that organizations depend on each other for financial resources and political authority. Resource dependency helps to create policy sectors, which are a 'cluster or complex of organizations connected to each other by resource dependencies and distinguished from other clusters or complexes by breaks in the structure of resource dependencies' (Benson, 1983: 3, cited in Hill, 1997: 170).

While interorganizational relations are formed to carry out specific bureaucratic functions, they are not mere administrative entities. Different relations of power linked to distinct interests at the same time are built into these networks. Those who hold dominant positions in organizations are in a position to control the direction of events and enforce their conception of reality over others. The level of interorganizational power is determined by three factors: first, the size of groups which may support the organization; second, the degree of mobilization of these supporting groups; and third, their social status. Interorganizational power may also be linked to coalitions and interest groups in wider society. Such differentials in interorganizational power hold significant repercussions for the promotion of particular courses of policy. Certain departments or agencies in government are able to secure support for their policies or programmes simply because they are linked to powerful professional groups and senior officials (Benson, 1975: 234). The health service and health service agencies is one example.

The relations of power in organizations at the same time reflect the wider rules of structure formation in organizational networks.

These rules are a reflection of the capitalist system, and are thus principally concerned with maintaining profit. As Benson (1977: 19) notes: 'Organizations constitute important instruments of domination in the advanced industrial societies. Any efforts to change these societies must deal with the organizational dimension.' State organizations and the networks that form policy communities function to main an economy structured around capitalist relations.

Benson, though, is careful not to fall into a deterministic trap. He acknowledges that these structural rules do not determine every policy or institutional detail. At an individual level, participants in organizations are not constrained to act in specified directions: 'The consciousness of organizational participants is partially autonomous from the contextual situations ... They are not in any simple sense captives of the roles, official purposes, or established procedures of the organization' (ibid. 7).

At an institutional level, Benson maintains that the administrative organization and the various structural interests are to an extent independent from wider relations of power:

> For each policy sector, then, it would be necessary to explore the impact of deep rules of structure formation. These would not determine the structure of the sector in every detail. It is reasonable to assume some measure of autonomy for ... administrative organization and structural interests. (Benson, 1983: 31, cited in Hill, 1997: 170)

In fact, Benson argues, adopting Weberian ideas, that administrative bureaucracies can develop independent institutional mechanisms. Ham and Hill point out, however, that there is a certain lack of clarity in Benson's analysis over the issue of administrative independence from structural constraints. It is noted that Benson does not make clear under 'what circumstances bureaucratic action is determined by deep structures or is independent of these structures' (Ham and Hill, 1993: 178). Although asserting a certain level of independence, Benson argues that events at the organizational level must be explained in terms of these rules.

Despite the lack of clarity on this point, Benson has given due regard to interorganizational relations in the policy process. His analysis of this area highlighted the dependent ties that exist between organizations within the public sector. At the same time, Benson regarded the setting in which administrative functions are performed as being of vital importance in understanding the nature of organizational relations and policy outcomes. In particular, he pointed to interest groups located across organization and policy networks. In addition, he took into account the structural rules established by the wider relations of production. These considerations and views will provide an important benchmark for the case study in Chapter 7, which examines the relationship between central and local organizations within the health service.

3.4   Conclusion: an interdependent coupling between agency and structure

This chapter has focused on the macro level of the policy process. This has entailed an analysis of the structural properties that form the setting in which policy is made and implemented. The structural context offers both constraints and opportunities to those agents engaged in the policy process. However, social scientists and policy analysts, as this chapter has shown, have tended to stress particular features of the structural setting while underscoring others. The main division has followed these lines. On the one hand, there are those who emphasize the influence of social and economic factors that are external to political institutions and policy actors. Functionalist and Marxist accounts exemplify such ideas from quite diverse positions. Both these theoretical positions argue that the behaviour and actions taken by governments should not be analyzed as isolated processes.

The problem in both functionalist and Marxist accounts is that the political sphere and government institutions are expressions or epiphenomena of external process – there is little room for manoeuvre outside the requirements and expectations established by external forces. Undoubtedly, the state in a capitalist society does assume a particular economic position that may support capitalist accumulation. Nevertheless, it would be a mistake to conceptualize the government system as functionally determined and mechanically subservient to these forces. The Marxist and functionalist positions fail to give proper consideration to the independent mechanisms and properties of the political system.

The theories considered in the second part of this chapter focused more readily on the political system as an independent sector. These approaches examined the intermediate structures that are particular to the political sphere where policy is directly produced. Elite theories underlined the fact that political power need not be economic in its origins, as political elites are products of the system of government. Policy-making, according to this approach, is not an inclusive process, it is often dominated by small sections of the population that gain control of political power. The corporatist position examined the inclusion of major interest groups, particularly those representing labour and capital, in the policy process. The interorganizational network characteristic of the government machine formed the main contribution of those policy analysts drawing from organizational sociology. This is a particularly useful form of analysis. For a start it highlights the interdependent relations between different government institutions in the policy network. As Benson's work demonstrated, this approach can accommodate wider structural considerations. Policy-making in these networks reflect power differentials within this institutional structure and patterns of domination found in society.

The issue that needs to be addressed is this: Where does the concept of agency fit into the present discussion about the role of structural forces in the policy process? This chapter has examined those theoretical positions that address policy from a macro level of analysis. The aim in all this has been to demonstrate the depth of structural forces that impact on the policy process. The structural forces that impinge on the policy process can be located external to political institutions. But, at the same time, they also form part of the internal political milieu where policy is formed. While this chapter has surveyed literature concerned with structural aspects of policy, this does not mean that agency has no significance.

There are good grounds for this. The second chapter in this theoretical section demonstrated the vital influence of purposeful actors. The theoretical approaches covered in this chapter show that agents are not mere dupes of institutional arrangements or wider structural arrangements. Policy agents are capable of acting in an intentional, purposeful and creative manner in policy contexts. They are able to remould government action during various stages of progress. Another significant detail is that structures, whether external or internal to the political context, are not entirely independent of human activity. Structures are the outcome of human activity, conducted over a protracted time-scale. However, it should not be presumed from these observations that structures are the same thing as human activity, just as agency is not a reflection of structural for-mations. These are distinct levels of social organization relevant to the policy process.

While distinct, these levels are also interrelated. It is for this reason that this review of theoretical literature on policy has been separated according to the emphasis placed on either structure or agency as the main driving force in policy. The point to be argued here, as maintained in the introduction, is that the two are distinct entities, with unique properties and mechanisms. Yet in the actual terrain of social life these levels are interdependent. Thus the ana-lytical framework used to study policy should not prioritize one sphere at the expense of the other. It is for this reason that in the introduction a sociological approach was advocated – one which would adopt an inclusive, multidimensional emphasis where the interconnections between structure and agency in policy-making are readily accepted. This means that government action must be viewed as expressing the intentions of agents at various levels of government. However, the ability of agents to act within the politi-cal sphere is narrowed by institutional arrangements and by external events.

Notable proponents of this form of analysis are Ham and Hill. The authors advocated the concept of analyzing policy in terms of different levels. This concept, though, is related to a more general and largely more significant 'issue of the relationship between action and the structure in which it occurs ... which is relevant for the whole of the policy process' (Ham and Hill, 1993: 175). Ham and Hill draw upon and highlight a body of literature referred to as radical organization theory, which is associated with such authors as Burrell and Morgan, Clegg and Dunkerley, and Benson. This literature accommodates different levels of analysis by considering the way society impinges upon organizations. For example, Benson notes how administrative organizations may be effected by societal factors, or by the rules of structure formation. This is not to say that these rules automatically determine organizational life. In public as well as private organizations, individuals and groups of agents will have some influence in responding to the pressures exerted by these rules.

Ham and Hill make similar observations about the policy process. The authors maintain the importance of locating the social context of political activity. The main strength of Marxist theory, according to Ham and Hill, is that government behaviour is not examined in isolation but in terms of the wider setting of the capitalist economy. The difficulty arises over the deterministic treatment of government and policy as a functional outlet and reflection of broader economic relations:

> Yet a rejection of structural determinism does not mean focusing solely on the role of political actors in seeking to explain public policy. Rather ... it is necessary to recognize that actors, in mediating structural influences, behave in ways that are meaningful to themselves. (Ham and Hill, 1993: 185)

Hence, policy should be informed by different aspects of reality that are linked but at the same time possess distinct properties. The attempt to link these spheres of social life should be characterized by rigorous analysis; it should not involve an unprincipled eclecticism where seemingly incomputable theories are combined without due consideration and proper analysis (see Layder, 1994: 222).

Such views, as conceded by these authors, owe a debt to that theoretical tradition, exemplified by Weber, where the political system is seen to have independent significance in society. Of particular import in this formulation is Weber's analytical regard for human action, motives and meanings. Another Weberian influence is the concern for bureaucracy and the idea that organizations are not instruments of capital but derive an independent standing from political, legal and financial resources. One of the characteristics of public bureaucracies is the position of political elites. These have access to wide-ranging powers, but they also have a role in mediating between key social groups in society. It is at the political level where internal and external structures intersect, setting parameters and also providing opportunities for policy agents. As Held (1989: 74) notes: '[S]tate power expresses at once the intentions and purposes of government and state personnel ... and the parameters set by the institutionalized context of state–society relations.'

Similar concerns and arguments inform the analysis of policy in the subsequent chapters. This analysis takes the form of policy case studies. As summarized in the introduction, the studies are organized into two sections. Each of the case studies in the first section is organized to represent distinct levels of analysis to explore the tension and interrelations between agency and structure. The analysis does not just look at the constraints posed by broad societal forces on the operations of policy agents. From the points made above, it also examines the relationship between policy agents and the network of organizational arrangements, forming the immediate political and institutional arrangements where policy is made. The second part examines the way in which elements of these different levels are responsible for propelling the policy process from initial formation to implementation.

The main objective in all this is to develop an understanding and appreciation of policy as a highly complex, multidimensional process. To do this, inclusive forms of theoretical and empirical inquiry are needed. Such analytical tools are well equipped to explore policy in the terms established above: as an interdependent coupling of two distinct areas of reality – the emergent properties of social and political systems, and the dynamic qualities of human activity.

part II

Case studies

Levels and stages of analysis

Chapter 4

Case study analysis and public policy

4.1 Introduction

Policy-making is a dynamic activity. There are numerous variables and factors that influence the policy process which require careful consideration. In view of this, researchers have attempted to utilize appropriate methods to gain a fuller understanding of public policy. One useful method which forms the basis of the chapters in this part of the book is the case study. The aim here is to provide a detailed assessment of the case study method as a methodological overview for the chapters that follow. The concern is to demonstrate how this method is used in policy analysis and how in practical terms researchers can go about developing policy cases.

The case study is essentially a narrative-based account of a limited number of select instances, which belong to a social or behavioural phenomenon as it occurs in its *natural setting* (Hakim, 1992; Yin, 1994). A detailed case study can be furnished by recourse to a variety of information gathering techniques. Most commonly, case studies utilize qualitative evidence garnered from in-depth interviews and close observation. Indeed, it was initially popularized by American academic researchers during the 1920s and 1930s as a reaction against statistical surveys which attempted to replicate scientific methodology. For a growing band of researchers in this period, particularly those based at Chicago University, quantitative methodologies were deemed unsuitable for dealing with the complex and variable nature of society. Hammersley (1989: 93) writes: 'Advocates of the case study pointed out that such studies produced much more detailed information about a case than that available about each instance in a statistical aggregate.'

It would be justifiable to argue from the foregoing that the case study sits firmly at the qualitative end of the methodological spectrum. The case study can be used to explain the subjective life of individuals and the complex range of variables involved in shaping human behaviour and social phenomena. Certainly, for early proponents of the case approach, it was seen as a rival to statistically based methods. However, the development of case analysis since it was first used in the social sciences during the early decades of the twentieth century has shown it to be a flexible research tool. Researchers have shown that this method can easily accommodate both qualitative and quantitative research designs. In fact, the work of LePlay, purported to be the earliest use of the case study in social research, combined typological and statistical analysis (Chinoy, 1964: 74).

The case study has gained increasing prominence across a range of social science disciplines. Analytically, for research purposes, the case study can provide a highly flexible research strategy for investigating a limited range of instances related to a specific phenomenon of interest. One area of scholastic output where this has become evident is public policy analysis. Initially, the case study was popularized by American academics focusing on public administration (see Stein, 1952: xx–xxx). Later American researchers used the case method to explore decision-making in the policy process. One notable illustration of this is Allison's (1971) *Essence of Decision*, which focuses on the single case of the Cuban missile crisis of October 1962. Here, Russia and the United States stood on the brink of nuclear war. Three competing policy models are used to understand why this threat to international security happened in the first place and to explain the course of subsequent events.

British practitioners have also come to favour the case approach to furnish detailed studies of specific policy-making decisions. Case analysis affords a broad range of sources and multiple research designs. It is thus seen as an effective research method for understanding the complex influences that impinge on government, and the often context-bound, event-driven nature of policy decisions. Examples of how this particular methodology has been applied to the study of public policy will be outlined below.

The case method, when used by policy analysts, is subject to a variety of designs. For instance, Heclo and Wildavsky's (1981) contribution to policy analysis relied upon a single case study. The researchers endeavoured to provide empirical insight concerning the policy-making community within central British government. Their research focused on the interrelations between spending departments, Treasury officials and Cabinet members. The authors were particularly interested in how links between these various groups helped shape the pattern of public spending. Although this study is now outdated in terms of current trends in Treasury economic philosophy, it usefully illuminated the nature of relations between departments and their political and administrative representatives.

Not all efforts to research the policy process have focused on single cases: there are some instances where multiple case studies have been carried out. Hall *et al.* (1975), for example, used multiple case studies to highlight the development of policy since the Second World War. The authors identified three forms of policy change: first, the intervention of the state in a new policy field; second, developmental changes in public policy resulting from alterations in the existing level of provision; and finally, reforms involving changes to existing policies. To detail these three categories, the authors examined the areas of social security, health, education, penal reform and environmental protection.

In a later work, Cooper (1985) illustrated how multiple case studies can form the basis of comparative analysis. The study focused on local authority welfare services in Scotland, England, Northern Ireland and Wales. It concentrated specifically on the way local provision became public systems of integrated personal social services. For each region, Cooper carried out a detailed case study of these changes. From this analysis, three different models of local social provision emerged. These models were a variation of the dominant policy themes surrounding the rationalization of the boundaries and structures of local services.

4.2   Adopting case analysis

Like the academic studies mentioned above such as Allison (1971) and Hall *et al.*'s (1975) work, this text attempts to exploit the explanatory utility of case studies. The specific objective of chapters in Part II is to examine broad analytical features of the policy process through case analysis. For instance, different levels of socio-political organization relevant to the policy process are put under the microscope using actual case analysis.

There are various reasons why the case study format is pertinent to this type of analysis. These reasons evoke or are indicative of the inherent strengths of case study methodology. One of these strengths is the ability to provide detailed analysis, or what Guba and Lincoln (1981: 375) term 'thick description'. This level of detail is vital when researchers explore complex themes or theoretical issues. The case study can potentially explore a wide array of scenarios and situations that are relevant to theoretical discussions. For instance, when assessing the impact of a policy programme on a specific area, a case analysis can take into account a whole range of variables. This may include political factors like the role of political institutions. External factors such as the economy and social divisions may be considered at the same time.

Such openness to a range of variables means that the ensuing investigation is not dictated and constrained by prior assumptions. The case study is able to embrace a more inductive or grounded approach. Here, theoretically relevant details, concepts and ideas can emerge out of the process of conducting research. Explanation-building can grow out of simple narratives or more analytical case studies which attempt to reflect theoretically significant ideas (Yin, 1994: 110–11). In operational terms, this grounded approach to analyzing policy may display the following pattern: a statement about the policy process is introduced; this may be compared against initial findings from the case study; further theoretical statements or propositions may be introduced; these in turn are compared against further case evidence; this process continues as more detailed evidence is garnered from the case study. As Yin notes: 'the case study evidence is examined, theoretical positions are revised, and the evidence is examined once again from a new perspective, in this iterative mode' (ibid).

Derthick's (1972) *New Towns In-Town* (cited in Yin, 1994: 112) illustrates the way case analysis can be utilized to build emergent explanations. This particular study focused on the implementation of Lyndon Johnson's house-building programme. As part of the policy, local authorities were given surplus land in urban locations for housing development. Derthick carried out case studies of seven local authorities where progress had proven slow. This analysis was able to discount the commonly held view that the programmes failed because of limited local support. Derthick generated an alternative explanation: that federal government set unrealistic expectations, which meant failure was inevitable.

A similar strategy was used throughout the case studies in this text. Chapter 8 on the Tomlinson inquiry is especially typical of this emergent method. In this study, different theoretical models on the process of implementation are compared against case study material from the Tomlinson inquiry into London's health service. The chapter gradually refines a set of ideas about the process of implementation by integrating case data with rival explanations.

The opportunities and possibilities offered by case studies are seen by others to harbour methodological shortcomings and weaknesses. A significant criticism is that emergent theory-building and detailed narrative material fails to be sufficiently vigorous in scientific terms. Case studies require analysts to interpret and select information. This can oversimplify matters. In addition, the type of data used by case studies – interviews, documents and archives – are seen to lack objectivity and neutrality, leading to politically biased studies. What these arguments overlook is that even the natural sciences are imbued by the values and preferences of those individuals performing the investigation. This is something confirmed by numerous studies in the sociology of scientific knowledge. On the question of interpretation, this is an inevitable feature of developing cases. At the same time, it is possible to assess the adequacy of various components of the case study: 'One can talk about the validity and reliability of the instrumentation, the appropriateness of the data analysis techniques, the degree of relationship between the conclusions drawn and the data upon which they presumably rest, and so on' (Guba and Lincoln, 1981: 378).

Another significant objection raised against the case method is that when compared to surveys it lacks the force of generalizability to other populations. This type of research often provides detailed information on the back of highly partial accounts. This, in turn, circumscribes the ability to represent other populations. Hammersley notes, however, that generalizability is not the sole preserve of survey methods. A number of strategies are available to improve the power of generalizing from case analysis. Relevant information can be drawn upon from published research and documentation. These publications might include statistical information, which, as argued earlier is not entirely incompatible in case analysis (Hammersley, 1992: 189–90). It is also possible to select a case which contains attributes typical of other events or incidents. In these circumstances, it would be safe to make certain tentative generalizations. Another possibility is to conduct multiple case studies across different populations. One strategy used by Allison (1971) in *The Essence of Decision* was to integrate theoretical analysis into the case material. Hammersley (1992: 191) observes that these various strategies will not guarantee an instant route for generalization, 'but they can provide some evidence, and we should not scorn that evidence simply because it is not statistical'.

Now that the utility of the case method for policy analysis has been established, attention switches to the issue of collating evidence and data for case analysis.

4.3   Developing a policy case study

One of the strongest features of the case study is that it can accommodate different sources of information and data. The main sources that can be used in policy case study work include the following: interviews, documents, secondary analysis and historical-based studies and texts. The aim now is to provide practical guidance on the construction of evidence for policy case studies. The various case studies covered in this text are used to illustrate points and observations about the way information and evidence is used to develop case research.

4.3.1   Documents

The use of documents in developing policy case studies is ubiquitous. There is a range of documentary materials that are relevant and useful for this task. The government and various other public agencies are fruitful sources of documentary evidence for developing case studies. These documents can take a very wide array of forms. Parliamentary papers, Hansard debates and select committee reports are especially useful. It is common practice in the present climate for public agencies like hospitals, local authorities and even government departments to produce annual reports. The privatization of various strands of the civil service into independent agencies has created a veritable industry in new documentary sources. The prison service is a classic example. This particular agency now publishes a range of documents, including guidelines for the recently established performance monitoring regimes.

Non-governmental sources are also a rich source of documentary evidence relevant to policy analysis. There are consultancy documents which can provide a different version of events to the official view. Such evidence, though, is not always available or easy to obtain. Articles from newspapers and other periodicals, including professional journals and magazines, can provide both descriptive and analytical information (Yin, 1994: 81). There is a whole plethora of journals covering aspects of the public sector, from medicine to local government, from the prison service to teaching. Again, many of these journals will pour a more critical eye over government policy and will serve as useful accompaniments to official documents and government papers. Other documentary sources can include letters. There are also minutes of meetings and other personal reports of events such as diaries. In all probability it is very difficult to obtain such documentation, apart from published diaries, but if access is gained it can shed a great deal of light over proceedings.

Documentation can play an integral part in policy case analysis or any case study for that matter. For a start, such evidence is useful for checking factual information and corroborating evidence obtained from other sources. Documents may reveal certain implicit features about the topic under investigation. For instance, the presentation used and information that is excluded will betray certain characteristics about the organization or body publishing the document.

All the case studies covered in this text made use of different forms of documentary evidence. One example is the case study in Chapter 8 on the Tomlinson inquiry into the reorganization of London's health service. Much of the data collected and used to develop this case study is garnered from documents. There are the two main public documents central to the whole case. The first was the Tomlinson (1992) inquiry findings, *Report of the Inquiry into London's Health Service,* and the second was the government's strategic response to the recommendations made by Tomlinson, *Making London Better* (DoH, 1993). These sources provide an official overview of the whole case. Useful additional information came from the minutes of three Health Committee reports. These gave a critical insight into the events surrounding the inquiry. Here the main protagonists expressed their version of events. This proved particularly important when examining the difficulties and barriers that are encountered during the process of implementation. There were also numerous articles obtained from professional journals such as the *British Medical Journal* and the *Health Service Journal*. Articles from these periodicals set out the events prior to and after the Tomlinson inquiry had made its recommendations in a wider historical context.

The case study in Chapter 6 on contractual relations within the new unitary authority of Bath and North East Somerset relies in part on documentation produced by that organization. This includes the minutes and agendas from various committee meetings; the advisory reports written by officers for councillors; and finally the minutes of main council meetings. Much of this documentation was obtained from the local library during fieldwork trips. Indeed, researchers of case studies should keep in mind that a vital aspect of fieldwork is to carry out systematic searches of relevant documentation. Some of these searches are location specific, such as the one at Bath and North East Somerset.

The official documents from the local authority proved highly useful, but they were also written for a specific audience. As such, the information gathered tends to be selective and omits important observations about the way local government officials operated. Indeed, these points are relevant to any form of documentation. Thus, researchers should not rely on documentation too heavily. Their role should be to scrutinize the context in which the documents were written. Moreover, the investigator should be willing to develop alternative sources of information in addition to documents. One effective source which highlights those events and processes that are often overlooked by official documentation is the semi-structured interview.

4.3.2   Semi-structured interviewing

Interviews can form a highly significant and effective source of information in developing policy case studies. The type of interview can vary according to the way questions are presented. There are the highly structured forms of interviewing, where respondents are taken through a carefully chosen schedule of questions. This type of interviewing is commonly associated with surveys. In the context of a survey, questions of sampling and representativeness of the population being interviewed are vital issues.

There are less structured forms of interviewing which may be more appropriate to the case method. For instance, the open-ended interview, in which the respondent is allowed to talk at length with minimal prompting. Researchers may ask the respondent to provide an account of particular developments and his or her opinions about these events.

For those wishing to obtain specific pieces of information, the semi-structured interview might prove more useful. These interview situations might still be informal and open-ended in the way they are conducted but interviewers are likely to follow a series of questions. Such is the nature of the semi-structured interview that analysts can improvise or add further questions when interesting points emerge in the conversation. These interviews normally take place within a set time limit but they can yield in-depth information and data that provide vital evidence for case studies. As Yin (1994: 85) observes:

> Overall, interviews are an essential source of case study evidence because most case studies are about human affairs. These human affairs should be reported and interpreted through the eyes of specific interviewees, and well-informed respondents can provide important insights into a situation.

Interview transcripts should be treated as verbal reports. According to Yin this means that they can be open to inaccuracies, bias and ineffectual reporting. In fact, the interviews conducted for the case studies in this text tended, for various reasons, to vary in quality. Nevertheless, the interview, particularly in semi-structured form, is a vital tool for building and gathering findings for case analysis. This was especially so for three of the policy case studies included in this text. (It should be said that respondents, as with all those interviewed for the case studies, were given anonymity. As well as protecting the interviewees, anonymity is an important device for ensuring openness and for obtaining sensitive information.)

The case study on the Chelsea and Westminster hospital reorganization in Chapter 7 is based in part on five semi-structured interviews. Each individual was interviewed a number of years after the events had taken place. As such, questions could be raised about the reliability of the material obtained. Evidence from documents and secondary sources suggest, however, that the interview material was of a reliable nature. The participants provided valuable information about the political manoeuvres which accompanied this hospital reorganization. Indeed, it could be argued that with events having taken place some time in the past, the respondents could afford to be more candid.

Unlike the survey, those respondents involved in semi-structured interviewing are not representative of a particular sample. Rather, they are specially picked because of the information that they can furnish. Those interviewed for this case study were key players in the whole scenario, as opposed to a representative sample of those effected by the events surrounding the reorganization. The respondents included a senior health service manager, the head of the Community Health Council, a senior consultant who served on various medical boards in London, a leading trade unionist and a senior administrator.

Interviews form a significant part of the data collected for the case study in Chapter 6 on compulsory competitive tendering. The interviewing centred on five senior officials in the new unitary authority of Bath and North East Somerset. Each respondent was specifically chosen to be interviewed because of their involvement and responsibilities for various aspects of competitive tendering. An effort was made to interview officials representing both client and contractor functions of the local authority organization. In addition, those at the corporate centre responsible for coordinating contracting activities were interviewed. The study was concerned with the nature of agency, that is, the way individuals behave and act in policy settings. Thus it was necessary to obtain detailed opinions and insights from the participants themselves.

The third case study partly based around interview evidence is found in Chapter 9. The interview material in this case study was used to evaluate Dutch drug control policy. Altogether eight key players in the drug field were interviewed to express their views about the impact of Dutch policy. Because of their close involvement in various aspects of the drug field, these respondents were important to the whole process of evaluation. Their first-hand knowledge and experience of government efforts to deal with drug abuse made them especially qualified to deal with questions about Dutch policy. For instance, a senior government official from the Division of Alcohol, Drug and Tobacco Policies furnished significant insights about the current policy ideas and concerns circulating in the Ministry of Health. A meeting with a consultant on drug problems was particularly informative about the standing of government and police authorities from the viewpoint of drug users. This information, together with other sources, provided a framework for developing an in-depth evaluation of the impact of Dutch drug control policy.

4.3.3   Historical sources

Historically orientated commentaries are a useful tool in policy analysis case studies. Although not extensively relied upon, reference to historical commentaries appear in some of the case studies, especially those on urban policy (Chapter 5) and Dutch drug control programmes (Chapter 9). The sources are mainly secondary accounts. These accounts came in two forms: commentaries written in the past while the policy in question was emerging (see Edwards and Batley, 1978; Higgins *et al.*, 1983), or contemporary histories looking back at the development of the policy (see Leuw, 1991; van Vliet, 1990). Although the historical material in the case studies was predominantly lifted from secondary accounts, alternative source materials may be used to construct histories, most notably, primary historical data in the way of archive documents. This includes government documents stored at the Public Records Office at Kew, although thirty years have to elapse before records enter the public domain. It should also be kept in mind that the records sent to Kew are carefully selected in the first place. In the public sphere, parliamentary papers and departmental documents can span long periods of time.

Depending on the area under investigation and the questions being asked, a historical angle can add a great deal to policy case analysis. In particular, it highlights the way contemporary features of policy life have been influenced by longitudinal developments and processes. The historical survey of Dutch drug policy shows how the philosophy of harm reduction, developed in the late 1960s, continues to hold a major influence over present-day policy-makers. Historical analysis can also help to pinpoint the reasons why specific policy matters emerge. Chapter 5 uses historical analysis to show how figures in government responded to issues relating to urban poverty and deprivation, in part brought about by socio-economic developments beyond the sphere of government. There is a sense that a historical dimension adds reliability and extra depth to the data being used for case work. Layder (1993: 145) notes:

> This [historical dimension] will provide the research with additional
> energy inputs both in the shape of a further data source that adds

empirical depth to the analysis, and in the form of another potential source of concepts and theoretical ideas. At the same time, a historical dimension provides validity and reliability checks on both the substantive and formal theoretical elements that have already emerged from the actual field research.

An example of the way historical insight can increase the analytical weight of a study is shown in the case work on Dutch drug control policy. In the study, the concept of policy style is introduced to assess the impact of drug control policy on the problems it endeavoured to address. It is demonstrated that the postwar development of new 'policy styles' in government contributed to the emergence of new innovative programmes like harm reduction in the drug control field. The continuity and changes in the Dutch policy style on drugs are highlighted in this case study. On the one hand, the concept of policy style underlined the way that governments, through careful deliberation and thought, can influence social issues and problems. On the other hand, the changes in policy that were introduced in this period revealed the limitations that can sometimes be imposed on the policy process. Pressures can easily be wrought on governments by the tide of events and external forces, and, as a result, existing policy styles are forced to change – sometimes against the better judgement of the policy-makers.

From this discussion, historical analysis clearly adds an important dimension to, and can easily complement, contemporary analysis. The point for those compiling case analysis data is whether a historical analysis is strategically relevant to the issues that are being covered.

4.3.4   Secondary source materials

Historical analysis is dependent on secondary literature. Indeed, secondary analysis is vital to case analysis. If the objective, however, is to produce a narrative case study, the need for incorporating secondary literature, particularly theoretical contributions, is less important, unless the secondary material is a key source for developing the narrative in the first place. However, for those case studies seeking to explore policy issues, the inclusion of such data is vital. The type of secondary sources which are typically used in case work are research and academic commentaries on the policy area under scrutiny. Like historical research, these add depth and provide a strategic outlet for making broader points from particular cases. The advantage of secondary analysis is that it is cheap and easily available. But original input from primary data – interviews and documentary evidence – can add fresh insights to established ideas and research findings.

4.3.5   Other sources

There are other possible forms of data that can be used to develop policy case studies. These involve both direct and participant forms of observation. Observational methods are not employed in this text, as greater use is made of literary-based evidence. In addition, this source of data is not entirely relevant to the questions and issues that were being explored in the case studies included in this text. Even so, observation can furnish original material for case analysis. Direct observation, in which the researcher records behaviour and events as they are taking place, is a useful research tool. Such research can provide both primary and additional evidence for a case study. It might be especially relevant to case research exploring the implementation of a new programme by local officials. In a notable study of Whitehall by Heclo and Wildavsky (1981), the authors observed at first-hand, and recorded, the expenditure process in action. This observational case study illuminated aspects of British central government that would remain unrecorded in secondary and primary documents.

With participant observation, the researcher does not assume a passive role. They will be actively involved in the situation being studied. For instance, a case study based on participant observation could be devised on rehabilitation practices in Dutch clinics. To become an active observer, the researcher may become a volunteer or a worker in the centre to examine directly the experiences of addicts and staff alike. Goffman's (1968) work on asylums opened up to public scrutiny the workings of institutions that had remained under wraps for many years.

The main difficulty with any observational method is one of gaining access. There is also the question of resources, particularly of time, as long periods of observation are required to get a proper feel for the subject area being studied. Nevertheless, if an observational method is relevant to a case study, it does provide unique and interesting insights that are often denied to those carrying out desk research in libraries.

4.4 A multiple research strategy for case analysis

It is possible for each of these five sources of data to be used separately to develop a case study. In practice, this is not the strategy adopted in this text. Each case study made use of multiple sources of data. This ability to accommodate different types of evidence is a major strength of the case method. Yin (1994: 91) acknowledges this: '[A] major strength of case study data collection is the opportunity to use many different sources of evidence.' For Yin, a multiple research strategy, where different sources of data are employed, can address a wide range of social and political issues. More significant, though, according to Yin, is that this approach adds reliability to the findings. This multiresearch strategy produces a process of what is termed triangulation, where different lines of inquiry provide multiple corroborations about conclusions and findings. Denzin (1989: 244–6) points to different categories of triangulation. This includes data, investigator, theoretical, methodological and multiple triangulation. These might be associated with distinct aspects of the research process, but they are all concerned with ensuring reliability and validity (Layder, 1993: 121). The main forms of triangulation being considered at present are those focusing on data and methods, although the other forms are also significant.

The practice of triangulation or multiple methodology is fairly common in research. Silverman (1984: 191) used both quantitative and qualitative methods to explore the implications for policy regarding the 'onward march' of private medicine. The research itself focused on doctor–patient relations in both NHS and private oncology clinics. The mainstay of the analysis was qualitative in tone but this was supplemented with statistical evidence, such as length of consultations and patient participation (ibid. 193–7). Ken Pryce's study of the West Indian community in the St Paul's area of Bristol was mainly based on participant observation. This was supplemented by data from published books, by parliamentary papers, and by factual information obtained from local newspapers and local council documents. Such documentation furnished important background information on the local situation (Pryce, 1986: 298).

Policy case studies, as shown in this text, undoubtedly benefit from multiple sources of data. The study on the reorganization of the Riverside Health Authority (Chapter 7) used parliamentary papers, secondary texts and interviews to produce a fully rounded picture of events. This provided the necessary details for considering theoretical ideas about the interrelations between central and local institutions. A similar approach characterized the other case studies, except that different emphasis was placed on the types of data employed. There are those who argue that the use of multiple sources to triangulate evidence simply amounts to another form of positivism, in which there is search for a single version of the truth (see Silverman, 1985: 105). There might be a point to this argument, but it is based on the questionable premise that the endeavour to obtain a realist image in social research is unattainable. There is an additional purpose, apart from triangulation of evidence, which is afforded by the use of multiple sources.

The other main benefit of combining different types of data is that it begins to reflect the distinct levels that are evident in social life. One of the central themes pursued throughout this book is that the policy process is not driven by a single force. In actual fact, policy is driven by both individual dynamics and structural forces, which are distinct though still mutually linked. In the first part of the text, the case studies focus on particular levels of analysis. At the same time, the diversity of the material used points to the interdependencies that exist between these levels. The first study in Chapter 5 examines the influence of economic, ideological and political processes on the development of urban policy. The following study in Chapter 6 focuses specifically on the nature of agency in the policy process as expressed through contractual relations. This study, through openness to different data, was able to take into account the existing institutional procedures that constrain the actions of individuals in local government. Layder (1993: 123) observes: 'Different research strategies (methodological or analytic) "cut into" the data from different angles to reveal a variety of "slices" of the research site. Thus, the accumulation of perspectives will add to the picture that was originally revealed.'

The various 'slices' of social life implicated in the policy process may include the influence of socioeconomic forces, the manoeuvring of political interest groups, the institutions of government, or the drive of individual political ideology. And it is the case study approach to policy analysis, open to different forms of data, which allows analysts to embrace the multi-layered nature of empirical reality. Indeed, the case studies in this section attempt to make a number of different 'analytical cuts' into policy life. The specific areas covered in the case studies have been deliberately chosen and structured to underline particular features of the policy process. The structure and organization of these case studies is summarized below.

4.5   Organization of the case studies

The case studies below utilize material from various institutional settings. They focus on the policy activities of different units within the government machine. The analysis touches upon central government, local authorities and various other public agencies such as health authorities. The aim is not to provide wholly descriptive summaries of chosen policy areas. Rather the objective is to use these issues to examine significant mainstays of the policy process. Ham and Hill (1984) outline two general aspects of the policy process that analysis must focus upon. The authors argue that in order to gain a better understanding of government action it is necessary to examine 'both different stages of the policy process and different levels of analysis' (Ham and Hill, 1984: 17). In view of this, the case studies in this text are organized in terms of two separate analytical frameworks. In one framework, the case studies reflect different levels of the policy-making process. In the other, the case studies focus on distinct stages of the policy process. Before going on to detail how the case studies are organized in relation to each other, it is necessary to flesh out the details of each framework.

The first framework covers distinct levels of analysis. Potentially, a whole panoply of levels could legitimately be covered in policy inquiry. Ham and Hill (1984: 18) suggest that three levels will suffice:

> These comprise, first, the micro level of decision-making within organisations; second, the middle-range analysis of policy formulation; and third, macro analysis of political systems, including examination of the role of the state.

A similar approach is taken in this book, but there are some modifications to the levels noted by Ham and Hill. The first set of case studies in Chapters 5, 6, and 7 explore three main levels of analysis.

First, the level of agency, surveying the way policy agents make decisions and construct policies within institutional settings. Second, there is the intermediate organizational level which covers the immediate context in which policy is put into practice and implemented. The final level of this research map is the wider context of macrosocial organization. This level includes forms of social and economic organization, together with forms of power (Layder, 1993: 72). What is important about these levels is that they reflect the dualistic concerns of structure and agency. Notably, these levels of policy organization enable analysts to investigate the mutual links that exist between agency and structure in the policy process.

The second set of case studies found in Chapters 8 and 9 are organized along the lines of a stagist framework. The case studies in this section will focus on some of the main phases of the policy life cycle. Several stages of development have been identified as central to the policy process. Hogwood and Gunn (1984: 4) offer a nine-point list of policy stages: the setting of a policy agenda; deciding which issue to focus upon; defining an issue; forecasting future developments; establishing objectives; examining a range of options; implementing policy, which involves monitoring and control; evaluating the achievements of a policy; and finally, decisions regarding whether a policy should be maintained, developed or discontinued. Jenkins (1993: 36) offers a seven-point list of stages, which includes the following: initiation, information, consideration, decision, implementation, evaluation and termination. Malpass and Murie (1994), following Smith (1976), maintain that it would be more useful to adopt a circular model for the policy process. According to these authors, government action and state intervention in particular areas may generate information which leads to reappraisals of the original policy objectives. Subsequently, this may result in new policies and implementation strategies (Malpass and Murie, 1994: 217).

This stagist model suffers from several shortcomings. The main difficulty is that such a framework often bears little or no relation to the actual reality of policy-making. In fact, the policy process is messier and more complicated than suggested by stagist models. The problem in using a linear framework is that analysts may fall into the trap of portraying the development of policy in overly rational terms. Parsons (1995: 79) observes: 'The idea of dividing up policy-making in such a way greatly overstates the rational nature of policy-making and gives a false picture of a process which is not a conveyor belt.'

From another point of view, Anderson (1975: 25) argues that frameworks like the stagist model should be dispensed with altogether:

> Generally, one should not permit oneself to be bound too rigidly or too dogmatically to a particular model ... It is my belief that the explanation of political behaviour, rather than the validation of a given theoretical approach, should be the main purpose of political inquiry and analysis.

Criticisms surrounding the stagist models do make valid points. Nevertheless, it is still vital to provide some sort of framework for organizing and adding clarity to the analysis of government activity. Burch and Wood (1983: 19) note: 'But it is undoubtedly useful to sectionalize the policy-making process. It helps in handling material and it aids comprehension.' Parsons (1995: 80) makes a similar point. Although he maintains that caution should be exercised when adopting a stagist approach, this sort of framework does have certain plus points. The main one is that it renders complex materials and issues more easily managed.

A similar view is taken in the present investigation. The later case studies in Chapters 8 and 9 are organized around a stagist format, the key phases being the emergence, the implementation and the evaluation of policy. In contrast to staid, mainly textbook versions, of the stagist model, attempts are made to understand the movement from one phase to another. Such analysis can highlight the relative significance of both structure and agency in policy development. Moreover, there are also considerations of the barriers that can hinder the progress and development of a policy issue.

STUDY GUIDE

A reading schedule

There are some useful books and articles on the case approach which are worth consulting. Hakim (1992: chapter 6) and Hammersley (1992: chapter 11; 1989: chapter 4) are general articles on the use of the case study in social science research. Yin (1994) is a detailed book on the case study and provides a

▶▶

▶▶
great deal of practical advice on developing case studies for research purposes. With the growing popularity of the case method in social research, there are now a number of good examples of case-orientated policy research. One notable example is Allison's (1971) study of the Cuban missile crisis, and closer to home, there is Heclo and Wildavsky's (1981) study of the Treasury. For an informative overview of the research process and the different strategies that can be used, Layder (1993) should be referred to. Silverman (1985) is a good overview of qualitative research methods.

Issues for revision and further consideration

Having studied this chapter you should be familiar with several key concepts relevant to policy analysis. These are as follows: the case study method (section 4.1); policy case studies (4.1; 4.2); an inductive approach (4.2); generalizability (4.2); a multiple research strategy and sources (4.3 and 4.4); triangulation (4.4); a stagist model (4.5).

▶   Compare and contrast the different ways in which case research has been used in policy analysis.

▶   Why do you think researchers might adopt case analysis in the first place? What are the advantages of this methodological approach?

▶   In methodological terms what problems does the case study present to researchers?

▶   Construct a research map of how a case study on a recent policy issue might be developed? Which sources of information might be used?

5

Levels of the policy process: the case of urban regeneration

5.1 Introduction: levels of analysis and urban policy

The objective of this chapter is to understand the links between agency and structure in the policy process. This is pursued by focusing on different levels of analysis. This requires a consideration of the main components involved in the formation and development of policy. As Ham and Hill note, there are a whole range of levels that can be used in policy analysis. This chapter focuses on distinct levels (the individual, institutional and external environment) which are relevant to exploring the links between structure and agency. (The subsequent two chapters, on the other hand, bracket specific levels for more detailed analysis.)

Analysts venturing along this path have usually adopted a single policy issue or a specific policy area. This chapter is not a break with past precedent. The policy area of urban and inner-city regeneration policy is used here to detail those issues involved in the analysis of the policy process. The first part of this case study outlines the historical evolution of urban policy from the late nineteenth century to the present day. Urban policy in this period passed through a number of distinct phases, which are documented. Studying different levels of the policy process demands that analysis needs to go beyond the chronicling of policy development. Description in itself is not sufficient. It is necessary to consider those factors that have influenced the general shifts in policy. Insights obtained from the social sciences, including sociology and political science, provide an informative framework for this analysis. Particular reference is made to Lewis and Flynn's (1979) behavioural model of policy-making.

5.2   Major phases of urban policy from the late nineteenth century to the 1990s

What follows is a historical summary of urban policy in Britain. Our period of coverage is relatively prolonged, covering the late nineteenth century through to the 1990s. The analysis endeavours to highlight different phases regarding the development of urban policy in this period. Distinguishing between policy phases is not a simple or straightforward matter. Urban policy to begin with is a complex phenomenon. Add to this its temporal evolution, and what we have is a process which is not easily subject to simple categorization. Robson *et al.* (1994: 2), in a similar vein, remark:

> [T]here is some difficulty both in determining unambiguously what government has aimed to achieve in developing its urban policy at any one time and in trying to characterise those aims over the course of the last two decades.

The authors point out that during a period such as the 1980s, policy objectives changed over time and a multiplicity of policy mechanisms were used by governments to address the urban issue.

Nevertheless, failure to broadly characterize policy shifts may undermine the ability of analysts to understand urban policy. Although it is important not to overlook such complexity, it is still possible to distil certain general features and characteristics of policy during specific historical junctures. With urban policy, four central phases can be detected, through which this issue has progressed. These are outlined below.

5.2.1   The formative, uncoordinated phase – from the late nineteenth century to the 1950s

In this early period, inner urban deprivation had not emerged as a distinctive niche within the government policy machine. Aspects characteristic of contemporary urban policy were subsumed under more general programmes. The impact of industrialization during the late nineteenth and early twentieth centuries is a prime example. In the face of growing urban poverty within industrial growth areas, governments intervened to tackle the generalized phenomenon of poverty, rather than urban deprivation *per se*.

It was among local authorities during the early decades of the twentieth century that formative interventions to address urban deprivation took place. By the interwar period, major towns and cities had developed a multifunctional system of local government. Growing levels of unemployment during the 1930s created opportunities for local authorities to add economic intervention to their list of municipal duties. Councils attempted to stimulate economic development through direct public works, the provision of industrial land, and in some cases the establishment of municipal banks. Central government also made a contribution to area-based initiatives. The Special Areas Act of 1934 gave special provision for developing industrial land and buildings (Mawson and Miller, 1986: 148–9).

By the postwar period, municipal intervention in the local economy faded into the background under the impact of nationalization and universal welfare provision. Central government during the early postwar years assumed a more direct role in relation to urban regeneration. However, government policy for urban areas was confined to the redevelopment of war-damaged industrial and residential locations, and the clearance of inner-city slums. This was achieved, in the main, by recourse to town planning mechanisms (Hill, 1994: 167).

The 1950s witnessed a modicum of change in central government intervention, as international competition began to bear down on staple industries. To assist the areas effected by these pressures, the government established Developmental Districts. The immediate aftermath of the Second World War had witnessed some progress in dealing with the ills of urban areas. Much of this intervention, though, was aimed at physical renewal. The urban locality as a matter of specific policy concern emerged in later decades.

5.2.2   The emergence of inner-urban policy – the late 1960s

It was in the 1960s that governments began expressing an explicit and specific interest in inner-urban regeneration. This constitutes one of the most crucial phases in the development of urban policy.

What gave rise to these concerns? The continued spectre of urban deprivation in the postwar period, despite the establishment of the welfare state, stimulated a great deal of interest around the inner city. The concept of the inner city became synonymous with the concentration of poverty around certain localities and social groups. Most notably, politicians expressed concerns over the levels of deprivation among immigrant communities, which tended to be confined to urban areas. Thus, from the late 1960s onwards, the related issues of urban regeneration and inner-city development became increasingly prominent in government policy circles. It was the Home Office that initially took charge and drove new policy initiatives.

One of its earliest forays was the Urban Programme – established in 1968. Of the initiatives that emerged during this early period, this was probably the most significant. Official powers were granted to the Home Office under the Local Government Grants (Social Need) Act of 1969. Here, extra funding was set aside for councils adjudged to be situated in the most deprived areas of the country.

Originally, 151 authorities were given Urban Programme status. Many of the early initiatives supported under the scheme had a welfare flavour, and were noted for services provided to local groups, such as immigrants. Indeed, the Urban Programme was seen as a direct response by the Labour government to Enoch Powell's 'rivers of blood' speech in the same year (Lawless, 1988: 531).

Around the same time, in 1969, the Community Development Project (CDP) under the auspices of the Home Office set up 12 inner-area projects. These were formed principally to provide a research base for government action. The research teams were asked to examine a broad range of socio-economic factors in urban deprivation. Even so, the individualistic view of urban poverty peddled by the scheme's progenitor, Derek Morrell, tended to prevail. The teams were plagued by operational difficulties, factional in-fighting among officials and a lack of leadership. By 1978, they were effectively wound-up.

5.2.3 Redirecting urban policy – the mid to late 1970s

A relative shift in Home Office policy for inner-urban deprivation was signalled by the formation of the Comprehensive Community Programme (hereafter, CCP) in 1974. Rather than viewing deprivation as an outcome of individual choices and decisions, the new scheme focused on improving the coordination of existing services and management structures. The CCP attempted to introduce a comprehensive programme of action, involving the coordination of different agencies in local areas (Higgins *et al.*, 1983: 86).

A similar project was undertaken during the early 1970s by the Department of the Environment (hereafter, DoE). The Inner Area Studies were established in Birmingham, Liverpool and Lambeth to develop a coordinated approach to inner urban intervention (ibid. 92). They were influential in the respect that they shifted attention away from individual malaise as the cause of deprivation. Instead, poverty was viewed as a problem of resources, power and techniques. The policy agenda set by the Inner Area Studies established a significant antecedent for a major rethink of urban policy in the late 1970s. This was ushered in by the Labour government's 1977 White Paper, *Policy for the Inner Cities*.

The Labour government's 1977 White Paper indicated a significant shift in the emphasis and nature of urban policy. First, as a DoE-led initiative, it demonstrated that this department had taken over from the Home Office as the prime mover in urban policy. Second, the document endeavoured to produce a strategy for pulling together and coordinating the various schemes and policy initiatives that had emerged since 1968. Third, in substantive terms, the focus was widened to address economic problems, especially unemployment, and the structural causes of urban deprivation. Finally, under this new policy regime, emphasis was placed on developing partnerships between local and central government. Such cooperation was seen as vital in tackling problems associated with the inner city, especially unemployment. Indeed, policy documents mentioned local authorities as the natural agencies for urban development. Moreover, the 1978 Act reformulated the Urban Programme so that extra funding was allocated to designated partnership and programme areas (Hambleton, 1981: 53–7).

5.2.4 The restructuring for the market and property-led development – the 1980s

Through successive Conservative administrations during the 1980s, urban policy underwent a pronounced, though gradual, transformation.

The policy orthodoxy that emerged in this period, like Labour's White Paper, emphasized economic development as the panacea of urban blight. In contrast to Labour's strategy of the late 1970s, this objective was pursued through private investment and property-led regeneration in urban areas. Successive Conservative governments peeled away planning regulations in urban areas as part of the renewed importance of the market. There was to be a special role for the private sector in all this. Partnerships between public and private sector agencies were encouraged, and private sector investment was secured through fiscal incentives. Several initiatives (Enterprise Zones, Urban Development Grants, City Grants) and specialist agencies were established (Urban Development Corporations) for the express purpose of levering private sector resources and expertise (Lawless, 1988: 533–7).

This shift in emphasis was very much at the expense of local authority engagement in the whole process. Symptomatic of this was the diminution of the Urban Programme, which was reduced down to 57 authorities in 1987 (Hill, 1994: 174–5). The Conservative government's strategy was far removed from Labour's 1978 Inner Urban Areas Act. Here local authorities were treated as natural agencies of urban redevelopment (Moore and Booth, 1986).

Following the 1987 election, and for much of the late 1980s, the newly formed government intensified its efforts to develop a private sector-led solution to the problems of urban deprivation (see Edwards and Deakin, 1992). Most of the schemes in this period, encompassed in the key policy document, *Action for Cities*, focused on the rejuvenation of the inner city. The document emphasized the need to cultivate an 'enterprise culture' within inner cities. It was envisaged that this entrepreneurial culture would be developed by specialist agencies, consisting of private and public sector representatives. The coordination of private sector resources and the attraction of investment into inner cities were also integral to the market-led assault on inner-urban deprivation. Thus existing organizations, such as the Urban Development Corporations, were expanded and new agencies – City Action Teams and Task Forces – were established to cultivate a dynamic economy within deprived inner-city areas.

5.2.5 A renewed emphasis on competition, targeting and communities – the 1990s

By the turn of the new decade, the policy orthodoxies of the 1980s came under mounting criticism. It was argued that public intervention in the urban arena throughout the 1980s lacked coordination and had detrimentally marginalized the capacities of local government for economic intervention. The new Conservative government under John Major responded by embarking on a new phase of policy. In certain respects, this involved consolidating aspects of earlier market-orientated policies. At the same time, overtures were made to the perceived weaknesses of the *laissez-faire* approach. This involved restoring the position of local authorities. Moreover, rather than focusing on property-led schemes, new policy initiatives attempted to fulfil broader social objectives.

The first major policy to emerge during this period of revaluation was City Challenge. The scheme was launched in 1991 by Michael Heseltine, who had just returned into government, at the DoE, after resigning in 1986. In contrast to what had taken place during the 1980s, the scheme did not deliberately attempt to marginalize the role of local government. Another shift with Thatcherite orthodoxies in urban policy was the emphasis on an inclusive strategy of intervention. City Challenge endeavoured to build partnerships between local authorities, local communities, business and voluntary groups, with government facilitating rather than directly controlling proceedings (De Groot, 1992: 205). In fact it was vital for bids to demonstrate partnership building potential.

The programme was created to target resources in specific areas through a competitive bidding system. In the first round, 15 of the 57 Urban Programme authorities were invited to make bids. After a series of presentations made to ministers and other senior officials, 11 bids were finally selected for the 1992–95 period. In the second round, all 57 Urban Programme authorities were invited to make bids. Out of these competitors, twenty programme bids were selected in July 1992 (Atkinson and Moon, 1994: 94–5).

After two rounds of the competition, City Challenge occupied the largest portion of the government's urban budget. The future of the competition, though, was thrown into severe doubt by the announcement in November 1992 that the third round of City Challenge for 1994–95 would not take place. Nevertheless, the system of competitive bidding and the endeavours made to improve coordination, continued to dominate the government's policy agenda for urban regeneration. An intimation of this was provided by the 1992 Conservative election manifesto. The document pledged to 'allocate a greater proportion of resources by competitive bidding' (Conservative Central Office, 1992: 39). The system of funding, though, was to be streamlined. The manifesto pledged that all the resources targeted for inner-city programmes would be confined to a single budget. However, research was revealing that local authorities were becoming disillusioned with the process of competing for funds (Oatley, 1995: 9). Authorities were finding that the competition was politicized and held only a tenuous relationship with social needs.

Nevertheless, following the 1992 election, the new Single Regeneration Budget (hereafter, SRB) was formally established. The new initiative, as its name suggests, merged several funding programmes concerned with urban regeneration. Altogether, 20 programmes, spanning five different government departments, were brought together, with a combined cost of £1.4 billion (Tilson *et al.*, 1997: 2–3). During the 1995–96 financial year the government made available over £100 million of uncommitted resources to be distributed by the SRB scheme. Bids, however, were not restricted to the 57 Urban Priority Areas, having been the case with previous funding programmes such as City Challenge and the Urban Programme. Here, local authorities in the main, but also Training and Enterprise Councils, private businesses and voluntary groups, were invited to make indicative bids. No restrictions were placed on those local authorities which could devise first-time bids. This effectively marked the end of the Urban Programme, which had targeted resources in the most deprived local authorities.

The task of overseeing the competitive bidding process was devolved from central Whitehall departments to the newly formed regional Government Offices. This structure brought the former English regional establishments of four major Whitehall departments – the Department of Trade and Industry, Department of Environment, Department of Employment, and the Department of Transport – under 10 regional Government Offices.

Significantly, the flexibility afforded by the SRB gave agencies, particularly local authorities, a central and influential role within the process. Local authorities were in a position to devise SRB bids according to local needs, although these were ultimately assessed by officials from within the Government Offices. Hence, the SRB constitutes a further shift, with certain qualifications, towards involving local authorities as central actors in the policy process. This contrasted starkly with many of the inner-city policy measures which prevailed throughout the 1980s.

The first competitive round of the SRB was announced formally on 14 April 1994, with the 10 new Government Offices for the regions responsible for overseeing the competition. Bidders were asked to place outline bids to respective Government Offices. The Government Offices on the strength of these initial bids either encouraged or discouraged partnerships to make final bids. The number of bids that finally succeeded in gaining SRB support for the 1995–96 period, following the final deadline for bids in September 1994, totalled 201 partnerships.

5.3　Urban policy and levels of analysis: the 'behavioural model'

Studying the policy process demands that describing or documenting changes within a specific policy area is not sufficient. Analysts also need to identify those factors and influences that have shaped the development of this policy issue. The concern now is to construct an explanatory framework by which this exercise may proceed. The thesis followed here is that the policy process cannot be reduced to a single factor. Neither can it be explained in terms of a general theoretical schema which attends to particular aspects of social reality. The underlying thesis here is that the policy process is driven by a number of factors which relate to different, interrelated levels of analysis.

Lewis and Flynn's application of a behavioural model of policy-making to urban and regional planning provides a framework which addresses these concerns. This model acknowledges the significance of decision-making and purposeful action. Individual action in policy-making is viewed to be an interactive process. Here, policy actors do not act in a neutral or homogenous manner; policy action, rather, is noted for conflicting demands, ideologies and interests. The reason for this is that actors in the policy process, as Lewis and Flynn (1979: 129) acknowledge, are very much situated within specific contexts:

> An individual situated within an organisation is faced with a dual set of concerns: the world outside the organisation which he is in business to do something about, and the institutional context within which he works ... The actor is constrained by the existence of these two sets of concerns which are relatively fixed, but at the same time there is some flexibility and variation because the person is not a robot, but perceives situations and possible courses of action in different ways.

Actors are constrained by these forces, but they are in a position to mediate between both external and internal forces. As such, this may lead to the introduction or reformulation of government plans to effect change in wider society.

The case of urban policy brings to the fore several factors that have shaped the development of this policy area. These can be accommodated within Lewis and Flynn's behavioural model of policy-making. In accordance with this model, the framework used to explain the development of urban policy includes three levels of analysis: (1) The first level of analysis focuses on the role of individual political agents, especially the influence of ideological priorities. (2) The second examines the institutional context, focusing on the delivery structure of urban policy. (3) The final level is concerned with the world outside urban policy institutions, especially the impact of uneven economic development. This roughly corresponds with analytical levels suggested by Ham and Hill (1984: 17). The objective now is to examine how these different levels of analyses can be used to understand the development of urban policy.

5.4   Policy agents and urban regeneration

With urban policy, the most significant policy actors have been located in central government. This is not to deny the importance of so-called policy implementers that belong to local authorities or to extra-governmental agencies outside Whitehall. Chapters 6 and 7 will show the level of influence exercised by such actors over the formation and development of policy.

This case study brackets those senior ministers and officials in government departments as primarily setting the direction of urban policy. They have been responsible for establishing the priorities and the substantive details of urban policy. The reason for this is simple. In the postwar years, the urban issue has been the preoccupation of politicians and officials in central government.

The most significant actors in this respect are those that have occupied senior positions within relevant government departments. Initially, the Home Office housed the prime movers behind urban policy but this position was later occupied by the Department of Environment (DoE). Ministers within these departments have not made decisions about urban policy simply on the basis of their organizational position. (Closer scrutiny will be given in later sections to the institutional context in which policy actors operate.) As Lewis and Flynn (1979) note, decisions are given shape by the ideas and principles held by individuals. This is especially pertinent to urban regeneration. This area of policy is driven by a clear and explicit objective: to solve the problem of urban deprivation and poverty. Ideas in this respect play a significant role.

In the post-Thatcher age of New Labour, where party policy is seemingly driven by the demands of focus groups and image consultants, ideological commitment seems to have been divested of its power. Tony Blair on the eve the 1997 election announced that this election would be the last fought on ideology and politics (Bevins and Boggan, 1997: 1). This is far removed from actual reality. Even the most pragmatic or non-ideological of political parties implicitly hold on to particular ideas or principles. The reason for this is that political ideology is not necessarily related to formal political theory or to a strict set of belief systems. Ideology is a diffuse phenomenon that can assume a variety of guises; its influence can often be implicit and remain unacknowledged. Leach's (1995: 15) definition of the concept goes a long way towards capturing the nature of ideology: 'Here the term is employed in the relatively comprehensive and neutral way ... to mean any loosely linked ideas, values or perspectives that inform political judgements and behaviour.'

Ideological assumptions held by policy agents have effected urban policy in three main respects: (1) ideas have shaped the way urban problems are identified; (2) the development of solutions and remedies to inner-urban deprivation have been influenced by prior assumptions; and (3) the formation and implementation of urban policy has been informed by ideological notions about the best way for a policy to proceed.

An important caveat should be added to these points of observation. Ideas can have a definite influence over policy-making, but this is not a one-sided affair. 'The relationship between political ideas and public policy is complex and often two-way. Ideas constrain and in some senses determine public policy, yet public policy may in turn influence the ideas that people hold' (Leach, 1995: 14). With urban policy, ideas and policy action clearly exist in a dialogic relationship. In this analysis, it will not be practical to cover the ideological basis of every new policy nuance in the urban arena. A selection of central policy developments in urban policy will suffice to illustrate the symbiotic links between ideas and action. More specifically, comparison shall be made of policy developments between the second and third phases identified above.

As already noted above, it was in the late 1960s that governments began making specific and explicit provisions for dealing with inner-urban deprivation. Several urban 'policy experiments' emerged at this historical juncture. Two of these experiments – the Community Development Project and the Urban Programme – were guided by policy actors with distinct ideological agendas.

The CDP was a ground-breaking event in urban policy – it made special provision for inner-urban development within the government policy machine. The origins of this early foray into the urban arena can be traced to the heart of Whitehall – to the Home Office, to be exact. Derek Morrell, the assistant under-secretary in charge of the Children's Department at the Home Office, could lay claim to be the main inspiration behind this innovation. Morrell had a reputation for being a highly proactive official. He joined the Home Office in 1966 and was a prominent figure behind the 1969 Children and Young Person's Act. Following close behind this programme was his other major achievement, the CDP. As Higgins *et al.* (1983: 14) note, Morrell's ideological outlook, his values and beliefs, had a 'profound influence on the original conception of the CDP'.

The CDP emerged during discussions between key officials about children's law, which included consideration of community development. Morrell asserted that community development had to go beyond the narrow confines of children and young offenders. By the end of 1967, an interdepartmental working party was established to examine Morrell's ideas. The working party's final report, published in June 1968, provided practical flesh to Morrell's vision for inner-urban areas. The Community Development Project was the key recommendation, centring around 12 action teams which would explore and initiate community growth in needy areas.

The report provided a range of significant details. However, its most interesting facet concerned revelations about Morrell's personal philosophy on social reform. The report showed that for Morrell urban poverty was a product of individual, family and community pathology. While early CDP documents encouraged local teams to examine socio-economic factors, Morrell's moralistic conception of urban poverty tended to prevail.

Once the CDP moved into operational mode, perceptions of

deprivation, and its underlying causes, began to shift away from Morrell's pathological aetiology of urban deprivation. The Coventry CDP team provides a case in point. The team's remit was to scruti-nize personal social services. By 1975, the team was making recommendations from its analysis that were not in the Morrell book of preconceived notions (Coventry CDP, 1975: 5–8). Rather than viewing maladjusted behaviour as the cause of poverty, this was regarded as a symptom of deprivation. In effect, the team was arguing for a move from 'social pathology' to one which stressed the 'structural causes' of poverty.

This ideological shift in the CDP became replicated in urban strategy. One important factor in all this was the emergence of the DoE as a major player in urban policy-making. Although the Home Office had stamped its authority on urban policy, the DoE by the early 1970s was beginning to rival its position in this area. Part of this was due to a distinct lack of urgency on the Home Office's part to pri-oritize urban deprivation. The Home Office was more preoccupied with its traditional responsibilities of penal law, prisons, police and new issues such as immigration. In addition, Roy Jenkins, Labour's new Home Secretary after the 1974 election, generally showed little interest in urban matters during his tenure at the Home Office (Higgins *et al.*, 1983; 109–10). This was so despite the early promise shown with the Comprehensive Community Programme in 1974.

The DoE, with its responsibilities for local government and areas such as housing, had a close affinity with urban policy. By the early 1970s, this department was beginning to offer significant initiatives. These rivalled those of the Home Office and provided a new con-ception of urban policy. An important shift was ushered in by Peter Walker in 1972, the Conservative Secretary of State for the Environment. Under Walker's guidance, the DoE formed three Inner Area Studies in Lambeth, Liverpool and Birmingham. Walker's Inner Area Studies were the harbingers of change for urban policy, not only institutionally but also theoretically. These studies showed a greater structural appreciation of inner-urban deprivation than the CDP had done originally. Most significantly, they provided a theor-etical framework for what was to become a pivotal turning point for urban policy in 1977: this was to be the overhaul of the 'traditional' Urban Programme.

The Urban Programme was established in 1968 by the Home Office. It is widely argued that this initiative was established because of the government's growing preoccupation with race relations, fuelled in part by Enoch Powell's 'rivers of blood' speech (Lawless, 1988: 531). The Urban Programme was an arrangement where local authorities or voluntary agencies would receive a grant covering 75 per cent of costs for community – or social-based projects in needy areas. Those initiatives coming under the auspices of the Urban Programme had a welfare flavour. The programme was very much influenced by the idea of targeting resources for the most deprived areas, which tended to coincide with localities containing a high ethnic concentration. Once off the ground, the Urban Programme used its resources – modest in scale – among 150 local authorities. Ultimately, this early initiative was more a funding mechanism than a strategic plan for urban intervention. This was to change by the mid-1970s, following the ground-breaking of the CCP.

The policy agent that acted as a catalyst for this major policy shift was Peter Shore, who was appointed Secretary of State for the Environment in 1976. This new incumbent at the DoE gave a high priority to inner-urban regeneration. His early public pronounce-ments made it clear that the problem of inner-city poverty required a new policy response (Higgins *et al.*, 1983: 126). Immediate action was taken. A Cabinet Committee was formed, chaired by Shore, to review urban policy. Under Shore's guidance a new theoretical approach to the urban question emerged within government. Shore in very definite terms defined the inner-urban problem as a conse-quence of structural economic factors. Moreover, prevailing government responses to urban decline – in particular the Urban Programme – provided only short-term succour. To address the underlying structural causes of urban deprivation, governments had to utilize major policy and fiscal instruments.

These new policy ideas were presented by Shore in April 1977 and subsequently elaborated in a White Paper in June. The new strategy for inner areas, *inter alia*, involved the transfer of the Urban Programme from the Home Office to the DoE. Most importantly, specified local authorities, separated into different categories, were to be the beneficiaries of a bolstered Urban Programme, expanded from £35 million in 1977–78 to £165 million per year in 1979–80. All this amounted to a major strategy of systematic intervention, the aim being to tackle the structural causes of urban deprivation (Hambleton, 1981: 56).

The changes in policy witnessed between the late 1960s and the late 1970s reveal the importance of ideas in policy-making. Possibly the most potent example of the way that the realm of ideology can shape policy responses is the development of urban policy during the 1980s. This, of course, was the era of Thatcherism. Here modern Conservatism adopted the ideas of neoliberal economics and embraced the policy prescriptions of New Right thinking.

The aim now is to provide a cursory summary of how Thatcherite ideas began to filter through to urban policy. Much of this summary deals with the period from 1979 to 1986. More detailed analysis of this phase, and the changes that took place in urban policy under Conservative stewardship, are left to section 5.5. The Thatcher governments are famous for their distinct ideological 'style'. In these terms, the following axioms were espoused:

> The Thatcher Government entered office intent upon reducing the role of the state and the size of the public sector in Britain ... Reducing the welfare state would increase entrepreneurial drive in the economy, and replace notions of collective welfare protection with individualist and familial self-reliance and self-help. (King, 1987: 133)

The impact of New Right thinking in the urban policy arena was not immediately evident. Michael Heseltine, who was Peter Shore's successor at the DoE, indicated in September 1979 that policy was under review. Yet the Urban Programme, Heseltine assured, would in the meantime enjoy the same level of funding in 1980–81 as it had done in 1979–80. An intimation of a new ideological course for urban policy was provided in the first Urban Programme circular issued by the Thatcher administration. The document suggested that funds 'should be used for schemes which will assist in wealth creation rather than consumption' (cited in Hambleton, 1981: 58).

The valorization of wealth creation became translated in terms of an emphasis on economic regeneration and property-led development, mainly at the expense of social schemes aimed at alleviating deprivation. The Conservative government introduced a number of measures in accordance with this economic, property-led focus. An early innovation was the Urban Development Grant, established in 1981. This measure used developmental grants, administered by local authorities, to lever private sector investment in urban areas. Using a similar fiscal strategy, the government introduced the Derelict Land Grant to encourage public and private organizations to redevelop disused land. New policy structures were added to these financial initiatives. In 1981, 11 Enterprise Zones were formed to attract private investment and entrepreneurial activity to mainly inner-urban areas. The Enterprise Zones were not subject to local rates and planning regulations in a bid to create the unfettered market environment seen as crucial for wealth creation. By the 1990s, around 27 Enterprise Zones had been created.

The 1980 Local Government, Planning and Land Act which had created the Enterprise Zones was also responsible for Urban Development Corporations (hereafter, UDCs). In 1981, the first two were established in Liverpool and London Docklands, and by 1992 there were 12 UDCs. These bodies, packed with private sector appointees, were given powers for redeveloping land, without having to obtain local authority consent.

These were the early products of the new Conservative strategy for deprived urban areas, one that was further built upon, as will be shown, during the course of the 1980s. The ideological basis of Conservative thinking was distinct from that which had guided earlier Labour and even Conservative administrations:

> Clearly, the assumptions and expectations which guided this strategy in the 1980s were far removed from the ideas which inspired and shaped the Urban Programme and the Community Development Project in the decade before. Then local industry and commerce were defined as part of the problem; in the 1980s they became the solution ... Urban policy was guided by an economic imperative that elevated the importance of growth and diminished the value of equity. (Barnekov *et al.*, 1989: 215)

This analysis of urban policy from the mid-1970s through to the 1980s highlights the role of individuals in policy-making, and the beliefs they take into the whole process. Ideology, loosely defined here, shapes the direction and practical strategies for dealing with issues such as urban deprivation. Even so, policy is not driven *tout court* by purposeful actors, influenced by specific ideological commitments. Such action takes place in specific institutional settings. As will be demonstrated in the following section, institutional structures can have a significant bearing on the direction of policy.

5.5   The institutional context of urban policy

Ideology, as shown, closely informs the policy process. Ideas and beliefs set the priorities for those operational tasks that are attended to by policy-makers. The question that concerns this section now is: How do policy-makers enact their priorities and goals?

Clearly, policy agents do not operate in splendid isolation. They make their decisions and enact policies within existing institutional settings. This means that agents have to deal with a range of other policy actors (ministers and officials), fulfil certain responsibilities and build links with other institutions within the policy network. Initiating a course of policy action is not necessarily something which is unilaterally imposed from a single figure, occupying a powerful departmental position. Rather, it involves careful manoeuvring and jockeying within and between different organizations. Lewis and Flynn (1977: 133) observe:

> All organisations therefore have to develop strategies or 'modes of action' in relation to the other organisations within their environment in order to fulfil their aspirations. What emerged ... from ... this project were the variety of modes of action available to organisations in government.

Urban policy as Lewis and Flynn note, is dependent on a structure of interdependent relations between various organizations in the state machine. Thus central government is very much reliant on local authorities or external agencies of central government, such as the regional arms of central departments, to implement policy. Urban policy, throughout its various phases of development, has shown that such institutions can be used in a variety of forms. Changes to the institutional mix can, and are often intended to have, a distinct influence over the delivery of policy. The development of urban policy in the postwar period has displayed three dominant organizational paradigms. These models are generally specific to particular historical junctures, although there is a certain degree of continuity from one phase to another. The three central institutional models are: local-authority-centred model; a centrally directed model; and a regional model.

5.5.1 Local authorities as the 'natural vehicles' for urban policy

The first institutional paradigm adopted by governments in the postwar period focused on local authorities as the main conduits for delivering urban policy. It is the Urban Programme which has most closely embraced this particular model. This is significant as the Urban Programme came to dominate government inner-city policy during the 1970s.

Although of central importance, the level of discretion afforded to local authorities tended to change during the history of the Urban Programme. Originally, the Urban Programme was introduced as a centralized policy: priorities were set by the Home Office, broadly following a national strategy. Control of the Programme rested with the centre – local authorities, as such, were simply responsible for implementing policies established from above. A mechanism of grant funding allowed the centre to dictate the terms of local authority projects. In this arrangement, central government provided a grant, covering 75 per cent of the capital and revenue costs for projects established to alleviate stress in areas of special social need (Higgins *et al.*, 1983: 49).

The role of local authorities in all this was to submit proposals to the Home Office. Those submissions congruent with Home Office priorities were then selected for grant support. A high level of financial support was generally regarded within the Home Office as integral to the maintenance of central control (Edwards and Batley, 1978: 125). Thus, early initiatives reflected the concerns of the Home Office, and, more importantly, of the then prime minister, Harold Wilson. As demanded by Wilson, early projects were directed at immigrant communities and at the provision of welfare for children and education.

The Home Office was, at the same time, willing for local authorities to set the agenda for projects once the Programme was up and running. The second programme circular, issued in February 1969, requested local authorities to indicate their preferred areas for programme support. This latitude, though, was provided as a matter of administrative convenience. The official view was that 'in essence the Programme was largely centrally determined' (ibid. 125).

Gradually, local authorities demanded greater sensitivity from the centre towards their stated priorities. By 1973, the Home Office conceded ground on this issue, assuring local authorities that their first priorities would gain approval within financial parameters. Central departments could still recommend project types within circulars. And in practice, it was not always possible for local preferences to gain central support. Nevertheless, the Home Office in the mid-1970s attempted to enhance local authority influence and autonomy over the direction of urban policy.

Labour's reformulation of the Urban Programme in 1977 held overarching repercussions for local government involvement in urban policy. As shown above, the Programme, *inter alia*, became a protectorate of the DoE. As part of the DoE's responsibilities, local authorities were given a significant role. Indeed, the 1977 White Paper reiterated that local government was to be the natural vehicle for inner-urban projects.

Labour's revised Urban Programme bolstered local government's contribution to urban policy in three main respects. First, special partnership arrangements were formed with local institutions in selective areas. Here, the DoE would cooperate with both tiers of local government and various local bodies, such as health authorities and voluntary groups, to reverse inner-urban decline. Seven special areas were in the end chosen for these special partnership arrangements. Second, there were to be extra resources available for the Urban Programme. Resources for the Programme were increased from £30 million to £125 million per annum. The seven Partnership Areas would receive £66 million. The next largest share went to 14 'second tier' deprivation areas, known as programme authorities. The remaining monies were distributed to various designated districts under traditional Urban Programme arrangements. Finally, the Inner Urban Areas Act of 1978 gave additional powers to select local authorities for locally directed forms of economic intervention. This included powers to assist industry, such as the ability to declare industrial improvement areas (Hambleton, 1981: 56).

Throughout the life course of the Urban Programme, local authorities gained increasing autonomy in dictating the direction of urban policy. However, the change of government in 1979 ushered in a distinct approach in relation to local involvement in urban policy and in relation to the sovereignty of local government in general.

5.5.2 Organizational centralization and fragmentation of urban institutions

There was no immediate sign that the new Conservative government was about to revolutionize urban policy. The traditional Urban Programme reformed by Labour was maintained. Nonetheless, a new institutional model for delivering inner-urban renewal began to evolve. The emphasis on the market as a panacea for urban ills was accompanied by a growing disregard for local authority involvement. Several initiatives, throughout the 1980s, meant that local government became less a natural vehicle than a peripheral agent in urban renewal. Three developments stand out.

First, the Urban Programme, although it survived the 1980s, was reduced in scope and capacity. Under the reconstructed Urban Programme of the mid-1970s, local authorities became the natural vehicles for directing intervention in urban areas. Successive Conservative governments mapped out a less prominent role for the Urban Programme, and, by implication, local authorities. In the summer of 1987, the government reduced the number of authorities that could apply for Urban Programme grants from 150 to 57. Second, in a related development, central funding for the Urban Programme was redirected into other initiatives, in particular the Urban Development Corporations. In 1991–92, the Urban Programme received £242 million while the Urban Development Corporations were given £501 million in the same financial year (Willmott and Hutchison, 1992: 74). Third, these shifts in institutional arrangements form a part of wider developments in central–local relations. Throughout the 1980s central government imposed several punitive measures on the spending and tax-raising powers of local authorities. There have also been a number of changes in the grant provision for local authorities – with needy areas receiving proportionally less government support than other authorities.

The declining influence of local government was not matched by a waning interest in urban renewal. For a government committed to reducing the frontiers of the state, it was ironic that a whole panoply of measures were introduced throughout the 1980s. New Conservative ideology maintained that state intervention was not sufficient. Governments in this period focused on the private sector and the market as vital to inner-urban development. Entrepreneurial activity, liberating planning regulations, financial match-making, property development, private sector involvement: these were the chief means for bringing prosperity to inner cities. A distinct institutional structure emerged around these new policy concerns; a structure which reserved a less prominent part for local government.

The organizational framework that emerged after 1981 had contradictory features. On the one hand, urban policy was directed and controlled by central Whitehall departments, especially the DoE. Centralization was reinforced by restrictions placed on local authority finances and the creation of programmes that bypassed local authorities. On the other hand, there was increased fragmentation in the organizational framework for delivering urban renewal. A whole range of initiatives, originating from different departments, came to the fore. The DoE was the leading department, overseeing the Urban Development Corporations and City Grant; the Home Office controlled Section 11 funding; the Department of Employment established the urban Task Forces for inner cities and Technical and Enterprise Councils.

The Urban Development Corporations typified the organizational framework that was emerging under the Conservatives. The UDCs were launched in 1981. Two such bodies were originally established, with the numbers swelling to 12 by 1992. The UDCs were given planning powers for specified areas. This provided a means for 'bypassing the bureaucratic inflexibility of local councils by promoting a more entrepreneurial spirit' (Hill, 1994: 184). Most UDC boards were packed full of ministerial appointees, mainly local business leaders with local government being minimized to token representatives. Birmingham Heartlands UDC, created in 1992, was the first such body to have equal local and central government appointed representation (ibid.).

Initiatives like the UDCs led to an upward shift, from local to central government, in terms of control over urban policy. It would be a severe oversight to argue, however, that local authorities were completely stripped of their powers to intervene in urban areas. Local authorities – curtailed in number – could still apply for Urban Programme support, certainly up until 1992 when the programme was scrapped. But, Urban Programme monies were increasingly dependent on councils establishing partnerships with other agencies. The City Challenge scheme was typical of this partnership-dependent funding project.

A number of authorities endeavoured to weaken dependency on central financial support. This was evident in the proactive, interventionist economic policies embraced by several authorities during the 1980s. In the early part of this decade, a number of Labour-controlled metropolitan or large city authorities reacted against these policy orthodoxies. An alternative urban strategy was pursued to that of central government's preference for divesting powers to the private sector. This locally emergent strategy involved a policy of what Goodwin and Duncan term 'restructuring for labour'. Emphasis was placed 'on using firms for the development *of* an area *for* its people, to be contrasted with using an area for the development of firms *in* an area' (Goodwin and Duncan, 1986: 19; original emphasis).

New organizational arrangements were put in place to implement these policies. Second-tier authorities like the Greater London Council and the West Midlands, Lancashire, West Yorkshire and Merseyside County Councils established 'Enterprise Boards' during the early part of the 1980s. These were created for the main purpose of intervening in the local economy and for investing in local industry. Interventionist authorities at district level developed internal structures to aid economic development. Sheffield formed an employment department and Leeds established an industry and estates department (Mawson and Miller, 1986: 146).

This interventionist approach pursued by these councils was antithetic to the dominant urban policy of central government. This obviously rancoured with the government. In subsequent reforms, the Conservatives abolished the mainly Labour-controlled metropolitan tier of local government, where this alternative strategy was prevalent. The government's urban strategy, prioritizing as it did quangos over local government, attempted in part to remove such opposition. They also placed resources into the hands of agencies that were more amenable to central policy demands.

5.5.3   The regionalization of urban policy

Successive Conservative administrations during the 1980s demonstrated that policy institutions are not static entities. The institutional arrangements ushered in by successive Conservative administrations differed markedly from those adopted in the 1970s, although vestiges of the old system such as the Urban Programme were maintained for some time. The diaspora of schemes and bodies that characterized the organizational network under the government encountered criticism. The Audit Commission (1989: 1) in a report of urban policy observed as follows:

> Government support programmes are seen as a patchwork quilt of complexity and idiosyncrasy … The rules of the game seem over-complex and sometimes capricious. They encourage compartmentalised policy approaches rather than a coherent strategy.

To address these problems the report argued for local government to be more closely involved in urban policy and for central government to attach greater importance to the coordination of intervention.

The City Action Teams formed in 1985 and 1988 went some way towards bringing greater coordination. The teams consisted of the Regional Directors of the Departments of Employment, Environment and Trade and Industry. Their task was to coordinate government expenditure for inner areas. The main break with the 1980s orthodoxy came later in 1991, with the introduction of City Challenge. As already seen, City Challenge incorporated social as well as economic goals. More importantly, the organizational structure introduced by the new scheme gave a more pronounced role for local authorities. At the same time, central government in the form of the DoE still retained a high level of control over the whole process: given that the DoE administered the competition, ministers and senior officials were in a position to direct funding into desired areas. As shown, however, after two rounds City Challenge was disbanded.

Yet this scheme and the earlier City Action Teams initiative were the precursors to the Single Regeneration Budget (hereafter, SRB), the most recent development in urban policy. With this policy, came a new organizational structure. For all intents and purposes, the institutional framework introduced by the SRB is essentially a regional structure.

To administer the new integrated budget, ten regional offices for England were established in April 1994. These integrated offices were formed by merging the regional units of the Department of Environment, Department of Trade and Industry, Department of Transport and the Department of Employment; it was also planned that offices should also work closely with the Home Office and the Departments for Education, National Heritage and Health. Directors headed each of the four main departments represented within the Government Offices, known as directorates. This is very much in keeping with the structure that existed before the introduction of the Government Offices (see Keating and Rhodes, 1982: 54–5). But in contrast to the preceding system of authority, the lines of responsibility for these directorates converged onto a single Regional Director.

The central responsibility of the Government Offices in relation to the urban policy was that of overseeing the SRB process. A crucial part of this responsibility involved regional officials liaising closely with relevant external parties: namely, local authorities, businesses and voluntary groups. The SRB allowed local authorities, in the main, to play a leading role in the development of bids. Yet the Government Offices were integral to the assessment of bids and thus played a significant role in shaping local initiatives. In one questionnaire, 55 per cent of respondents claimed that Government Office assessments of outline bids were critical in shaping their eventual strategies. Moreover, 42 per cent made similar observations about the regional office guidance on geographical targeting (Mawson *et al.*, 1995: 23). In the capital, officers at the Government Office for London were involved in establishing and developing the East Thames Side Partnership, led by Barking and Dagenham, Havering and Newham councils. This partnership was encouraged because it tied in with central plans for the redevelopment of the East Thames corridor (Davies and Tym, 1993).

The Government Offices of the regions are essentially the bureaucratic and administrative functions of central departments. Such a development has been termed by the Association of Metropolitan Authorities as *creeping executive regionalism* (AMA, 1995). This refers to the way in which the new regional structures have, by and large, further extended rather than devolved executive power. With a limited pot of money available, the Department of Environment established a number of stringent conditions for bidders, which the Government Offices are entrusted to implement. The government has expected that proposals would have to meet one or more of seven main objectives: enhance employment prospects, encourage sustainable economic growth, improve housing, promote benefits to ethnic minorities, tackle crime, protect the environment, and enhance the quality of life for people (DoE, 1994: 4–5).

The argument here is that the structure of the Government Offices, and the lines of responsibility between Regional Directors suggest that their main priority is to do the bidding of central departments on urban policy initiatives.

5.6   The wider socio–economic context and urban regeneration

Ideological and organizational factors undoubtedly make a prominent contribution to the policy process. The day-to-day operations of policy-makers tend to be dominated by dealings within their own department or other parts of the government machine. However, the policy process cannot be separated from events taking place outside the institutional machinery of government. Social developments can have a profound effect on the actions of policy-makers and the institutions they inhabit.

It may not be relevant to include an examination of the wider social context in all policy situations. But this should not in any way diminish the significance of these external forces (Layder, 1994: 89–90). The 'world outside the organization', to use Lewis and Flynn's terminology, impinges upon the policy process, in one form or other; it is the analyst's prerogative whether to focus on these wider forces.

Marxist theoreticians, as shown, have made an important contribution to this whole debate. They have asserted, problematically in certain respects, that government action reinforces and protects the interests of those groups in society that hold wealth, property, and control economic forces in general. There are problems, as shown, in subsuming policy analysis under the general and functional precepts of Marxist theory (see section 3.2.2). Nevertheless, the workings of the capitalist economic system do present certain structural challenges to policy-makers. The issue of urban deprivation exemplifies this to be so.

Urban policy is intimately tied to the economic deterioration and decline of inner-urban areas. Such conditions within inner-urban areas are the result of forces beyond the immediate control of policy agents. Some conceptualize deprivation as a consequence of particular social or local pathologies. It is argued that there is a malfunctioning specific to urban areas which leads to economic malaise in these localities. In-depth analysis reveals the shallowness and analytical redundancy of this conception (Massey and Meegan, 1982: 123–4). Urban economic decline, more appropriately, is linked to general structural features concerning developments in the domestic and international economy. Harrison (1985: 47) notes: 'The inner city, like the depressed regions, is the inevitable result of the unplanned, destructive way in which the British economy adjusts to changes in the global economy.'

The unyielding drive towards commercial, financial, and productive interdependence of the global economy has been a prominent factor behind the decline of heavy, labour-intensive industries. For British society, these manufacturing industries were the basis of secure employment and financial security for whole regions. Within the context of the modern global economy, these industries found themselves under severe foreign competition. They were ill-equipped to sustain such pressure, because productive capacity was denied proper levels of investment, much of it destined abroad. In this integrated system, Britain together with America was a slow-growth economy and lacked the dynamism of Germany and Japan. Thus, when shocks to the world economy were administered – specifically in the mid-1970s and the early 1980s – Britain's economy, and especially its industrial base, was susceptible to deep recession.

In spatial terms the decline of the manufacturing base in Britain has proven to be unequal. The socio-economic standing of urban districts are intertwined with the fortunes of manufacturing and heavy industrial sectors. Historically, these have formed the mainstay of employment opportunities in these areas. Trends in manufacturing employment changed dramatically during the postwar period. Up to the mid-1960s, manufacturing employment grew steadily, reaching a peak in 1966. Indeed, the whole British economy in this period, like all advanced capitalist countries, grew steadily at a rate of 4 per cent, which brought a level of socio-economic stability (Harvey and Swyngedouw, 1993: 13).

By the mid-1960s, the economy as a whole, but especially the heavy industrial sector, began to slow down. Manufacturing industries were naturally embroiled in this downward turn – output and productivity in the manufacturing sector dropped. Nationally, this meant that manufacturing jobs at best grew slowly or, at worst, underwent rapid decline. If the rates of decline are broken down geographically, the winners and losers do not easily follow a crude north versus south dividing line (see Fothergill and Gudging, 1982). On the other hand, once the rates of decline are broken down subregionally a significant pattern emerges. Large urban subregions – the capital, large industrial conurbations, free standing cities, industrial towns – have experienced a marked decrease in manufacturing employment since 1966. In London, there was a 5.1 per cent decrease in manufacturing employment between 1971 and 1975. In the same period, large industrial conurbations such as Birmingham, Manchester and Clydeside saw a 2.2 per cent decrease. By contrast, rural areas and county towns have faired much better, seeing growth, albeit modest, in the manufacturing sector (Fothergill and Gudgin, 1982: 23).

These disparities can be partly explained by the postwar New Towns programme, promoting the movement of industry from cities to more rural locations. This decentralization of industry was seen to combat overcrowding. But the general decline of the manufacturing sector created few alternative sources of employment in large industrial towns. Areas such as the South East, generally regarded as prosperous, saw a diminution of manufacturing unemployment in the 1970s; the rate of decline in traditional industrial areas like Scotland was even more rapid. According to Fothergill and Gudgin (1982: 20). 'much of the blame must be placed on the declining competitiveness and employment of British manufacturing industry as a whole.'

Commentators are generally agreed that the decline in manufacturing could have been alleviated by greater investment in new technology. This would have enabled the manufacturing sector to resist foreign competition and maintain a reasonable level of labour productivity. Britain, historically, through its early industrialization and colonial interests, has developed a strong orientation towards investing in the international market. This tendency was exacerbated by the move towards global integration during the postwar years. As such, the needs of financial capital on the world markets rather than the needs of domestic manufacturing industry have prevailed (Judge and Dickson, 1987: 9–12).

Manufacturing decline leads to growing levels of unemployment in large urban areas. This in turn holds deleterious social consequences for these localities:

> The deterioration in the economic bases of Britain's cities is the single most important parameter of decline, which has an impact across the board. Reduced income affects the ability of individuals and indeed of entire communities to operate effectively within a range of private and public markets, such as retailing, education and transport. (Lawless, 1986: 24–5)

Historically, these periods of socioeconomic decline, and their concomitant impact on jobs, have shaped the development of inner urban policy. The Urban Programme of 1968 partly emerged as a result of the rediscovery of poverty in the 1960s. Despite the strides made towards welfare provision, the spectre of poverty, especially in urban areas, was still in evidence. The Urban Programme responded to such developments. Peter Shore's bold effort to reform the Urban Programme in the mid-1970s was preceded, and very much influenced, by a sudden economic downturn. Between 1974 and 1976, the British economy entered a deep recession. In this period, manufacturing employment across all regions fell by 8 per cent (Fothergill and Gudgin, 1982: 18). A speech given by Shore in January 1977 intimated that his developing strategy for cities was informed by the recession's impact on inner-urban economies:

> The first objective in my list would be to improve the local economies of the inner-city areas. In present-day conditions, when there is not very much brand new commercial and industrial development, our top priority must be to preserve the jobs that at present exist. (cited in Higgins *et al.*, 1983: 126–7)

The recession of the early 1980s ensured that urban regeneration remained a pressing and urgent issue. All indicators, especially levels of unemployment, suggest this was a particularly intensive period of economic decline. The rate of unemployment between 1977 and 1982 had doubled to around 12 per cent. Urban areas have done worse than other parts of the country. Unemployment levels in Scotland stood at 14 per cent, in the West Midlands at 15 per cent and around 17 per cent in the north of England (Barnekov *et al.*, 1989). Inner-city areas could be described as high concentration unemployment zones, such was the intensity of the recession on manufacturing and heavy industries. During the spring and summer of 1981, a number of these inner-city areas witnessed social disturbances and rioting. Subsequent public inquiries blamed aggressive policing for the civil unrest. Even so, declining economic conditions and job prospects could not be ruled out as contributory factors.

Whatever the reasons, events in the early 1980s provoked further responses from the government in relation to the inner-urban problem. Barnekov *et al.* (1989: 181) note that the recession of the early 1980s not only led 'to a concentration of national policy on economic issues, it had a profound effect on the implementation of urban policy and the role of local government.' As outlined above, the 1980s, under successive Conservative administrations, gave rise to a whole variety of urban measures. These were underpinned by a specific ideology – one that upheld the market, entrepreneurial activity and property-led development as vehicles for reversing urban decline.

The argument pursued here is that the policy-making process is not a phenomenon whose main reference points are wholly specific to the government machine. Events and movements outside policy institutions can influence the priorities, programmes and agendas of policy-makers. Urban initiatives have tended to intensify during periods of economic decline, mainly because these recessions have proven to be especially damaging for urban localities.

Although governments have stepped-up their programmes during periods of recession, the pressure for regenerating cities has proven to be ongoing. Urban policy initiatives have endeavoured to tackle problems which are deeply embedded in the socio-economic structure of society. The historically entrenched economic decline witnessed in urban areas has given rise to entrenched cycles of deprivation. A number of studies have chronicled the disadvantaged position of those social groups within the inner-urban context.

Willmott and Hutchison (1992) conducted a survey of socio-economic conditions in 32 major urban centres identified as deprived by the government. Statistical evidence between 1977 and 1991 was used to 'examine how far economic, physical and social conditions in deprived areas are improving or deteriorating (in absolute terms or relative to the rest of the country)' (ibid. 1). There are certain positive trends identified in the survey. Conspicuous examples include improvements in infant mortality and the falling number of children taken into care (ibid. 80). However, the aggregate picture from key life-chance indicators seems to be bleak: 'in general the gap between conditions and opportunities in deprived areas . . . remains as wide as it was a decade and a half ago. In some respects the gap has widened' (ibid. 82).

The growing inequalities can in part be explained by government policy, especially those pursued during the 1980s. Most notably, the fall in financial support being directed from the centre to deprived areas and the decline in social housing have been responsible for growing levels of deprivation in urban areas. At the same time, the relative fortunes of the economy, and the effects of this on industry and employment opportunities, have exacerbated levels of deprivation.

In terms of unemployment, those urban areas in the survey experienced greater rises in unemployment up to 1986. Large conurbations like London and Manchester experienced particularly high levels of unemployment. These areas did share in the general employment increases brought about by the boom years of the late 1980s. However, their share of new jobs was proportionately less than in other parts of the country. Birmingham is a case in point. In 1983, unemployment in travel-to-work areas of this city stood at 74.2 per cent and in 1991 this increased to 75.9 per cent (Willmott and Hutchison, 1992: 16).

Unemployment, in turn, effects poverty levels. Poverty, as measured by the proportion receiving income support, has fluctuated according to movements in the economy. Those families in poverty within urban areas grew more than in other areas. For instance, those people of working age receiving income support within 23 urban English areas were higher in 1989–91 than in 1983–85 (ibid. 40).

Focusing on external developments should not divert attention from the fact that government policies can in their own right effect the social impact of the wider economy. This has been especially evident during the Conservative-dominated 1980s. Certain policies, such as privatization and the stringent conditions placed on welfare claimants, have added to the burden of deprivation experienced within urban areas. Thus it seems ironic that in certain respects the government has added to the social problems wrought by the workings of the national and international economy.

5.7   Conclusion

The first case study in this text has attempted to provide a general overview of the different levels of analysis required in studying the policy process. Indeed, analysis of the policy process entails an assessment of the various influences on policy-making. This exploration was pursued through a case study of urban policy. Lewis and Flynn's behaviour model was used to identify those general levels of social and political life that have influenced the development of urban policy in Britain. The behavioural model is generally congruent with the sociological framework advocated in this text.

Significantly, it takes into account the role of the individual, the institutional context and the world outside those organizations responsible for policy. In this case study, the role of the individual is most evident here in the way agents influenced the ideological agenda of how to address the problems of urban deprivation; the institutional context was analyzed in terms of the way it has been used to shape the delivery of urban policy; and the most relevant aspect of the external context in relation to urban policy has been the global economy and levels of socio-economic deprivation.

The levels of analysis covered in this case study are quite separate entities. In reality, though, there are a series of linkages between all three levels. This is to be expected, as the three levels of analysis are parallel in certain respects to the dichotomy between agency and structure. Agency and structure do have distinct properties, yet there are mutual and significant links between these two features of reality. Similar mutual links are evident in the three levels of analysis covered in this chapter. They are apparent for instance in the way the problems of urban deprivation emerged. The socio-economic forces, together with the actions of politicians such as Enoch Powell, Harold Wilson and Peter Shore, contributed what Hogwood and Gunn (1984: 88–90) call the 'issue filtration' of the urban question in government. In developing an interventionist response to this perceived problem, individual policy agents and the institutional machine at their disposal assumed equal significance.

The next two case studies in this section each focus on a single level of analysis within a specific policy field. This will not deny the importance of the other levels of analysis. Such a practice involves what has been termed the bracketing together of particular levels of analysis for more detailed examination.

STUDY GUIDE

Chronology of events surrounding the development of urban policy in the postwar period

1967:   At the end of this year, an interdepartmental working party was established under the chairmanship of Derek Morrell, a senior Home Office official. It was formed to discuss ideas about promoting a coherent strategy for community development.

1968:   Early in this year an interdepartmental working party, chaired by the Home Office, is established to review immigration and race relations policy. The working party considered a support scheme for helping the integration of newly arriving immigrants.

1968 (April):   Enoch Powell delivers his racist 'rivers of blood' speech, warning against further increases in the immigrant population. It is argued that this provided the event for the announcement of the Urban Programme, a funding support mechanism for inner-urban areas, especially those localities with high immigrant populations. Before the speech, however, the Home Office was looking into the possibility of greater financial assistance for immigrant communities.

1968 (May):   Harold Wilson, the prime minister, formally announces the Urban Programme. The decision to form the Urban Programme was influenced by the results of the interdepartmental working party. The task of managing the Urban Programme was given to the Home Secretary. The Home Office was chosen to oversee the Programme because of its proximity to race relations – the issue which provided the immediate stimulus for the Urban Programme. Two days after Wilson's announcement, a new working party was established to develop the programme. The working party and the interdepartmental committee announced that local authorities would be used to administer the Programme. The early projects conducted at a local level were very much proscribed by the centre.

1968 (4 October):   The first Home Office circular is sent to local authorities, inviting bids for Urban Programme support funding.

1968:   The Report of the interdepartmental working party, entitled *Community Development – An Experiment in Social Growth*, was published in June. Details were included of the Community Development Project, revolving around 12 community-based research teams. These were to be given a £60,000 budget to conduct research into social growth. This was not a programme about poverty essentially, but a means towards encouraging personal and moral growth through what were termed community experiments. The scheme was accepted by the Labour government, although it aroused little interest in the parliamentary Labour party. Some politicians, in fact, were suspicious of the scheme.

1969 (July):   The Community Development Project (hereafter, CDP) was formally announced. The following year, in 1970, the CDP came into being. The original enthusiasm that greeted the scheme in 1968 was less evident by 1970.

Indeed, some local authorities and academics hindered the progress of the scheme by arguing over the placement of projects.

1971:   There were calls from local project directors for less centralized control over the teams by the Central Research Unit at the Home Office. Gradually, in this period, the Home Office's control over the projects began to wane as CDP directors turned to the Consultative Council, within the Centre for Environmental Studies, for advice.

1972:   The Coventry CDP team began arguing for a more structural rather than personalized appreciation of urban deprivation.

1972:   Final decisions over the location areas for the research teams were finally accomplished in this year.

1972:   Following the Conservative election victory of 1970, Peter Walker, then Conservative Secretary of State for the Environment, established three Inner Area Studies (hereafter, IAS) in Lambeth, Liverpool and Birmingham. This began the Department of the Environment's (hereafter, DoE) close association with urban policy. A number of working papers and reports are produced by the IAS over the course of the next four years. These seem to indicate a move towards a more total approach in which greater emphasis is given over to the structural causes of urban deprivation.

1974:   A new Labour government is elected.

1974:   Following a Home Office management review of the CDP in this year, cuts were administered to the project. At the same time, a number of teams began to publishing reports through the Information Intelligence Unit (hereafter, IIU), established in 1973. The closure of the IIU contributed to the eventual abrogation of the CDP.

1974 (July): see above examples. The new Labour Home Secretary, Roy Jenkins, announced in this year a new strategy for inner-urban regeneration, the Comprehensive Community Programme (hereafter, CCP). This came to dominate government urban intervention between 1973 and 1975. The CCP attempted to introduce a comprehensive strategy for tackling inner-city blight and thus acted as a significant forerunner to the inner-city policy announced by Peter Shore in 1977. The attempt to develop a more coordinated approach in tackling urban deprivation grew out of a wider movement to adopt a 'joint approach to social policy'. The Cabinet Office think tank, the Central Policy Review Staff, was at the forefront of these discussions, issuing a report, *A Joint Framework for Social Policies* in 1975.

1974 (February):   The Home Secretary is confirmed as the minister responsible for coordinating urban policy. There is confusion at the appointment of Charles Morris as minister for urban affairs by the DoE. It was unclear how this would impact upon the Home Office's role. This seemed to be a misunderstanding over the Home Secretary's role in these matters. As a result, the Home Secretary was once again confirmed as the minister in charge for urban policy development. The minister for urban affairs was given certain responsibilities in the DoE but the position was subsequently scrapped.

1974 (July):   The Home Secretary unveils plans for the Comprehensive Community Programme. An interdepartmental subcommittee was formed to receive regular reports on the progress of CCP. Six local authorities were chosen to run the CCP: Bradford, Gateshead, Wandsworth, Wirral, Merthyr Tydfil, and Motherwell. There were difficulties in focusing on single deprived areas within these authorities. This was a point of concern for officials at the Home Office. The CCP was subsequently reformulated. Local authorities could propose more than one area for CCP support.

1975 (July):   Ministers announce further progress towards the implementation of the CCP before Parliament went into recess for the autumn. However, there was also opposition from the Treasury against further spending for the CCP. Little progress was made by the following year. The CCP was enacted in two local authorities but the scheme was no more than a coordinating exercise.

1975 (August):   The CCP may have been losing momentum, but political events in this month gave a much needed fillip to urban policy. In August, the Cabinet met at Chequers to review public spending. It was decided from the meeting that high priority should be given to tackling inner-city deprivation. This task was entrusted to an interdepartmental committee under the chairmanship of the DoE's chief planner, Wilfred Burns. The DoE gained responsibility because of its close involvement with local government. This indicated that responsibility over urban policy was moving in the direction of the DoE. The Burns committee, whose report was never published, recommended the continuation of the Urban Programme and the CCP. It argued that these programmes should be progressively adapted. It was noted that progress could be made providing there was the political will. It was decided that a group of junior ministers, under the chairmanship of a cabinet minister, would reappraise the whole area of urban intervention. This was subsequently achieved under Peter Shore.

1976:   Two CDP projects are closed in this year because of local troubles.

1976 (September):   Peter Shore replaces Anthony Crosland as Secretary of State for the Environment. Under Shore, urban issues are given higher priority in the DoE. In the same month, a Cabinet Committee, chaired by Shore, is formed to examine inner-city problems.

1977 (April):   The government announces reduced funding for new town policies. The following day, Peter Shore outlines the government's new strategy for urban regeneration. It is revealed that the Urban Programme will be transferred from the Home Office to the DoE. In addition, the Programme was to be expanded from £30 million to £125 million per annum. Local authorities eligible for such funding were separated into three different categories.

1977 (June):   This strategy is explained in greater detail in the DoE White Paper, *Policy for the Inner Cities*, published in this month. The White Paper details how urban policy will adopt a more unified and coordinated approach.

1977 (November):   The first Urban Programme circular under the DoE is issued in this month. At this stage, authorities have not been separated into tiers and as such the programme continues in its original form.

1978 (August):   The new tiered arrangements come into effect in this year.

1978:   The remaining 10 CDP teams are wound up in this year.

1979 (May):   The Conservatives under Margaret Thatcher gain power.

1979 (May):   Michael Heseltine, the new Secretary of State at the DoE, embarks on a review of urban policy.

1980 (March):   The review initiated by Heseltine is completed. In April of this year, the minister for local government, Tom King, declares that the Urban Programme may be disbanded. This suggestion is heavily criticized and is subsequently dropped.

1980:   The Local Government Planning and Land Act of this year allowed central government to form Urban Development Corporations (hereafter, UDCs). The UDCs were created to regenerate specific urban areas by endeavouring to attract private sector funds. The agencies had powers to clear, service and act as the development controllers.

1980:   In addition to the UDCs, the 1980 Local Government, Planning and Land Act established Enterprise Zones. These zones covered specific derelict, mainly urban, locations. Within these areas certain planning regulations were relaxed and financial incentives were provided, including dispensation from local rates for a period of time. Eleven Enterprise Zones were formed in 1981.

Altogether 27 Enterprise Zones were created up to the 1990s. Not all of these were found within inner-urban areas.

1981:   Two UDCs were introduced in this year. These were established in the docklands of London and Liverpool.

1981 (February):   Heseltine confirms that the Urban Programme will not be disbanded and that some procedural simplifications would be made instead.

1981 (spring and summer):   There is a spate of inner-city rioting in areas such as Brixton, Toxteth and Moss Side. Subsequent inquiries blame heavy-handed policing, but urban deprivation is an underlying factor in this breakdown of social order.

1981:   The Secretary of State for the Environment, Michael Heseltine, creates the Merseyside Task Force following the riots in Liverpool.

1982:   Michael Heseltine announced the formation of Urban Development Grants in this year. The objective of these grants was to use public subsidies for levering private sector resources for inner-urban development. There was no actual restriction on the type of projects that could be funded. After 1984, greater emphasis was placed on private sector-led, physical regeneration projects.

1985:   In this year, six City Action Teams were formed in Urban Partnership areas of Liverpool, Birmingham, London, Newcastle, Gateshead and Manchester. Two more City Action Teams were formed in Nottingham and Leeds. Each team was headed by Regional Directors from the DoE, Department of Employment, and Department of Trade and Industry. Their task was to direct government expenditure worth £850 million per annum. In addition, the government established inner-city Task Forces, consisting of teams of civil servants and private sector secondees. By 1988, there were 16 of these Task Forces.

1985:   In this year, closer monitoring of projects is introduced through the Urban Programme Management Initiative. The monitoring system used several numerical output measures against which projects would be assessed. The programmes supported under the Urban Programme began to prioritize projects with an economic emphasis.

1986:   The traditional Urban Programme through which a large number of authorities outside major conurbations received small funds was discontinued.

1987:   The local authorities eligible for Urban Programme funding was redefined. At this point, 57 authorities became eligible for support funding, a reduction from 150 authorities previously covered by the Urban Programme.

1987:   Five more UDCs were created in this year – these were found in the Black Country, Teesside, Trafford Park, Tyneside and Cardiff Bay. Three smaller UDCs were formed at the end of 1987 in Bristol, Leeds, and Manchester. A further UDC was formed in 1988 in the Lower Don Valley in Sheffield. It was calculated that by 1988–89, the UDCs controlled over 40,000 acres of land and would receive £200 million in central grant support.

1987:   The new Urban Regeneration Grant is introduced, in part to overcome the perceived weaknesses of the Urban Development Grant. The new grant system did not require developers to make initial applications to local authorities, who were regarded as too bureaucratic and cumbersome in their handling of grant requests. Instead, contractors would apply for subsidies direct to the DoE. The grant support was made available for development projects covering substantial tracts of land – 20 acres, or more – or large concentrations of existing buildings. Only five projects were approved by the time the government introduced a new grant system in 1988.

1988:   The government announced a new grant scheme for inner urban development to replace the Urban Development Grant and Urban Regeneration Grant. The new City Grant is detailed in the government document, *Action for Cities*. The City Grant was specifically designed for capital development projects which could not take place without central subsidy. Priority was given to projects within the 57 Urban Programme authorities, although local authorities would not be involved in devising and assessing bids.

1990 (November):   After John Major's election to the leadership of the Conservative Party, Michael Heseltine was appointed Secretary of State for the Environment. At Heseltine's behest, a review was undertaken of the DoE's urban initiatives.

1991 (March):   At this point, Heseltine indicated his preference for a new urban funding scheme based around a competitive bidding system. The new scheme was to be called City Challenge and its was introduced publicly at a speech to the Manchester Chamber of Commerce on 11 March 1991.

1991 (May):   City Challenge was formally launched in this month. Fifteen out of 57 Urban Programme authorities were invited to submit bids for additional funding. Of this number, only 11 authorities would end-up being successful. Later another six Urban Programme authorities were allowed to make bids.

1991 (July): The DoE announced the 11 successful bidders, who would claim £7.5 million per annum over a five-year period.

1992 (February): A second round of City Challenge is launched. Here 54 Urban Programme authorities participated in the competition, where £750 million was available to all successful authorities over a five-year period. The 20 winners of the second round are announced in July 1992.

1992: There was a growing realization that the new Secretary of State at the Environment, Michael Howard, was not entirely enthusiastic about City Challenge. Because of public sector cuts, there was a danger that the scheme would be scrapped. Hence, there was no City Challenge scheme for 1993–94.

1992 (April): An election is called in this month. The Conservative party manifesto emphasized the benefits of City Challenge and the competitive bidding system adopted by the scheme. The manifesto pledges to further extend the competitive bidding system. It also outlines details for greater coordination of government policy through the commitment to bring resources together under a single integrated budget.

1992: A new UDC is formed in this year – the Birmingham Heartlands UDC. This agency was significant because it was the first UDC to have equal central and local government representation on the main board. Up to then most UDCs were mainly filled with business representatives appointed by central government. Calculations show that the proportion of inner-urban spending committed to the UDCs increased from 31.4 per cent in 1987–88 to 62.9 per cent in 1990–91.

1993: The Leasehold Reform, Housing and Urban Development Act of this year established the Urban Regeneration Agency (hereafter, URA) in England. The URA, termed English Partnerships, began in November 1993. The new scheme combined the existing funding programmes of Derelict Land Grant, City Grant and English Estates. The UPA had responsibility for upgrading derelict land in partnership with local authorities and the private sector. Local authority regulations could be side-stepped by the agency, although the URA was instructed to work alongside local groups.

1993 (November): The new Secretary of State for the Environment, John Gummer, announced a major reorganization of the urban policy with the introduction of the integrated offices for the regions and the Single Regeneration Budget (hereafter, SRB). The new budget was to be made available throughout the English regions and merged 20 separate programmes, worth £1.4 billion, across five different departments. Like City Challenge, the new SRB was to be distributed through a competitive bidding system administered by the various integrated Government Offices. This initiative effectively marked the end of the Urban Programme as all English local authorities could apply for SRB money.

1994 (April–September):   The bidding period for the first round began. This involved local partnerships making submissions to regional offices. This was a two-tier process, involving outline bids followed by the submission of final bidding documents in September.

1994 (December):   The first successful bids under the SRB are announced. Altogether 201 bids succeed in gaining SRB support across the 10 regional offices.

A reading schedule

To find useful literature concerning the idea of levels of analysis it is important to venture outside policy analysis. The arena where these issues have been given a great deal of consideration is in sociological thinking. Layder's (1993, 1994) two texts are especially useful for theoretical and methodological discussions pertaining to debates about micro and macro levels of analysis. There are some texts in the policy field where such issues are examined. Look, in particular, at Ham and Hill (1993: chapters 1 and 10) and two respective articles by Degeling and Colebatch (1984) and Castles (1981).

As far as urban policy is concerned, the extensive policy initiatives of recent years have given rise to a veritable cottage industry in both academic research and government documents on the subject. For an excellent overview of urban policy, check articles by Lawless (1988) and Edwards and Deakin (1992). There are many different books on urban policy, but Barnekov et al.'s (1989) collective effort is a comprehensive overview and covers policy developments up to the mid-1980s. Hill's (1994) solo piece, on the other hand, covers contemporary developments. There is also some excellent official documentation on this policy area. Robson et al.'s (1994) effort is excellent and the Audit Commission's (1989) review is a very revealing, critical account of Conservative urban policy. There are Environment Committee reports (22 November 1995, Session 1995-96), included in the Parliamentary Papers, that provide a useful analysis of the Single Regeneration Budget.

Issues for revision and further consideration

Having studied this case study you should be familiar with several key concepts relevant to policy analysis. These are as follows: levels of analysis (sections 5.1 and 5.3); policy agents (5.4); ideology and the New Right (5.4); institutional context (5.5); centralization and fragmentation of policy (5.5.2); regionalization of urban policy (5.5.3); the socio-economic context (5.6).

▶ To what extent do you think that multiple levels of analysis are applicable to other policy areas? Use some examples.

▶ In urban policy, how far are these three levels of analysis linked?

▶ What does the historical overview of urban policy show and why is such a historical dimension useful in policy analysis? (See Chapter 4.)

▶ What is Mrs Thatcher's legacy in an area like urban regeneration? Does this extend to other areas of policy? (See Chapters 6, 7 and 8.)

Chapter **6**

The essence of agency: policy agents and contractual relations in local government

6.1 Introduction

How do policy agents in public institutions behave? How do they influence and shape policy? On the other hand, is it possible to dictate the action of agents operating in public institutions?

These points of discussion will inform the present chapter. Such issues focus predominantly on a micro level of analysis. This level of analysis encompasses decision-making, relations between policy actors and the idea of the purposeful and creative policy actor. Focusing on the micro level does not exclude issues relating to the institutional context in which agents operate. It should be reiterated that the micro- and macro worlds are interdependent. Nonetheless, the strategy of the present chapter, as outlined previously, is to methodologically bracket the level of agency. Methodological bracketing just means deliberately leaving aside aspects of the structure–agency divide in order to concentrate on the level of analysis in question (Layder, 1993). This chapter omits a detailed analysis about the world economy and social trends in pursuing a level of analysis concerned with agency. Focusing on an aspect of organizational and social life relevant to policy-making like agency is done to detail its contribution to the whole process.

The development of contracting and contract relations in local government is used to develop a case study which goes some way to addressing this objective. The study is based on a specific location, the new unitary authority of Bath and North East Somerset. It centres on those officers across different service departments who have been implicated, and engaged, in forming contractual programmes.

(See Chapter 4, section 4.3, for details about the methodology employed in this case study.)

Contractual systems that form the basis of this case analysis have been ushered into local government through competitive tendering legislation. This has required local authority officers and politicians to compare the costs of specific in-house services with those of private contractors. Legislation throughout the 1980s and 1990s extended this financial discipline to various local government services, from blue-collar to professional services. This has resulted in the formal delineation between those officers responsible for purchaser functions and those responsible for provider functions.

The objective of this legislation has not simply been to reform local authority services and organizations. At its core, like many of the market reforms of the public sector introduced in the 1980s, is an attempt to dictate the behaviour and norms of bureaucrats working in local government. Competitive tendering has sought to promote a form of calculative rationality, reminiscent it seems of the idea of 'economic man' (*homo economicus*), where the maximization of financial targets figures centrally in actors' behaviour. The aim in this chapter is to explore the extent to which contracting has created such a person in practice.

The case study has three main sections. The first charts the formation of Bath and North East Somerset (B&NES), and outlines the more general position of central government in contemporary society, following 18 years of dramatic upheaval. The second part deals with one crucial aspect of recent local reforms – the introduction of competitive tendering being a prime concern. This has redefined the role of local government officials. The final section focuses on the way officers from B&NES have dealt with contractual relations; the decisions and actions that have been taken by officers to operationalize a contractual system of service provision. Although this study is set in a particular context, examining a specific aspect of the public sector, it is hoped that more general observations about the micro world of the policy process will become apparent.

6.2   A new unitary authority in a new era for local government

One of the most significant, yet little heralded, structural changes in local government in the 1990s has been the selective reform of

English county and district councils. The Conservative government of John Major formed the Local Government Commission for England in 1992 to oversee this programme of reorganization. The intended replacement of the two-tier county and district council system was a matter for gradual reform, as the Commission undertook a rolling programme of reviews. Altogether the Commission was scheduled to produce reviews of 10 counties by January 1994, including the Isle of Wight and Derbyshire. It was envisaged that in the wake of these reviews the necessary structural changes would be carried out between 1994 and 1998.

Among the counties considered for review were Avon, Gloucestershire and Somerset in the west country, which formed part of 20 authorities in a two-tier county and district system. The Commission began its review on 28 September and subsequently published its recommendations in June 1993 for public consultation. The Commission proposed the replacement of Avon, Gloucestershire and Somerset, including 20 authorities in a two-tier system, with eight new unitary councils that would provide all local government services. It was estimated that the changes would bring annual savings of £19 million, mainly in administrative costs. These proposals were subsequently approved by the Secretary of State and work was soon under way in all the authorities to create unitary structures.

One of the new authorities to be created was Bath and North East Somerset, combining the former district councils of Bath, Wansdyke and relevant elements of Avon County Council. Following local elections in April 1995 for a 'shadow authority', working groups were formed to oversee the creation of full joint arrangements. And thus Bath and North East Somerset (hereafter, B&NES) formally came in to being on 30 April 1996 – an occasion known as vesting day. Although preparations for joint arrangements had been in place for some time, officers and members were still grappling with the new arrangements long after vesting day. The most significant changes in creating a new unified structure was the transfer of services from the county council to unitary district councils. A senior official from the Corporate Strategy Group commented about the magnitude of this change:

> The county council's biggest functions were education and social services, and it effectively meant that if you take a council like Bath or Wansdyke the council's budget actually doubled again because the costs of education and social services are massive ... So the cre-

ation of new unitary authority was a massive change. And we are
still dealing with the cultural change in the organization. (*Fieldwork
Interview*, B&NES Policy Unit, 16 May 1997)

The creation of new unitary authorities constituted one of the
first major redrawings of local authority boundaries in England
since the 1974 reorganization of local government. The authorities
created by the Royal Commission of 1992 were confronted with a
completely different political milieu to that faced by two-tier authorities emerging out of the 1974 reorganization. Local government
had undergone dramatic changes as a result of concerted legislative efforts on the part of Conservative governments during the
1980s and 1990s. The legislative thrust initiated in this period not
only attempted to transform the role of local government, but also
the operations of local authorities (Stewart, 1989: 171). The aim
was to remodel the organizational arrangements and practices that
had become a part of local government throughout the postwar
years.

The postwar years witnessed unprecedented expansion and
growth in local government. True, local government was stripped of
several functions as a result of peacetime reconstruction. Industrial
nationalization meant the loss of control for local government over
electricity and gas supply. The Water Act stripped away the responsibilities for water supply from many local authorities. Under the
National Health Service Act all local authority hospitals (1,700) and
voluntary hospitals (1,300) were transferred to Regional Hospital
Boards.

At the same time, major service functions were devolved down
to local authorities. Education, social services and housing became
key service functions for local government. Local authorities
expanded existing responsibilities, such as environmental health,
engineering and leisure facilities. Such was the rate of expansion
that central government support and grants grew dramatically in
this period. As a proportion of local government income, central
government grants grew substantially: 15 per cent in 1913, 34 per
cent in 1950, and 50 per cent by 1980 (Byrne, 1990: 225).

The dominant practice that emerged was for local authorities to
act as the direct providers of those services and functions for which
they had become responsible. This required authorities to directly
employ people. While local authorities did use external agencies
from the private and voluntary sector, 'the dominant approach has

been directly to employ the staff necessary to do the work' (Walsh, 1991: 1). Service departments came to oversee the hiring, organization and management of service staff, as well as key ancillary workers attached to functions. Teachers, social workers, refuse collectors, engineers and support workers such as cleaners and caterers are among those groups that came under the direct employment of local authorities.

The principle of direct service provision came to be deeply embedded in local government, governing the way members and officers related to each other. This direct service function dominated the local authority organization. Such functional self-sufficiency has traditionally been organized through hierarchical structures and according to professional principles. Chief officers and managerial staff, normally professionals in a relevant field, direct the operations and conditions of service and ancillary staff workers. On the political side, service provision was organized around committees, wholly involved in running services. The principle of self-sufficiency assumed such importance, according to Stewart (1989), that it steered reforms to create large local authorities.

Most notably, the 1972 Local Government Act reorganized local authorities in England and Wales, creating a smaller number of larger councils in a two-tier system. The Act abolished all county boroughs and reduced the number of county councils in England and Wales from 58 to 47. Within these counties the 1,250 municipal boroughs and urban and rural districts were replaced by 333 district councils. Under the Act, the functions and responsibilities of new local authorities also changed. For example, in the metropolitan areas, most service functions – education, housing, social services, libraries, museums, planning, refuse collection, and environmental health – were allocated to the metropolitan district councils. All this added to a growing movement in the postwar period towards local government as a direct service provider.

This prevailing orthodoxy of local government as the direct provider has been fundamentally challenged in the past 18 years. Successive Conservative governments endeavoured to restructure traditional institutional arrangements in the public sector. The emergence of what is termed 'new public management' witnessed a series of major reforms across central and local institutions of the state. The movement introduced market disciplines and private sector practices in public sector services and organizations. This was done to invigorate what were perceived as moribund, producer-dominated, public institutions.

Local government, seen as a haven for sectional interest groups and politicized factions, was a prime target for change. As part of the government's strategy of remodelling the way public institutions are managed, competition and market-styled procedures were introduced in local government. The emergence of market disciplines here has assumed different forms. A prominent vehicle for these reforms concerns the privatization of local services. The 1980 Housing Act provided the legislative ground for hiving off local authority housing stock to the private sector. The principle mechanism for this was the right to buy. Central government subsidies for rent were also cut, providing added incentives for tenants to purchase their homes through higher rent increases (Stoker, 1991: 209). Although local authorities – successfully on certain occasions – resisted implementation of the right to buy, this was a notable and highly effective privatization mechanism in local government. Privatization also moved into local authority transport provision. Successive Transport Acts in 1980 and 1985 made it easier for private sector operators to provide local bus services, and forced local authority operators to form into separate companies (ibid. 216–17). These privatization measures have circumscribed the traditional role and function of local government as a direct and autonomous provider of services. But more was to come from the government.

One of the most highly effective privatization mechanisms has proven to be the system of competitive tendering. There is nothing particularly new about the use of competitive tendering in the public sector. Several non-medical activities in the NHS, such as engineering and building maintenance, window cleaning and security, have long been contracted externally. The election of the Conservatives in 1979 produced more intensive and politically driven efforts to contract out across the public sector. The NHS was a prime target, with cleaning, catering and laundry services being subject to external competition. Even the Civil Service was not spared exposure to the contracting culture. For instance, by the early 1980s the Home Office had contracted out domestic and catering services, security and cleaning, and in the Department of Environment, cleaning and security (Perkins *et al.*, 1986: 14–15). But it is in local government where the expansion of competitive tendering is most notable.

A range of legislative provisions were introduced at various points throughout the 1980s and 1990s, with the ensuing changes holding significant repercussions for local government.

The first legislative foray into competitive tendering territory came with the Local Government Planning and Land Act of 1980. The Act specifically required local authorities to compete for building maintenance and highways. This meant local authorities had to compare the costs of their in-house building and maintenance services with those of private contractors. The objective of the comparison was to identify the most competitive bidder. Where local authorities did carry out these areas of work directly, separate trading accounts had to be kept for each category of work. Commercial pressure was applied as trading accounts were required to make a rate of return on capital employed of 6 per cent. The force of the legislation was blunted as exemptions were granted to emergency operations and work valued below a specified financial limit. Moreover, under the Act, the comparison of bids was compulsory, but not the contracting out of services to the bidder offering the most competitive contract.

Because of these caveats, the extension of competition following the Act proved limited. By 1985, only 41 out of 456 local authorities in England and Wales brought in private contractors (Patterson and Pinch, 1995: 1443). Most of these were located in the south of England and only a single authority was Labour controlled. It took the government some time before it addressed the sluggish progress of competitive tendering under the voluntary terms of the 1980 Act. Backbenchers, think-tanks such as the Adam Smith Institute and private sector representatives implored the government to act (Walsh, 1995a: 29). Consequently, in 1985 a discussion paper was published that outlined the government's plans to make competitive tendering compulsory across a range of core services. The period after the 1987 general election saw matters proceed apace (Walsh, 1993: 108).

The subsequent Local Government Act of 1988 widened competitive tendering to seven additional services: refuse collection, street cleaning, building cleaning, school and welfare catering, other catering, vehicle maintenance, and grounds maintenance, while management of leisure facilities was added in 1990. Rules of competition proved far more stringent. The range of exclusions from the competitive process was limited. Activities deemed as anti-competitive were prohibited. This notably included: the packaging of large contracts, likely to deter private contractors; and the rejection of lower, competitive bids without sound justification. This added an element of compulsion which was missing from the previous legislation. Indeed, these services had to be subject to competition according to a strict timetable established by the government, between 1989 and 1992.

Up until 1988 most of the services covered by competitive tendering were in the blue-collar bracket. The 1992 Local Government Act changed all this. The legislation modified the provisions of the 1988 Act to extend compulsory competitive tendering (hereafter, CCT) into 'white collar' areas of local authority services. Covered by this was the provision of professional advice and other services involving the application of financial or technical expertise (computing, finance, legal services, personnel, architectural management, engineering). With these services, local authorities were obliged to maintain an internal trading account of all professional services, even if they remained in-house. The 1992 Act also enabled the government to add other white-collar and manual services at a later date – housing management became a target for CCT in June 1992 (Burton, 1992).

This engineering of competition was not exclusively reserved for local government legislation. The National Health Service and Community Care Act 1990 compelled local authorities to contract out elements of social care to the private and voluntary sector. The local management of schools introduced in 1988 left individual establishments with the choice to purchase services such as catering and building maintenance from the private sector, putting further market pressures on local authority in-house contractor units.

Clearly, by the time Bath and North East Somerset was formed in 1996, competitive tendering had become firmly entrenched in local government. This was reflected in the fact that a range of organizational and administrative preparations for competitive tendering had to be made by the new unitary authority. During the shadow year, the Policy Committee sat in August to consider a report on key CCT issues. These meetings set out the main CCT-related tasks for the first 18 months of the council. It was subsequently decided at a full council meeting in September to retain manual services in-house for the next round of CCT (B&NES, 1995a: 44). The new council took advantage of an exemption given under new CCT rules, allowing new authorities to take manual DSO services back in-house. This meant continuing with direct service delivery previously undertaken by council departments (DSOs) in Avon, Bath, and Wansdyke.

White-collar CCT had not progressed to the same extent in organizational terms as manual services. There were two responsible factors. First, blue-collar CCT structures were already in place when the new authority was formed. Second, unitary authorities like B&NES were exempt from the legislative timetable, and were thus able to delay the tendering process for white-collar services by 12 months. Nonetheless, definite preparations were made for white-collar services in the interim period and once the council was officially established. Client-side committees began developing contract strategies for each defined activity. The Chief Executive's Policy Unit was given the task of coordinating CCT for professional services during this formative period (*Fieldwork Interview*, B&NES Policy Unit, 16 May 1997). The unit in consultation with heads of directorates, *inter alia*, attempted to pinpoint those services which would retain in-house status as core services and those that would be subject to competition (B&NES, 1997a: 3).

On the member side of the CCT fence, a CCT Strategy Working Party was established during the interim period. The purpose of the group was to support and define the role of members in relation to the competitive process. The Working Party continued after the interim period but was having to deal with issues that went beyond its remit and status as an informal consultative body. As such, by the middle of 1997, the Working Party became a subcommittee of the Policy and Resources Committee: 'The Working Party has revised its Terms of Reference. It is apparent that the scope of the issues that are being addressed . . . are not appropriate for consideration by an informal Working Party which is not Minuted' (B&NES, 1997b: 4). The new subcommittee is responsible for overseeing the council's competitive strategy and CCT timetable programme. Crucially, the subcommittee can determine contract-packaging across different services.

These developments exemplify the way competition impinges upon the task of managing local government. However, it is the objective of this case study to dig beneath these surface institutional changes to consider the effects of competitive tendering on local agents. The remainder of this case study focuses on such matters.

The experiences of senior officials from B&NES forms the basis of this discussion, which, at the same time, seeks to go beyond the confines of CCT and local government to assess the general role of agents in the policy process.

6.3   CCT and local government agents: the imperative of acting efficiently and rationally

In the postwar period, structural reorganization was seen as the key to improving administration in local government. In fact, most of the major postwar reforms in local government up until the mid-1980s concentrated on such features. The introduction of larger local authorities and a corporate departmental structures following the 1974 reorganization perfectly exemplifies this approach (see above, section 6.2).

The public sector reforms of the 1980s witnessed a quite different emphasis. Private sector forms of management were adopted for specific reasons. Market-based reforms like CCT did not seek primarily to create new organizational formations, although these remained important. Rather, the central animus of such reforms is this: to influence the behaviour, relationships and views of agents operating in key public sector institutions like local authorities. As Walsh (1995b: 31) acknowledges:

> The new market-based institutional framework that is being put in place is seen as leading to the change in values and attitudes that is desired. Public sector managers, it is hoped, will not simply operate different systems, and work within different structures, they will also act and think in a new way.

The new values that these reforms have attempted to inculcate throughout key public institutions are those associated with the private sector – a sensitivity to finances, innovation and entrepreneurship. In certain respects the form of behaviour required by these reforms is reminiscent of the ideas propounded by rational decision-making theorists (see Chapter 2).

The introduction of competition in the public sector was viewed as an ideal vehicle for producing particular behavioural outcomes. A hierarchical system of public administration, based around self-sufficiency and monopoly service provision, exerts few demands on the actions and values of bureaucrats. Competitive tendering, on the other hand, requires politicians, bureaucrats and in-house staff to adopt the behavioural traits associated with the commercial environment.

It was on such grounds that in the late-1970s, think-tanks, academics, politicians and private sector associations began mounting a strong case for competitive tendering in the public sector. In local government especially, competition was seen to provide a mechanism for reshaping relations, values and modes of behaviour that had become entrenched in such organizations throughout the postwar period. Competition, the argument went, could potentially effect two general changes in the way key agents – politicians, officials and in-house staff – performed their duties in local government. First, to create a greater sensitivity among staff in relation to matters of efficiency and financial prudence. Second, to clarify responsibilities among individuals in a manner which favours and bolsters the authority of managerial officials. Both points will be analyzed below. Again, research from B&NES illustrates the extent to which officials have accommodated to the type of behavioural patterns required by contracting legislation.

6.3.1   The economies of competition

It is considered that a sensitivity towards efficiency and financial probity is a prime behavioural trait encouraged by competition. The Adam Smith Institute was an early and staunch advocate of competition in local government on these very grounds. One policy document published by the Institute in the 1980s argued that substantial expansion had taken place in local government. This was mainly due to pressures exerted on members and officials by sectional interest groups, especially unions. Such expansion, it was argued led to higher local taxes and rates (Perkins *et al.*, 1986: 9).

These observations hold a great deal of resonance with, and echo the views of, public choice theory. Key features of the Conservative reform agenda for the public sector have taken their cue from this theoretical approach. Public choice theory is commonly referred to as an 'economics of politics' or a theory of rational choice and behaviour in government. It offers a microeconomic analysis of political behaviour. Buchanan (1978: 17) notes: 'In one sense, all of public choice or the economic theory of politics may be summarised as the "discovery" or "re-discovery" that people should be treated as rational utility-maximisers in *all* of their behavioural capacities' (original emphasis). These are the characteristic features that shape the actions of political and bureaucratic agents. Politicians, for instance, are not wholly concerned about the needs of society. Rather, they use their position to pursue their own interests and those of sectional interest groups, which leads to an inefficient use of public resources.

As Olson (1982: 41) points out, in modern society small sectional interest groups 'have disproportionate organizational power for collective action' and it is a power base that remains in stable societies. Interest group politics tends to be dominated by questions of distribution as opposed to questions of productive efficiency. Organizations are unlikely to pursue the interest of their members 'by making the pie the society produces larger' (ibid. 42). The reason for this, argues Olson, is that interest groups are likely to gain far more when attempting to secure redistribution, 'larger slices of the social pie' (ibid.). With efficiency gains, the benefits are thinly distributed throughout society. Those responsible for efficiencies have to bear the full cost of the action and yet they receive only a meagre portion of the gains made. Hence issues of redistribution dominate collective political behaviour. But there is a cost attached according to Olson: the resources that are redistributed will only reduce the social output and transform the system of incentives so that production levels go into decline. Thus it is in the interests of politicians to align themselves to such concerns, as calls for redistribution are more likely to enjoy support than are demands for increases in productivity.

Niskanen (1973), a major proponent of public choice theory, argued in a similar vein about public officials. These agents were regarded as being responsible for the productive deficiencies of the public sector, as they prioritized their own sectional interests. Officials endeavour to maximize their status, earning power and authority, according to Niskanen, less by making economies than by attempting to secure higher institutional budgets (ibid. 22). Niskanen acknowledges that not all bureaucratic behaviour is dominated by the selfish pursuit of interests. There are those bureaucrat that attempt to serve the public interest. However, such individuals are not in a position to inculcate a pursuit of the public interest.

> He cannot acquire all the information on individual preferences and production opportunities that would be necessary to divine 'the

public interest', and he does not have the authority to order an action that is contrary to either the personal interests or the different perceptions of the 'public interest' by other bureaucrats. (ibid. 23)

These theoretical discussions informed policy discussions in the late 1970s and early 1980s among the rightward leaning intelligentsia, about efficiency in local government. Out of these debates came policy prescriptions. Competition was regarded by the likes of the Adam Smith Institute and the Public and Local Service Efficiency Campaign as a key policy for improving efficiency at the local level. The Confederation of British Industry (hereafter, CBI) formed a working party in 1981 for examining the scope of achieving efficiency savings in central government, local government and the NHS. The working party's final report, published in 1984, argued that the exposure of in-house service managers and workers to market forces can maximize efficient working patterns in two respects: first, external competition pressurizes the staff of in-house services to cut their costs and work harder; second, if such savings are not made, managers can contract such work out to private contractors who are prepared to perform the service for less money (Perkins et al., 1986: 7–8). The argument used by the pro-competition lobby was straightforward: that exposure of local government to the market instils a greater sense of economic rationality among key agents in local authorities.

The dire economic situation of the mid-to-late 1970s brought intense pressures on the public purse. It forced the Labour government to consider the option of creating efficiency savings through competitive tendering. But it was Conservative governments in the 1980s which demonstrated a political commitment towards implementing the sort of recommendations made by the CBI working party. A government-commissioned report was published in 1986 scrutinizing the use of competitive tendering in six departments. The report observed that the prime aim of competitive tendering should not be the reduction of manpower *per se* but 'value for money'. The report found that '*competitive tendering* is improving efficiency by … exposing outdated and restrictive practices and pointing up opportunities to deliver better services at lower cost' (HM Treasury, 1986: 3). As such, it recommended that the government should seek to extend competition.

Over time, local government, as shown above, became a conspicuous candidate for exposure to the rigours of competition. Legislation was passed requiring local authorities to expose specified services to the competitive tendering process. All of this contributed towards a progressive though calculated drive to impart a more pronounced concern for efficiency among officials and politicians. This proved to be a principal feature of the 1988 Local Government Act (see section 6.2). One draft circular from the DoE (1995: 9) noted: 'The purpose of compulsory competitive tendering is to stimulate greater efficiency and secure better value for money by requiring fair competition between local authorities' own in-house teams and private contractors'. Under the Act, officials compare tenders and they cannot reject lower-priced bids by private contractors without good reason. This competitive element within the legislation was seen to prioritize economic efficiency and rationality. Indeed, it could be argued that it forcibly requires officials to maximize financial savings above other courses of action in the competitive tendering process.

With reference to B&NES again – the subject authority for this case study – several provisions were made to ensure that officers and politicians complied with the legislative demands for efficient conduct. The new unitary authority's Statement of Vision and Values gave an express commitment to seek value for money: 'Responding to competition to promote improved value for money in services and ensuring that the authority's services are efficient and in the best position to compete' (B&NES, 1995b: 5).

This part of the B&NES Statement was an implicit reference to the legislative requirements of CCT. But response to competition went beyond grand vision statements of future intent. The core group of senior officers were careful to submit advice to the CCT Working Party as the new authority prepared for white-collar CCT. These officials drew the Working Party's attention to the legislative requirements for efficiency. While the local authority can dictate how competition is conducted, the officers noted that it is incumbent on officials and politicians to act in a manner that does not hinder the search for greater efficiency. They quoted directly from the DoE Circular 10/93. This document insisted that when different service functions are combined in one contract, private contractors should still be given the chance of bidding for each type of work separately. Accordingly, 'this may secure a better competitive response and result in better value for money' (DoE Circular 10/93, cited in B&NES, 1997a: 4).

This emphasis – an unequivocal reference to competitive tendering – affected both sides of the competitive divide within the local authority organization. The head of Leisure Services, the client in relation to grounds maintenance, found that the 1988 Local Government Act made exacting demands for services to be operated in a rational, cost-effective fashion. For a service such as grounds maintenance, this meant that price was prioritized above quality. This was especially evident in drawing up a list of tenderers. The head of Leisure Services acknowledged the following about the process:

> Companies were evaluated at the pre-tender stage to see whether they could get onto the selection list. But ... the legislation states you must have a minimum number of contractors invited to tender. And if as part of your invitation to tender you didn't get sufficient numbers, then all companies irrespective of their suitability at that stage had to be included, which then made it very difficult if those companies came in with a bid to discount them despite the fact there were serious concerns about their capability ... Blue-collar legislation was horrendous in that respect. A lot of the quality of the services that many councils have had, particularly in the area of grounds maintenance and floral decorations, I think has deteriorated. (*Fieldwork Interview*, B&NES Leisure Services, 12 November 1996)

On the internal contractor side for B&NES, the question of value for money and efficiency is a prime regard for key officers. As a result of legislation, the Commercial Services Directorate has a separate trading account for its various Direct Service Organizations. Significantly, the various services are required by law to make 6 per cent return on the capital employed. This produces a commercial ethos but is a demanding requirement for a local authority organization, as the head of Commercial Services acknowledged:

> It's just like running any business. How good your estimates are, or how good your operation managers are ... If you are bad there's penalties, maybe it is an independent district auditor. So there is always a threat there on the DSOs and the workforce – if you drop below a threshold performance level you will be forcibly tendered. (*Fieldwork Interview*, B&NES Commercial Services, 17 March 1997)

These observations illustrate the new commercial regime that local officers such as those at B&NES have to comply with. It is a regime that necessitates agents to function predominantly as rational, profit-maximizing operators.

6.3.2   Separating responsibilities and management discretion

The other behavioural features of local authority life which competitive tendering has sought to influence are the relations between officials. To establish a competitive or quasi-competitive system, officers have to perform distinct roles. These reflect the specialized market-style relations between buyers and sellers. In the technical language of the legislation, local authorities have been required to separate the client and contractor side of the organization. 'The *client* has the role of service planning, defining the work to be delivered by the *contractor*, and letting and managing the contract. Thus the traditional service provider . . . became the client, and the contractor . . . delivered services as defined by the client' (Audit Commission, 1993: 1; original emphasis). Walsh's research on the impact of the 1988 Act showed that extensive measures had been taken to institutionalize the client–contractor split in local authorities. Of the 40 organizations studied by Walsh, most of the local authorities had adopted a client–contractor split, and much of this had taken place prior to the services being tendered (Walsh, 1991: 77–8). Shaw *et al.*'s (1994: 207) sample of 23 northern local authorities found that in the 1988–92 period 90 per cent had formally established a client–contractor split.

For those advocating competitive tendering in local government, the separation of client and contractor functions holds definite advantages. The split helps to clarify the responsibilities of different officers, and renders the costs and standards of services increasingly transparent (Walsh, 1993: 115). Thus information systems that allow client officers to oversee and scrutinize the implementation of contracts have to be established. In addition, officials have to operate more sophisticated financial mechanisms. Direct Labour Services, under CCT, are in a position of managing their own accounts; invoice and payment procedures come to the fore; and budgeting is shaped to accommodate the advanced tender prices. All this creates an accountable organizational structure. As Harden (1992: 33) explains, the contract resolves 'the old dilemma of "independence versus control" . . . by using the former to promote accountability'.

This clarification of duties does augment the position of managers. The Adam Smith Institute made this very point in an early policy statement on competition in local government. A clear split between the client and contractor functions, in theory, allows managers to devolve certain activities to the contractors. This enables the client to concentrate on the task of managing the service contract. A cross-departmental study of competitive tendering found clear evidence among managers that a client–contractor split adds to their personal control. A Departmental Security Officer made the following observation: ' "My day-to-day involvement in management problems has significantly reduced, and I have more control: if a guard is not working properly I can get the contractor to replace him at once" ' (HM Treasury, 1986: 8).

This split also has significant political repercussions in terms of the relationship between management and the in-house workforce. Michael Forsyth, an early and vociferous supporter of contracting in local government, maintained that the split empowers officers acting as client managers in relation to in-house teams. As some commentators have noted, this was an intentional feature of competitive tendering in local government. The origins of this policy is the winter of discontent in 1978–79, where local authority manual workers were at the forefront of strike action (Stoker, 1991: 218–19). Client officers, under competitive tendering, can pressurize in-house teams by setting service standards and by opting for external contractors over Direct Labour Organizations. This without doubt strengthens the hand of client officers. Indeed, one of the consequences of contracting in local government has been an intensification of working conditions for manual staff. The Public Services Privatization Research Unit found 19.7 per cent of full-time manual jobs and 5.5 per cent of part-time manual jobs were lost in the period between 1988 and 1991 (Patterson and Pinch, 1995: 1454).

Competitive tendering for defined services may be compulsory, but the actual form of the client–contractor split is not proscribed by legislation. Local authority officials and members have considerable leeway over how they separate client and contractor responsibilities across the authority organization (Vincent-Jones and Harries, 1996: 188). The actual form of the client–contractor relationship between local authority agents can assume one of two general forms.

First, there is the hard-split or quasi-market arrangement. Here, those officers responsible for client and contractor responsibilities are located in separate departments. This has involved the creation of a single contractor department, containing all the defined functions under CCT. Typically, there will be a head of department managing officials responsible for different contractor functions. The officials in standard service departments are then left to act as clients, setting and overseeing contracts. This type of arrangement will encourage a more commercially orientated set of relations between agents in the same authority.

For blue-collar services, Bath and North East Somerset adopted a hard quasi-market arrangement. This resulted in a major reorganization of officers and departments responsible for the contracting functions. Parts of all the sections of the County Council Direct Services Organization (hereafter, DSO), covering cleaning, catering, grounds maintenance, highways and transport, became the responsibility of the new authority. These services were amalgamated with the existing DSOs of Bath City and Wansdyke Council. The combined DSOs formed the Contract Services Directorate, later renamed Commercial Services, one of B&NES's five main directorates. Commercial Services is responsible for strategically managing the five service departments, which are akin to traditional departments in local government. Each service department is responsible for different contractor functions. Hence, Environmental Services oversees refuse collection, cleaning and grounds maintenance, while Amenity Services is responsible for catering and the cleaning of leisure buildings. The client functions – that is, those components of the organization that purchase and monitor services – are found in separate directorates. For instance, the client for grounds maintenance is found in the Leisure Services Department, which is responsible for parks and open spaces.

The decision to opt for a hard over a soft split for blue-collar services emerged from the influence of Wansdyke Council. The former Wansdyke Council had successfully managed to retain its services in-house using a hard-split formula. The new unitary authority of B&NES was committed to retaining services in-house and it was logical that it would follow Wandyke's example. One official noted:

> The former Bath CC had more of a soft-split approach to it. The former Wansdyke council had more of a hard-split approach. In bringing the two together the contracting side in Wansdyke was very strong and was able to influence members that this was the

right way to go. Whether it will remain that way I don't know.
(Fieldwork Interview, B&ANES Leisure Services, 12 November 1996)

The contractor side at member level was dealt with by the Commercial Services Committee. However, the council, well into 1997, had not agreed upon appropriate committee arrangements for the other service functions that came under CCT legislation. Various other client and contractor-side functions were embedded within various service committees. There was a sense that a more deliberate system was needed for dealing with these functions at committee level as opposed to the ad hoc arrangements that were in existence. One official report on this matter suggested the possibility of a resources sub-committee which could act as a client for all the services located in the Resources Directorate (B&NES, 1997b: 4).

The second major style of client–contractor relations is the soft-split or soft quasi-market arrangement. Here, client and contractor agents are located in the same department. For instance, those officials and staff responsible for housing maintenance are not hived off to a separate contractor department but remain in the department responsible for housing. This may require officers to perform both client and contractor functions. Or it may be that dealings between officials in a soft quasi-market arrangements will encourage collaboration between the different parties.

Contractor–client relations, as already mentioned above, were less well developed among the white-collar services in B&NES. Nevertheless, there seemed to be a fledgling movement towards a soft quasi-market arrangement. The preparation for housing management CCT is an apposite example. As with all new authorities, B&NES was exempted from housing CCT for 18 months. It was given a further six months' abstention for housing management as the former Wansdyke Council's housing stock was regarded as too small for CCT. Consequently, housing contracts had to be in place by 1 April 1998. By the time the new council was formed in April 1996, the previous Bath Council had already placed specifications for managing its 10,300 domestic properties (B&NES, 1996: 1). The new council continued the work, consulting with tenants and establishing a strategy for officers. Rather than creating a separate Direct Service Organization for housing management, officials on each side of the competitive fence remained in the Area Housing Management unit. One official was appointed in July 1996 to carry out client functions. This entailed setting out contract specifications which were in part based on a consultation exercise with tenants and tenant groups. The contractor side of housing management, on the other hand, was the responsibility of a seconded official.

Thus what emerged in housing during the pre-contract letting stage was a distinct soft split. Similar scenarios were also evident in other functions like computer and legal services. At the same time, opinions were being expressed that client–contractor arrangements for white-collar services could potentially change in the future once the contracts had been settled. A senior official from the Chief Executive's Policy Unit, in part responsible for the corporate coordination of CCT across the authority, acknowledged this: 'At senior level it's most likely that a single manager will be twin hatted and deal with both. But at a level below that senior manager, and the advice here is that it can happen at a level below, there will need to be a split' (*Fieldwork Interview*, B&NES Policy Unit, 16 May 1997).

6.4   The behavioural consequences of competition

The issue that needs to be pursued is whether the introduction of competitive tendering in local government has produced the type of behavioural patterns outlined above. As shown, competition sought to encourage two main traits in the actions of local government agents, especially officers. In part, competitive tendering was regarded as a means for making agents aspire to the goals of organizational and financial efficiency. Second, the institution of a quasi-market system has required local authority agents to deal with one another in a more formal manner. In particular, the client–contractor split has demanded that agents operating as purchasers deal with internal providers at arm's length, replicating commercial relations and patterns of interaction.

It has been shown above in our case authority – Bath and North East Somerset – that various organizational provisions were instituted to ensure that these very behavioural traits were reproduced. However, the development of contracting in B&NES witnessed forms of behaviour which were not entirely congruent with the results envisaged by legislation. The patterns of action displayed were reminiscent of traditional patterns of behaviour in local government. On the one hand, as will be shown with reference to B&NES, agents continue to rely on hierarchical forms of administra-

The creation of new unitary authorities such as B&NES has enabled these organizations to actively circumvent the rules governing competition and the externalization of services. Those councils included in the reorganization could set aside CCT arrangements during the period of change. Moreover, these authorities were allowed to take back in-house those contracts made with the private sector that had come to an end. This allowed authorities like B&NES to protect and have greater control over the quality and standards of those services brought out of the commercial relationship.

A draft circular of 1995 to chief executives from the DoE witnessed a further significant shift from the price-orientated rationality of the 1988 Act. The document allowed client officials to take into account factors other than price when evaluating bids, providing these points were explicitly stated. Officers could legitimately consider quality issues, environmental standards and equal opportunities, alongside tender prices (DoE, 1995: 12). The senior officials from Leisure Services at B&NES, which performed the client function in relation to leisure management and grounds maintenance, were given an ideal opportunity to reflect this new policy. Early after the formation of B&NES, client managers from Leisure Services had to oversee the renewal of their contracts. Reflecting the change in emphasis, the client managers at Leisure Services developed an assessment model for the tendering process. The model was designed to be applied flexibly across different contracts and used a range of non-financial criteria to develop an assessment formulae. The head of Leisure Services noted:

> But what we are looking to highlight is anything from 8–13 main areas to evaluate a contractor on. Such things as experience, equal opportunities policies, whether or not they have put in sufficient resources into the bid, their understanding of our operational plans, emergency operating plans, and the role of sports development. All that type of criteria in a sports and leisure context will be utilized. (*Fieldwork Interview*, B&NES Leisure Services, 12 November 1996)

Even though the tendering process is now more inclusive and less dominated by financial rationality, officers still have to prioritize monetary value:

> I think price will normally be the dominating factor and I would

imagine evaluation models to operate on a 60 : 40 per cent, 65 : 35 per cent, 70 : 30 per cent with price being dominant ... Price is still a major concern, but there is a little bit more flexibility. (*Fieldwork Interview*, B&NES Leisure Services, 12 November 1996)

6.4.2   Hierarchies and contracts

This section continues to examine the actual behavioural consequences that have emerged from the establishment of competitive tendering in local government. The argument, as above, is that, in practice, there is a chasm between what the original legislation intended and the actual patterns of action which emerged in the local context. Above it was shown that the inherent economic rationalism of competitive tendering, as applied to local government, is not entirely feasible. Much of this has to do with the nature of local government. Local authorities are in a democratic relationship with various constituencies, and these cannot be properly addressed by operating services in a wholly commercial manner.

Attention now shifts to consider the way competitive tendering attempted to transform relations between local government agents. The institution of a competitive system for specified services led to the formal institutionalization of a client–contractor split in local authorities. The contractual relationship, whether involving internal or external providers, was seen to act as the harbinger of new organizational relations. In particular, the power to externalize services would in theory require a move away from hierarchical to market-styled organizational relations. These would involve networked links between independent agents located in distinct sections or units within the overall organization.

Research has shown, however, that competition has not dismantled completely existing organizational relations. In fact, research on local government, including the present case study, has shown that prevailing organizational cultures and procedures are integral to the development of contract relations. The examination here focuses on the persistence of hierarchal authorities in contract relations.

A certain level of hierarchical control and authority is necessary in managing contracts. Much of this is due to the fact that contracts are not definitive entities. For the smooth running and administration of the contract process, it is vital that the various parties involved are able to deal with unforeseen and problematic events. These can include different interpretations over specifications or a demand by either the client or contractor to change conditions. Provision for such difficulties can be made by the inclusion of clauses in contracts which deal with the possibility of variation.

It is also usual for these problematic features to be managed by recourse to 'authoritative methods'. It is unusual, especially in local authority contexts when dealing with internal contractors, for such methods to take the form of legal action. Authority is more commonly manifested in the guise of organizational hierarchy, where one party in the relationship determines features of the contract. Usually it is the client which determines the work of the contractor, and deals with issues of incompleteness and unexpected events. Stinchcombe (1990) acknowledges that contracts can lead to relationships which are similar to prevailing hierarchies in an organization. Hierarchical features can address a range of issues:

> Features of hierarchies (authority systems, incentive systems, standard operating procedures, dispute resolution procedures, and non-market internal pricing) are useful when a client may want to change specifications, when a contractor or a client cannot predict costs very well, or when performances are not easily separately measured. (ibid. 233)

In the relatively short time that B&NES was in existence, relations between contractors and clients effectively had already began to adopt elements of hierarchy. This was most evident in the blue-collar sector, where contracting was firmly established. The contractor side of manual services, as already shown, was brought under the auspices of a single directorate – commercial services. Members of this directorate were in a position of having to deal with client officers spread across a range of directorates. Although dispersed in this manner, the client officers used their authority to implement contractual changes. Client actors are better placed to take action in these situations because of their role in writing-up the contract, overseeing the tendering process and monitoring progress. As one client officer notes:

> [A client is in a strong position]. I don't mean a dominated client, I mean a client that sets out its strategy, sets out its policies, sets out a framework in terms of what is needed to be achieved and then works in partnership with the contractor in order to achieve that.

But it's very clearly focused in terms of what direction it's going in and what it wants to achieve, that's the important thing. (*Fieldwork Interview*, B&NES Leisure Services, 12 November 1996)

Client reliance on hierarchical authority at B&NES were evident when budgetary deficits emerged. The experience has been that in these situations adjustments are made to the contract at the client's behest rather than disbanding the contract altogether. One senior client officer noted: '[The contract continues when there are reductions in the budget] unless we renegotiate the terms of the contract. It can happen. Generally what happens is that if you have a contract . . . you don't expect to kill that contract. It is not usual that happens' (*Fieldwork Interview*, B&NES Development and Environmental Services, 18 March 1997).

One side of the Commercial Services that has experienced the contractual vicissitudes from the client-side is grounds maintenance. In 1997, the client, in response to budgetary pressures, introduced a reduction in the number of times council lawns and parks were cut from 22 to 8 times a year. However, these adjustments can be the source of much consternation for contractors. These client-induced reductions in the grounds maintenance contract has proven to be particularly difficult for the contractor:

> What I do end up with is a lot of people with not a lot to do with some of their time. All planting equipment that I have got is now useless because it is not man enough to cut the grass when it is growing more than three inches. I've got to sell that. I've then got to buy new planting equipment to cut the long grass. So this marvellous saving which was supposed to come up has actually reduced the service quality dramatically and increased the cost. (*Fieldwork Interview*, B&NES Commercial Services, 17 March 1997)

Another feature of the contracting relationship which reveals hierarchical elements is the monitoring of the contract by clients. This function can take a number of different forms. The parks and grounds maintenance contract at B&NES is typical of the way contract monitoring is conducted in local government. The monitoring of this contract, as one senior client officer noted, is 'not a case of people going round with a clip board and checking things'. Nevertheless, there are occasions when officers need to be physically present to witness the contractors in operation. A specially assigned supervising officer is responsible for monitoring. This officer meets with a relevant contract manager on a fortnightly or monthly basis to discuss the work that will be carried out over the following weeks. At the same time, the parties review the work that has been carried out, including the various issues that arise. It is on the basis of such discussions that payments are made.

The Leisure Services Department, which acts as the client for grounds maintenance, is looking to extend the system of self-monitoring. Part of the reason for this has to do with the lack of client supervisors. But at the same time interventionist supervision by a large army of client officers can prove intrusive and prove harmful to the client–contractor relationship. As a client official observed: 'With too many client managers, you end up with a scenario where people go out to justify their existence ... You end up with people going out with clipboards watching the contractor's every move. And that's not good for relationships' (*Fieldwork Interview*, B&NES Leisure Services, 12 November 1997). Officers from both the client and contractor side of the divide at B&NES are considering methods of placing responsibility for monitoring on the side of the contractors. One possible route is the quality accreditation systems, such as 'Investors in People' or the ISO 9002. Indeed, Commercial Services is seeking to have the whole Directorate accredited by the ISO 9002 quality scheme, although only a select number of functions have been accredited to date.

Also symptomatic of the fledgling moves towards a self-monitoring system are the plans of client officers at Leisure Services to move from input- to output-based contracts. Whereas an input-based contract specifies the procedures to be accredited out, the output-based contract specifies the end results while leaving detail of how these are achieved to the contractor: 'In the output specification you write the general flavour of the service you want. It gets round some of the problems and stops you from being anti-competitive' (*Fieldwork Interview*, B&NES Policy Unit, 18 March 1997). The increased use of self-monitoring highlights a significant facet of contracting relations in practice – the building of cooperative relations.

6.4.3   Cooperation and trust in contract relations

Above, it was shown that existing organizational procedures and mechanisms – namely, the use of hierarchies – still perform a significant role in contracting. But managing a contract wholly by recourse to hierarchical authority would in all probability sour relations between purchaser and provider. Ultimately, this could result in a breakdown of relations, ending in conflict. As shown with regard to self-monitoring, a certain level of close cooperation, trust and mutual adjustment is a necessary part of any contract relationship (see North, 1990: 55–7). The institutionalization of competitive relations in local government, though, created a significant barrier to the development of cooperative, trusting relations between the parties involved. The barrier is a consequence of the formalization of the client–contractor split.

The manual service sector at B&NES pursued the most formal arrangement that is possible – the formation of a hard split between contractor and client. As shown (see section 6.3.2), each party is placed in separate spheres of the organization. This, as insiders within the authority have testified, has generated complications and impediments to the client–contractor relationship. A senior official from Commercial Services acknowledges: 'What the CCT legislation has done is almost say, "You don't work together". Working together you'll be accused of fiddling it. It's focused people: you are either a client or a contractor' (*Fieldwork Interview*, B&NES Commercial Services, 17 March 1997).

Complaints about the formalization of contractor–client roles are especially conspicuous on the contractor side of the relationship. The contractor dealing with highways maintenance has complained of too frequent monitoring. Another criticism is the lack of communication channels between client and contractor. This has been exacerbated by the reorganization, involving the amalgamation of three separate local authorities. Most notably, the formal separation of roles can potentially result in conflicting objectives between client and contractor officers. One senior official from the contractor side of the divide noted:

> The client officer is held to account for not overspending the budget ... And the contractor is coming from the point of view that they want to provide a good quality of service ... Really those two people should be sitting together and they should be saying, 'We are jointly responsible for quality of service and value for money'. (*Fieldwork Interview*, B&NES Commercial Services, 17 March 1997)

Vincent-Jones and Harries' (1996) study of competitive tendering, specifically building cleaning, in two metropolitan areas confirms this point. The authors found that the authority which had adopted a strong, formal split between contractor and client resulted in excessive contractual conflicts (ibid. 204). On the other hand, the Eastmet authority, which pursued a flexible system of soft contractual splits, contributed to the cultivation of close, trusting relationships between contractor and client (ibid. 200).

The results from Vincent-Jones and Harries' study show that the contracting system does not inevitably lead to a remote and distant attachment between client and contractor. Walsh (1991: 73) observes: 'Though contracts necessarily lead to formalisation, this does not mean that informal procedures and approaches are abandoned. Authorities emphasised the importance of informal procedures for the resolution of difficulties, whether with internal DSOs or external contractors.' A soft split is more likely as shown in the study to encourage close cooperation between relevant agents.

Yet even in a hard-split scenario, as in the manual service sector at B&NES, officers from both sides of the contractor–client split still endeavoured to cultivate collaborative ties. They are in part able to achieve this because a contemporary feature in local government is the growing use of informal channels of communication among local agents. Laffin and Young (1990) found that officials, in response to the growth of partisan politics in local government, have increasingly displayed the traits of a bureaucratic politician. The bureaucratic politician according to the authors is 'more willing to allow political factors and tactics to influence their involvement in the policy process ... and believe in, and relish, close involvement with the politicians in developing and carrying out council policy' (ibid. 51). Officers, especially in larger authorities, are accustomed to and have worked in a culture where close collaborative ties are the norm; indeed, they are integral to the overall running of the organization. Certain aspects of manual contracting at B&NES has, by the admission of those officers involved, become too formal. Nevertheless, there are those agents that have endeavoured to encourage closer affinity across the contractual division. One client officer notes:

> I think in some respects on the grounds maintenance side we got the balance between contractor and client just about right. We set out from the outset not to police the contractor but to work with the contractor to achieve our objectives and our targets and our quality standards that we required. And we recognized fairly quickly you

can achieve far more and the contractors were likely to be more flexible in terms of their approach. Consequently we have been able to go to contractors and get extras carried out without any additional costs because there is a quid pro quo. (*Fieldwork Interview*, B&NES Commercial Services, 12 November 1996)

Research has shown the importance of close informal contact between clients and in-house contractors in blue-collar competitive tendering. Walker's (1993) DoE-sponsored analysis of 19 Direct Labour Organizations in local government found that all but one of the authorities instituted regular contact with internal DSOs. Significantly, this characterized relations with both internal and private contractors: 'The sorts of issues which arose in the course of undertaking a particular job were, in all authorities, handled quite informally ... and this contact was viewed as a normal part of the working relationship in the case of both private contractors and the DLO' (ibid. 43).

The development of white-collar competitive tendering in B&NES has so far witnessed those parties involved opting for a soft-split relationship. Preparations for housing management have been typified by a 'very informal split' between the officer responsible for the client side and the officer performing the contractor role. Such informality became manifest in close collaborative links between client and contractor officers. The client officer, for example, was able to attend contractor meetings. What is more, officers from the area management teams – effectively, the DSO for housing management – were closely involved in the writing-up of the contract specifications. The client did not impose a list of obligations on the contractors. Rather, the in-house contractor was consulted throughout the drawing-up of the contract. The client official noted:

With the specification it was sent round to all the area teams and we set up working groups maybe on lettings, or rent arrears and staff doing the job who would form the DSO. They would actually contribute to looking at that specification and saying what we would do and if there are any problems. It was very much to try and involve them as much as possible so that when we came to letting the contract they would know what was in it ... as opposed to what I thought they might do which I think has been the problem elsewhere. (*Fieldwork Interview*, B&NES Housing and Social Services, 16 May 1997)

There was less certainty, however, over how the client–contractor relationship would develop once the letting process was complete. Although matters were still to be finalized, it was unlikely according to officers that the relationship would assume the form of a hard, formalized division between purchaser and provider.

6.5 Conclusion

Competitive tendering in local government was in part introduced to create an arm's-length relationship between internal contractors and those officers acting as clients. The rationale here was that such distance would create suitable conditions for commercial transactions. In fact, competitive tendering has contributed to a formalization of relationships between officers. The experience of agents in local government is that arm's-length relations can hinder the operation of contracts. Effective and constructive relations are dependent on modifying the formal distance between those assigned as either clients or contractors. Harden (1992: 34) observes: 'Although the separation of interests is vital to the contractual approach, many contracts for public services involve relationships in which ... the parties have a long-term commitment to each other.' This, in part, can be achieved by utilizing informal procedures and channels of communication that are now integral to local government organizations. These relations of trust, which to a certain extent were impeded by the increased formality required by competitive legislation, are integral to social relations: 'Our perception of collective order as stable is sustained by rule-following behaviour, which makes our world predictable, reliable and legible. All these rules rest on actors' trust or expectations of "things as usual" ' (Misztal, 1996: 97).

The legislation in theory seemed to be imposing a mode of behaviour and operation which is generally antithetical to human modern societies. Misztal (1996: 9) argues that changes in contemporary society have made the attainment of trust between social groups an urgent matter. With global integration and growing inequality undermining social cohesion, the active development of trust can secure communication and dialogue and reconcile distinct interest between social groups. Even from the economic perspective of rational choice theory, trust is regarded as an efficient lubricant for economic exchange and transactions (Scott, 1995: 90–1).

Overall, effective contracting is very much dependent on types of relationship and modes of action that competitive tendering attempted to render superfluous. Hence, the continued use of hierarchal authority, the attempts to introduce quality measures as a way of neutralizing the emphasis on monetary criteria and the concern for informal links were integral to the operation of contracting. The case example of B&NES illustrated the way existing procedures and patterns of action among officers were not entirely redefined by competitive tendering. Rather, they provided the basis from which competition was modified and integrated in local government.

STUDY GUIDE

A chronology of major legislative developments in the restructuring of local government – from direct provider to contractor

The restructuring of local government and local government services

1957–60:   The structure of local government in London is reviewed by a Royal Commission under the chairmanship of Sir Edward Herbert. The Commission made several proposals concerning the establishment of a two-tier structure for local government in Greater London: (1) the London County Council and Middlesex County Council should be abolished and replaced by a Greater London Council; (2) within the area covered by the GLC, the existing local authorities should be reduced from 95 to 52, and these were to be called Greater London boroughs (apart from the City); (3) the Greater London Boroughs were to preside over local services, such as housing, welfare and libraries. The GLC, on the other hand, would be responsible for the broader functions of fire, ambulances, main roads and refuse disposal.

1963:   The government responded positively to these recommendations and included many of them in a modified form, following an independent consultation, in the London Government Act of 1963. The London County Council (LCC), which had been created in 1888, was replaced by the Greater London Council (GLC), covering an area slightly smaller than that recommended by the Commission. The area covered by the GLC was divided into 32 London boroughs, instead of 52 as put forward by the Herbert Commission.

1966–69:   The government established two separate Royal Commissions on the reorganization of local government, one for England (led by Lord Redcliffe-Maud) and one for Scotland (chaired by Lord Wheatley). Both presented their respective reports in 1969. The Redcliffe-Maud Report criticized the structure of local government in England, arguing that there was too much overlapping of functions between authorities and a lack of coordination. The report proposed that England should be divided into 81 new authorities, with 58 unitary authorities, 3 metropolitan authorities, and 20 metropolitan districts. These would be responsible for all local government services.

1970 (February):   The Labour government largely accepted the recommendations of the Royal Commission Report, and a course of legislative action was set in motion with the publication of the White Paper, *Reform of Local Government In England.*

1970 (June):   The Conservative election victory saw Labour's planned course of reform scuppered as the new government was committed to retaining the two-tier system of local government in England. The Conservative government's White Paper of 1971, *Local Government in England,* proposed a two-tier system based on existing counties with a reduced number of district authorities for the second tier.

1972:   These recommendations were placed into the 1972 Local Government Act, which became operative from April 1974. The Act abolished all county boroughs and reduced the number of county councils in England and Wales from 58 to 47. Within these counties the 1,250 municipal boroughs and urban and rural districts were replaced by 333 district councils. In major conurbations, six metropolitan counties were established (Greater Manchester, Merseyside, West Midlands, Tyne and Wear, South Yorkshire, and West Yorkshire). Within the metropolitan areas 36 metropolitan districts were created.

Under the Act, the functions and responsibilities of new local authorities also changed. In the metropolitan areas, most service functions – education, housing, social services, libraries, museums, planning, refuse collection, and environmental health – were allocated to the metropolitan district councils. The six metropolitan councils were given strategic planning functions and responsibilities over a limited number of services, which were seen as requiring large areas of strategic control for efficient administration. These service functions included the police, fire service, public transport and refuse disposal. For the non-metropolitan areas, county councils were made responsible for major local authority services: education, social services, planning transport, highways, refuse disposal, fire service and police. The 'shire' district councils assumed control over housing, planning (development control and local planning), refuse collection, museums, paths, and municipal bus service. The Act of 1972 also gave all local authorities the power to spend up to a two-pence rate for the general benefit of their inhabitants.

1972:   In this year, the Conservative government passed the controversial Housing (Finance) Act which required local authorities to charge higher rents, but with planned reductions for those on low incomes. This was essentially a measure for reducing state expenditure. The Act was seen by some as undemocratic because it attempted to impose a rental policy on local authorities. With the election of a Labour government in 1974, the housing and rent powers of local authorities were restored. However, the provision that private tenants should receive rent allowances according to their income was kept.

1979:   Soon after the Conservatives' election victory, local government was subjected to stern criticism by Tory ministers. Initially, changes in the machinery of local government were not a priority.

1980:   The Housing Act of 1980 introduced new measures for the provision of council housing: (1) a major reduction in central government subsidy; (2) the Act gave council tenants the right to buy their own council homes at a considerable discount, 33–70 per cent, depending on the length and type of tenancy. Over one million council homes were purchased between 1981 and 1990. This constituted around 20 per cent of council house stock in Britain.

1982:   All seven metropolitan councils fall under Labour control at the local elections in this year. This leads to a series of conflicts between central and metropolitan authorities over central policy areas such as local economic development and the social services.

1983 (May):   The government introduced into its general election manifesto a pledge to abolish the six English metropolitan county councils and the GLC. The official line on this policy proposal was that these authorities had few functions and were therefore redundant. The Conservatives subsequently win the General Election on 7 June 1983.

1983 (October):   A White Paper produced this year, *Streamlining the Cities*, outlined the 1983 election manifesto pledge to abolish the six metropolitan county councils and the GLC. The functions of these metropolitan county councils, according to the Paper, would be devolved to a lower tier of local government – metropolitan district councils or London boroughs – or to a range of joint boards and central government departments.

1985:   The Local Government Act of 1985 abolished the GLC and the six metropolitan councils; this took effect from the 31 March 1986. As a result of the Act, London and metropolitan areas throughout England were left with a single tier of local government. Altogether there are 36 metropolitan districts and 32 London boroughs (and the ancient City of London). In the main, these are unitary or 'most purpose authorities', having responsibilities for areas such as education, housing, social services, highways, libraries, museums, planning, and economic development. The responsibilities of former metropolitan county councils, including the GLC, are transferred to the boroughs (for instance, education) and to various joint boards, such as joint police and joint passenger transport authorities, made up of appointed councillors.

1988:   The 1988 Housing Act introduced the concept of 'tenants' choice' which allowed new landlords (private, cooperatives, housing associations) to take over council housing following a ballot of tenants. This ballot was weighted against local authorities. But rather than challenging local authority ownership, councils have worked alongside housing associations and transferred their stock voluntarily.

1989:   As a result of the 1989 Local Government and Housing Act, all housing authorities were brought under greater central government control. The Act introduced stricter central government controls over the Housing Revenue Account (hereafter, HRA) of local authorities. The Act effectively reduced housing subsidies, thereby limiting the positive advantage of low rents afforded by council housing. The 1989 Act also required the HRA to become an independent trading account. Subsidizing the account from other areas was ruled out. A new HRA subsidy was given to local housing authorities based on a government-devised formula.

1992:   As part of the Local Government Act of 1992, a 15-member Local Government Commission for England, originally under the chairmanship of Sir John Banham, was established. The main objective of the Commission has been to replace the two-tier system of local government in England and Wales with unitary authorities. Towards this, the government directed the Commission to conduct reviews of specific local authority arrangements.

The internal restructuring of local government

1967:   A report by the Committee on the Management of Local Government, chaired by Lord Redcliffe-Maud, is published. The Committee was originally appointed to consider how local government might continue to attract and retain high-calibre members and senior officials. The Report found members were overly concerned with the details of the day-to-day administration rather than with strategic matters. Maud was critical of this situation and subsequently came up with a number of proposals. It suggested that in all but the smallest authorities a Management Board of between five and nine members should be appointed. The Board would have a wide range of delegated powers, including the ability to select those committee issues which make their way to the full council. The report also recommended a reduction in the number of committees and departments – around six was seen as sufficient.

There was a great deal of hostility to Maud. There were some who argued that it was an elitist measure, which would lead to the marginalization of elected members in local authorities. Nevertheless, the Maud Report stimulated some change: in many authorities, the number of committees was rationalized and the post of chief executive supplanted that of the town clerk. Despite the widespread hostility, the Maud Report was an important forerunner to those internal changes introduced in the 1970s with the publication of the Bains Report.

1972:   The Bains Committee was established in 1971 to provide advice on the future development of internal management structures in local government. The Bains Report of 1972 was more positively received than Maud. The Report argued that traditional departmentalization needed to give way to an authority-wide corporate structure. It made three main recommendations: (1) the appointment of a chief executive as leader of officers and general adviser on policy matters; (2) the creation of a policy and resources committee to provide coordinated advice to the council in setting plans, and in providing general advice on policy matters; (3) the establishment of a management team made up of senior officers, under the chief executive, to ensure the implementation of such plans. In 1974, following the 1972 structural reorganization, most councils followed the recommendations made by Bains.

1980:   Among its many provisions, the 1980 Local Government, Planning and Land Act introduced competitive tendering in local government for the first time. The Act specifically covered manual work areas, namely, construction, building maintenance, and highways. Competitive tendering was essentially a privatization strategy for local government services. It required local authorities to compare the costs of in-house services with those of private contractors in order to identify the most competitive bidder. However, under the Act, the comparison of bids was compulsory, but not the contracting-out of services to the bidder offering the most competitive contract.

1988: The Local Government Act of 1988 was the next major legislative initiative in the extension of compulsory competitive tendering or CCT. The Act extended CCT to various ancillary services in local authorities: building, cleaning, ground maintenance, vehicle maintenance, school meals, staff canteens, refuse collection, street cleaning, plus sports and leisure management (these functions were added in December 1989). The DoE issued a timetable for the phasing-in of contract awards. Parish authorities with budgets of less than £100,000 were excluded. For all the services, apart from grounds maintenance and sports and leisure management, competition was phased in over a 30-month timetable, from August 1989 to January 1992. A further element of compulsion was added by the fact that the Secretary of State was given powers under the Act (Section 13) which required authorities seen as anti-competitive to retender bids. In effect, this meant that following the bidding process local authorities would need to have very good reasons for not choosing the most competitively priced contract on offer.

1990 (September): The Audit Commission published a paper on the changing functions of local authorities and the role that councillors should play in the management of a local authority. In view of the internal changes brought about by the introduction of CCT, the paper wielded a certain amount of influence: it argued that the setting of strategy, policy planning, and reviewing of performance and organizational change should be the prime functions of elected members.

1991 (July): Michael Heseltine, who by this time was back at the DoE, produced a consultation paper, *The Internal Management of Local Authorities in England*. The paper put forward arguments favouring more elitist forms of management. The main underlying premise of the paper was that local authorities should increasingly look to become the enablers rather than the direct providers of services. It envisaged that local authorities should cultivate skills in setting up and overseeing contractual arrangements. Heseltine's document criticized the committee system as time-consuming and made a number of recommendations to overcome such perceived weaknesses: to promote more effective and business-like forms of decision-making; to enhance the scrutiny of decisions; to increase the interest taken by the public in local government; to provide the means whereby councillors could devote more of their time to constituency work. The 1990 Audit Commission and 1991 Heseltine papers were influential in moving the debate towards the terrain of local authorities as enablers rather than direct providers of services. This shift in the emphasis on the role of councillors and officers was further concretized by further CCT legislation.

1991:   The Conservative government, under John Major, made clear its commitment to expand CCT. In November 1991, the government published the consultation paper, *Competing for Quality*, which outlined proposals for extending competition in the provision of local services.

1992:   The basic precepts of the consultation paper were placed into the Local Government Act of this year. While CCT had only a minor impact prior to 1988, the government was convinced that CCT was the best way in which to secure the efficiency of service delivery at the local level. The 1992 Act essentially enabled the government to modify the provisions of the 1988 Act in order to extend CCT into 'white collar' areas of local authority services – the provision of professional advice and other services involving the application of financial or technical expertise. The 1992 Act enabled the government to add other white-collar and manual services at a later date. For instance, in June 1992 housing management became a possible target for CCT, with the publication of *Competing for Quality in Housing*. Moreover, local authorities were obliged to maintain an internal trading account of all professional services, even if they remained in-house. At the same time, the Act tightened the CCT mechanisms included in the 1980 and 1988 Local Government Acts by seeking to outlaw what are considered anti-competitive practices within local authorities.

1992 (November):   The then Secretary of State at the DoE, Michael Howard, published the Paper, *Extension of Compulsory Competitive Tendering*. This abandoned the centrally proscribed procedure of separate evaluation of bids according to price followed by quality. In this case, quality could become a more important factor as authorities would have the flexibility not to choose the lowest priced bid. The consultation paper also introduced other changes: police vehicle maintenance and police building cleaning and other services, such as fire service vehicle maintenance, were exempted from CCT.

1992 (December):   A certain degree of flexibility was introduced to CCT when the Housing Minister Sir George Young showed leniency over the timetable for placing housing management under CCT. He also proposed that small housing authorities would be exempt from CCT. (These events demonstrate that while the government was resolute about its CCT policy, there was a willingness on the part of some ministers to be flexible in extending competition to particular services.)

1993 (April):   The government outlined a timetable for introducing CCT to white-collar services: the first contracts (legal, construction, and computing services) were to be put out in October 1995 and the rest (computing, finance, personnel, corporate administrative) were to be placed under CCT no later than April 1997.

A reading schedule

The best textbooks on public policy have substantial sections or chapters devoted to the level of agency. Part III of Parsons (1995) provides an extensive overview of decision-making analysis and theoretical models. Sections 3.4, 3.5, and 3.6 of Parsons examine rational approaches to decision-making and recent market-orientated interpretations of the rational approach. Ham and Hill (1993; chapters 5, 8 and 9) provides an overview of various aspects concerning the role of agency in the policy process. Hill's (1993) series of edited articles on the policy process contains a whole section (part VIII) focusing on the influence of front-line staff. This section includes some important articles on the importance of discretion in policy situations. Refer to Dunleavy and O'Leary (1987: chapter 3) and, particularly, King (1987: chapters 5, 6 and 7) for useful summaries of the political ideas that underline the policy of competitive tendering. Walsh (1995b: chapters 1, 2, and 3) contrasts traditional forms of service provision with market models, while chapter 5 provides an insight into the debates about contracting.

There is a burgeoning literature on competition and contracting across different public institutions. Local government has attracted much analytical attention. Research by the late Kieron Walsh is highly informative. See Walsh (1991) for a comprehensive study on the impact of competitive tendering in local government. Patterson and Pinch (1995) is an illuminating article about CCT in local government. Stoker (1991: chapter 9) is a useful summary of privatization in local government. For an examination of competitive tendering in other public sector institutions the following journals, especially those printed after 1990, should be referred to: *Public Adminstration, Local Government Studies, Housing Studies,* and *Public Money and Management* contain a significant range of articles.

Issues for revision and further consideration

Having studied this case study you should be familiar with several key concepts relevant to policy analysis. These are as follows: the level of agency (section 6.1); public choice theory (6.3.1); compul-

▶▶

▶▶

sory competitive tendering (6.2); direct service provision (6.2); value for money/rational efficiency (6.3.1); contractor and client (6.3.2); hard and soft splits (6.3.2); quality criteria (6.4.1); hierarchical authority (6.4.2); cooperative contractual links (6.4.3 and 6.5).

▶ In what ways does competitive tendering strengthen the hand of local authority managers?

▶ Describe the possible ways that CCT can be modified to better suit the types of behaviour patterns found in local government?

▶ Why do informal relations between officials perform a significant function? Is this true also of other public institutions?

▶ To what extent has contracting transformed the behaviour of and relations between local government agents?

7

An interorganizational level of analysis: central–local policy action in the Riverside DHA

7.1 Introduction: an interorganizational level of analysis

Policy is not wholly determined and controlled by central government. As will be studied in this chapter, peripheral or local policy institutions, and the agents that operate in these contexts, actively engage in shaping and redefining policy set by the centre. However, this process is far from being entirely dependent upon bodies beyond the executive sphere. Central government still has a significant role in the policy process. These may be two separate and distinct spheres of the state machinery, but policy is the outcome of interdependencies that exist between them.

Hence, the final case study in this section focuses on an intermediate level of analysis – on interorganizational relations (see section 3.6). This particular level of analysis is concerned with the multiplicity of relations that exist between organizations in government. In particular, it examines the links between central political institutions and local governmental bodies or territorial service institutions. This intermediate level of analysis does not discount or belittle the contribution of policy agents. As Rhodes (1992: 316) observes, intergovernmental analysis does consider the relations between public officials. It is especially concerned with the politicized nature of these relationships. Interest groups, professionals, politicians and officials are continually engaged in a process of attempting to influence policy strategy or gain a particular share of resources.

This chapter uses the National Health Service (hereafter, NHS) to explore the intricacies and nature of intergovernmental relations. The analysis specifically examines events within the former London health authority of Riverside. The object of this study is a major restructuring programme. This entailed the closure of two district general hospitals and three specialist care units, and the subsequent construction of a new hospital on a single site.

These developments were intimately tied to a series of administrative, organizational and financial reforms pursued systematically over a period of time by central government. Significantly, restructuring in Riverside may have been unlikely without such central intervention. No attempt is made, though, to sustain the view that policy is a preordained matter, emanating from the highest authorities in government. Events show that crucial developments took place among local, territorial institutions. Here, local policy actors made crucial decisions that were carried out within Riverside. The study attempts to understand how this came about, and it assesses the repercussions of such action for the policy process.

7.2 The authority of the centre: central government restructuring and the Riverside Health Authority

There is, in the literature on government action, a distinctive approach which conceptualizes policy as a centralized executive function. A classic early statement of this position is Weber's formative work on bureaucracy. For Weber, policy decisions in modern democracies are the locus of those who occupy the highest and most authoritative positions in government. This has taken place because of the increasing scale and complexity of society.

While there are different emphases, advocates of this model, like Weber, generally view policy as the provenance of figures at the centre of the government system. These officials provide clear goals and guidelines for implementing policy. This is done to ensure that the actions of implementing officials do not waver or divert from the objectives originally established from above (Sabatier, 1993: 267). There are policy analysts who advocate the top-down approach as the most efficient method for enacting policy (see Chapter 8). Hogwood and Gunn (1984: 210–12), for instance, prescribe that decisions should essentially originate from the top. This should be done to minimize the exercise of discretion by local agencies and, thereby, ensure unadulterated implementation.

This view of policy is highly problematic. Top-down theories tend to overemphasize the role of the centre as the mainspring of policy, while overlooking peripheral institutions beyond the centre. Barrett and Hill (1984: 219) note how policy 'is modified and mediated over time in response to external circumstances or as a result of the actions and responses of those responsible for its execution or upon whom it is brought to bear'.

The case analysis in this chapter in no way seeks to develop a perspective orientated towards central government institutions. Policy is a continuous process, involving constant adjustment and redefinition by different levels of government. Berman (1978: 157) argues that 'policy passes through and is transmuted by successive levels of implementing operations. The net result is that the effective power to determine a policy's outcome rests with local deliverers.' Berman's view may be a little extreme. To argue that the centre is rendered powerless, by the complexity of the policy process and by its dependency on local implementing agents, is equally spurious.

The 1980s demonstrated the impact and scale of change wrought by top-down intervention, especially in the public sector. The health service figured prominently in these central reforms. Events which unfolded in Riverside, as shall be shown, owed a great deal to restructuring of the health service by the centre. By the same token, this analysis endeavours to avoid repeating the errors commonly associated with a centrally orientated approach: these central reforms did not determine or automatically lead to strategies that emerged within Riverside. The policy of reorganization pursued in Riverside was initiated and shaped by those operating in various institutional settings at the ground level, by managers, practitioners and interest groups.

For the moment, we focus on government policy, on the way it helped shape events in Riverside. There are two areas of particular concern. The first preoccupation are those changes to the system of resource allocation within the NHS. Second, the analysis focuses on those public sector reforms initiated during the 1980s. How these two central reform trends influenced events in Riverside will be examined in greater detail below.

7.2.1   Restructuring resource allocation: the 'emergent' policy framework in Riverside

The very conditions, which led to the restructuring programme in Riverside can be located to the development of health care in London. The provision of medical services in London has long been under the spotlight of central government. Difficulties centred around the large number of teaching hospitals, disproportionate when compared to the whole population. Community and primary care facilities, by contrast, are widely regarded as inadequate (see Tomlinson, 1992). Over the years there have been numerous commissions and reviews of London's health service and hospital institutions. Since the late nineteenth century up until the early 1980s, governments and various organizations attached to the health service have carried out around twenty different reviews (Rivett, 1986: 349–63). The overwhelming evidence from these reviews showed that the proportion of acute hospital beds, when compared to the diminishing residential population, had in actual fact increased. The case for changing the capital's hospital service – notably, systematic rationalization – was clear but somewhat complicated by the predominance of institutions engaged in medical research and teaching.

The problematic nature of health care in London was not properly addressed until difficulties emerged over resource distribution in the whole service. Since its inception, the question of NHS expenditure was a source of political concern and debate. Nevertheless, support for the NHS was entrenched. Thus funding continued to rise, both as a proportion of national income and in real terms, throughout the 1950s and 1960s. The political demands to rein in spending did not gain resonance in government circles until the mid-1970s. Moves to economize within the NHS, and in the public sector generally, gained urgency as the condition of the domestic economy began to deteriorate. Ministers responded by hauling back spending on the NHS. They sought, in addition, to introduce efficiency savings within the NHS. Integral to this task was the attempt to overcome the geographical inequalities which had emerged over health funding. Analysis showed that NHS funding was not wholly congruent with the actual needs of regions and districts. To ensure greater equity in the distribution of finance to the different regions, the Labour government introduced the RAWP (Resource Allocation Working Party) formula in 1977.

The RAWP system introduced a new formula based on mortality rates and demographic factors for assessing the health needs of English regions. Previously, funding very much followed patterns established by historical precedence. The outcome was that prosperous areas continued to gain, while less prosperous regions with major health needs were left to relative neglect (Baggott, 1994: 88). The London regions with many prestigious teaching hospitals had enjoyed a gilded past. The future prospects for London's hospitals in the wake of the RAWP exercise were less favourable. Such were the demographic shifts which had taken place in London that resources had outstripped the health needs of London's diminishing population. The RAWP formula showed that the four Thames regional health authorities of London were overfunded in comparison to the rest of the country. Consequently, London hospitals over time were poised to face significant reductions in funding in order to divert funding to more needy areas. This required a comprehensive review and reorganization of services across health authorities throughout the four main regional health authorities in London. A move of this sort would be politically sensitive.

Such plans were directed from within the London area. This happened even though central government had established the financial framework that had foisted restructuring onto the agenda. Attempts from the late 1960s to restructure London's medical schools provided the local impetus for these changes. Historically, these schools had developed within teaching hospitals rather than universities. This produced 12 highly independent medical schools, which provided a buffer against sweeping changes to the health service in London, including medical education. In 1968, Lord Todd's Royal Commission endeavoured to create six undergraduate teaching units through sweeping amalgamations. This particular initiative was successfully resisted by the 12 schools.

Under the 1974 restructuring of the NHS, the staunchly independent teaching hospitals were brought under the control of regional and district authorities. This made the prospect for change more likely. An embryonic attempt to orchestrate change across the London regions came in the form of the London Coordinating Committee, formed in 1975. This was followed in 1977 by the London Health Planning Consortium, a non-executive body which provided advice on restructuring the health service in London. The Consortium argued that the high level of acute medical facilities required to support London's medical schools could no longer be justified, on the grounds of London's diminishing population. The Consortium's final report did not emerge until 1981, but in the intervening period further pressure for reform came from the projected reduction of the University of London finances. The Vice Chancellor of the university, Lord Annan, was moved to form a working party on the matter. The working party, under the chairmanship of Lord Flowers, reported in 1980, and recommended that larger medical schools should be formed to keep within financial targets (Pettigrew *et al.*, 1992: 72).

When presented to the University Senate, these proposals were defeated by a narrow margin. Notwithstanding this, the momentum for change gathered pace in view of the fact that financial allocations in the Thames regions were due to fall in the 1980s, a consequence of the RAWP formula. As such, revised proposals were put forward in 1981. The University of London suggested that four independent medical schools should be maintained (the Royal Free, St Mary's, St George's and King's Hospital Medical School), while the remaining eight institutions would be merged to establish four medical schools. Amongst the recommendations was a proposed merger between Charing Cross and Westminster Medical Schools and the establishment of a joint school between the Middlesex and the Faculty of Clinical Sciences of University College (Rivett, 1986: 336–7). In December 1981, the University Senate finally accepted these recommendations (Pettigrew *et al.*, 1992: 73).

The Senate's decision led to the redrawing of those districts implicated in the school mergers. A joint venture, involving the medical schools of Middlesex and UCL, led to the creation of the Bloomsbury District Health Authority in 1982. Creating the combined Charing Cross and Westminster Medical School in 1984 was the catalyst, in the following year, for the merger of the Victoria and Hammersmith and Fulham Health Districts. The redrawing of these two boundaries led to the creation of the new Riverside District Health Authority. Riverside, like Bloomsbury, was created primarily to develop an agenda for the retrenchment of medical services. The future prospect of rationalization in Riverside, as in other districts, presented considerable logistical and political difficulties. Primarily, the responsibility for developing a retrenchment strategy was left to the district health authority. Central government would play a peripheral role in cultivating this strategy. However, it was the pursuit of public sector reforms by the centre which brought to the fore local institutional arrangements and a set of policy agents, in the relevant positions of authority, that could manage the necessary changes.

7.2.2 New public sector reforms: the 'emergent' policy agents in Riverside

New allocation measures and local responses to these policies, as demonstrated above, created the context for pursuing new arrangements in Riverside. The aim now is to account for the way this plan was executed. This will mean identifying those policy agents who formulated and enacted the programme. Health administrators-cum-managers played a central role in reorganizing the health authority. The reason for their prominence can be located to major structural reforms of the NHS. These changes typified, and were symptomatic of, reforms introduced throughout the public sector during the 1980s. According to Ferlie *et al.* (1996), the importance of these central reforms was their systematic nature and persistence over time:

> In the 1980s a new concept of radical shock, where the scale of the repetitive application of a single set of policy objectives, emerged as significant ... Post-1980 processes of reform may move through the various layers of the organization, reconfigure power relations within the organization ... It is the cumulative effect of the combination of all these factors ... which is significant rather than the effects of any one. (ibid. 37)

Conservative administrations in the 1980s, under the ideological and political guardianship of Margaret Thatcher, set about reshaping what was perceived to be an overblown, sectionally dominated and largely ineffective state bureaucracy. Central to this programme of reform was the transformation of public administration. The aim was to bring private sector models of management and greater financial discipline in public sector institutions and services. Such reforms were viewed as integral to engendering a more business-like approach.

Similar reforms have taken place throughout the public sector. However, the pace and extent of reform in the health service was particularly intensive. Ferlie *et al.* (1996: 88–9) argue that such reforms are of transformational significance: that is, fundamental and pervasive. Like other areas of the public sector, the health service was seen as too bureaucratic. The incoming Conservative government in 1979 immediately pursued its manifesto commitment to reduce the NHS bureaucracy. The reform document, *Patients First*, contained proposals for abolishing the middle tier of the NHS – the area health authorities. At the same time, there was to be a greater delegation of managerial responsibilities to those providing heath care at unit level – hospitals or community services.

These proposals came into effect in 1982. But concerns emerged that decentralization could weaken the ability of Parliament and the DHSS to monitor the health system. This early strategy was promptly replaced by an emphasis on devolved management. For Norman Fowler, the new Health Secretary who resided over this policy shift, administrative problems within the NHS were due to management; the relationship between the centre and localities was irrelevant (Baggott, 1994: 122). The vehicle for these reforms was the Griffiths Report. The Report was based around the views of a single adviser, the senior retail executive Sir Roy Griffiths. His conclusions put forward the case for major structural changes over incremental progress. Griffiths maintained that the malaise in the NHS was the product of consensus-style management. Members of health authority management teams were typically drawn from different professional backgrounds such as finance, nursing, medicine and administration. The ethos in such teams was more one of negotiation and bargaining than the imposition of decisions. This form of management was seen to be ubiquitous. According to Griffiths, it gave rise to procrastination in decision-making, a lack of clarity over responsibilities, and, ultimately, to inefficiency in service delivery. These observations were not shared by Griffiths alone. The Royal Commission of 1979 and research done at the time reached broadly similar conclusions (see Merrison Report, 1979).

In contrast to the earlier Royal Commission, Griffiths maintained that there was a clear case for reinventing NHS management. The Report advocated, *inter alia*, the replacement of consensus-dominated administrative teams by a system of general management. This involved placing responsibilities for planning and control of service performance under a single management figure. Such appointments, it was argued, should be made at all levels in the NHS.

The Griffiths Report gained wholesale acceptance by the government, which was determined to implement the recommendations without delay. Such was the haste of the government's timetable that general managers were in place throughout the NHS by 1986. Individual health authorities and their chairpersons were given the autonomy to make these managerial appointments, although such decisions could be overturned by the DHSS.

Ministers were concerned that most of the new cadre of general managers should be recruited from outside the NHS, particularly the commercial sector. Management within the NHS initially did not have the same attractions and fringe benefits as comparable positions within the private sector. Available data on the backgrounds of new general managers in the NHS revealed that most of those appointed by 1986 were former NHS administrators (Baggott, 1994: 127). Riverside was no exception. The incumbent general manager at Riverside was previously district administrator for Victoria Health Authority. In addition, he brought other managers from Victoria to join his 10-strong management team, consisting of medical and professional representatives (*Fieldwork Interview*, Senior Health Official, 26 June 1995). This nucleus of managers constituted the central policy actors in Riverside – those overseeing policy decisions of major strategic importance. Although many of them hailed from Victoria Health District, a clear effort was made to ensure that the creation of general management was accompanied by substantive changes in administrative style.

The aim for the remainder of this case study is to assess the impact of these new local arrangements in Riverside. The study focuses in particular on the reliance placed by central government on local territorial institutions, in this case the district health authority, and key agents within this organization, namely managers and members of the district's governing body. Local territorial bodies of the state machinery are often better positioned than the state machinery to deal with the panoply of interest groups, professional bodies, trade unions and community organizations. These local officials are also better equipped to deal with the complex interdependencies that exist within decentralized government institutions.

7.3 The significance of local organizations and their agents

The previous section examined the impact of centrally driven policy in the NHS. These observations do not provide a complete picture. The assertion of this chapter is that the formation and development of policy is not the sole preserve of central government. Governments depend on a diverse range of local organizations, consisting of officials, professionals and practitioners. These peripheral settings are not passive recipients of central government decisions. They are in position to influence the way such programmes are delivered, even redefining or making new policy on the ground. This can be seen even in those instances where governments set out unequivocal policy objectives, often accompanied by legislation. Researching the enforcement of environmental regulations on businesses, Peacock (1984) found that officials were often sensitive to the specific circumstances of individual companies. Thus in times of recession they were less rigorous when applying *statutory* requirements (ibid. 104).

At the same time, governments do not always provide clear policy guidelines; the responsibility for developing strategies in these circumstances belongs to organizations beyond the centre and their army of officials. The reorganization programme in Riverside falls into this category. On the one hand, central government determined crucial aspects about the health care system in London, certainly in financial and organizational terms. On the other hand, officials in regional and district bodies were left to develop a strategy of scaling down hospital services in response to new allocation measures. Such is the complexity, and sensitivity, of rationalization that those operating locally are ideally placed to oversee such a process. A programme of this kind cannot be imposed: it requires a strategy, based on local knowledge, astute management and political negotiation. The remainder of this chapter focuses on the procedures adopted by the Riverside District Health Authority to balance vested interests in the course of trying to usher in a programme of rationalization. The argument is that these procedures shaped the emerging policy. We begin by examining how financial imperatives in early managerial decisions and actions shaped Riverside.

7.3.1 Early responses to financial targets in Riverside

The prospect of retrenchment was not an issue that could be avoided or deflected for consideration at a later, more convenient date. Riverside was formed during preparations by the North-West Thames Region of its 10-year strategy. Publication of this document in October 1985 came to dominate the strategic considerations and plans of senior officials in Riverside. As the most overallocated region in the country, according to the RAWP calculations, the report noted that financial allocations to the region were projected to fall. Financial support had to be redirected from the centre, where population levels were in decline, to districts outside London where population growth necessitated an expansion of service provision.

The region's proposed strategy held serious implications for inner-London districts, especially Riverside. Riverside was the largest district with a budget of around £130 million. Thus it was expected to deliver savings of around £32 million by 1994. Cuts to priority and acute services were singled out as prime targets for savings. According to the region, acute bed provision in Riverside had to be reduced from 960 to 625 beds (later revised to 738).

By forming Riverside, the first necessary step toward achieving these savings had been taken. But it was not inevitable that reorganization would follow. The case of Bloomsbury is a prime example. This district, like Riverside, was established on the premise of rationalization. However, restructuring in this authority did not progress as expected; the formulation and implementation of a programme for the acute sector proceeded sluggishly. Management in the district proved largely unwilling to develop a strategy. They were also highly ineffective in dealing with attempts by professional groups to obfuscate retrenchment (Pettigrew *et al.*, 1992: 88).

Riverside's managers, by contrast, showed a greater willingness and urgency to restructure services. While Riverside was established three years after Bloomsbury, it achieved more rapid progress in forming a strategy for the acute sector. Three factors were prominent in this respect. First, the hospital network within Riverside was not overburdened, like Bloomsbury, by a dense and complex arrangement of units. Riverside had 12 hospitals and a further 17 health centres and clinics located within the district. Acute hospital care was concentrated, though, on six main sites (Charing Cross, Westminster and St Stephen's were general teaching hospitals, while

West London, St Mary Abbot's and Westminster Children's Hospital provided specialist acute care).

Second, Riverside's officials gained full assistance and cooperation from the regional health authority. This is hardly surprising as the region's 10-year strategy centred around reducing services within London. In response to the urgency shown at district level, regional officials did not force or expect speedy solutions; managers were afforded the time and flexibility to develop a strategy. An indication of this flexibility was shown when the region amended the projected target of future bed allocations. District managers insisted that the regional figure of 625 beds was not sufficient to maintain two viable teaching hospitals. A revised target of 738 beds was given, providing managers could deliver revenue savings.

A third pivotal factor was the part played by management. As we have already noted, the post-Griffiths reforms increased the decision-making powers of managers in health authorities. Managerial heads in Riverside possessed considerable authority over the formation and implementation of policy. Significantly, district managers in Riverside embraced restructuring as imperative to the future viability of the district. Planning and monitoring systems were put in place to ensure that managers at all levels in the district were prepared and geared for organizational change (Battle, 1989: 169). Riverside's new general manager had already presided over reorganization plans for acute services in the Victoria District where he was chief administrator. The plans for Victoria included the possible closure of both St Stephen's and Westminster, and the development of a new hospital on the St Mary's site. This was seen to be an attractive option in terms of location and, most importantly, in terms of generating long-term savings for the authority (Paton and Bach, 1990: 39).

No concrete decisions were taken following the publication of Victoria's framework strategy in 1984. Yet a precedent and strategy for retrenchment had been established. It is no coincidence that a year later the Riverside merger took place. The senior administrator who had moved over from Victoria to become general manager at Riverside was confronted by a new situation. The creation of Riverside had brought together three major teaching hospitals into a single district. The eastern part of the new district – the area formerly occupied by Victoria Health Authority – contained two of these sites, namely, St Stephen's and Westminster Hospitals. It was unlikely both could remain, especially as the teaching hospital in Fulham, Charing Cross, was a relatively new establishment. Riverside's management was left to create an appropriate plan of action.

Piecemeal tinkering and isolated closures of hospitals could not produce the required savings. An extensive programme of restructuring, previously mooted by managers in the former Victoria Health Authority, was the only realistic chance of meeting expected financial targets. As an option, it was highly precarious. Nevertheless, managers, especially under the leadership of the general manager, were keen to get results. The realization of this more ambitious project went through three main stages: first, developing a strategy; second, attaining consent by negotiating and bargaining with interest groups; and finally, attempting to execute plans with few delays.

7.3.2   Developing a long-term strategy

Managers at Riverside had long appreciated the importance of major structural changes. Soon after the creation of Riverside, researchers from the King's Fund College were employed to investigate the future configuration of acute services. The findings would ultimately contribute to an overall strategic plan for Riverside. These experts eschewed traditional cost-benefit analysis for a more sophisticated planning methodology known as multiscenario planning. This methodology, unlike quantitative models, took into account the nature of decision-making and the influence of political factors (*Fieldwork Interview*, Senior Health Official, 26 June 1995).

The presence of the King's Fund was not simply a technical matter. Such participation was expedient on two counts. First, the involvement of a renowned organization ensured certain *gravitas*, and, hence, possible support, for the strategy when it finally emerged. Second, a period of investigation under the auspices of the King's Fund gave district managers space to develop a plan of action on their own terms, freeing them from external timetables. The region was amenable to the proactive stance of Riverside's management, although this autonomy was granted on an understanding that concrete savings were part of the deal.

To ensure progress in reaching a final strategy, a planning team was established in 1985. Its membership consisted of Riverside's director of planning, a specialist in community medicine and a representative from the King's Fund. The deliberations conducted by the team aimed to plot different future scenarios. This was done by isolating possible factors that would determine demand for, and supply of, health care in future years. Population changes, epidemiology, and medical practice and technology were seen as the key determinants in shaping demand. By contrast, supply issues were seen to be determined by health policy, resources, medical practice and technology. The group concluded from its survey that future trends in medical provision were likely to see a move away from acute hospital provision to local, community-based services. This, once again, confirmed the importance of restructuring in Riverside (Paton and Bach, 1990: 43–4).

Managers in the district preferred to pre-empt and prepare for these changes, rather than have closures imposed upon the district by regional officials or government ministers. During the hiatus provided by the planning exercise in 1986, senior district authority managers considered the possibility of closing Westminster Hospital and retaining St Stephen's because of its central location and community focus. Such a plan was potentially very sensitive and extremely precarious. Westminster, as a hospital frequently used by politicians and even members of the Royal family, was protected by its political support and reputation. At this juncture, neither the health authority members nor the Health Secretary were prepared to make a final decision on such a plan.

Ministerial refusal to approve a radical shake-up was not taken as a definitive response. Financial pressures still meant long-term viability could only be attained by reducing acute services. In 1986, Riverside was given an allocation of £123 million, a reduction of 3.2 per cent. Managers, as result, considered the closure of West London Hospital in Hammersmith. Such proposals were met with vociferous opposition, which was exacerbated by an impending by-election. Management ultimately shelved the plan in 1987.

Despite the lack of a concrete scheme, advancement towards a definite strategy for restructuring moved on regardless. Central to the progress made was the planning team's completion, in 1986, of a strategic framework for Riverside. The document outlined various alternative futures, which were linked to five different policy options. All the options included the transfer of services from St Mary Abbot's Hospital and its eventual closure. However, five different possibilities were detailed over the prospects of Riverside's three district general hospitals: (1) retain all three district general hospitals; (2) retain Charing Cross and St Stephen's; (3) retain Charing Cross and Westminster; (4) retain Charing Cross and build a new site; (5) retain St Stephen's and Westminster (Paton and Bach, 1990: 49–50).

The first of these five options had the advantage of not leading to major hospital closures. At the same time, this seemed very unlikely as Riverside was facing cuts in resources. The second option to retain services at Charing Cross and St Stephen's was a distinct possibility. Nonetheless, it was problematic in that it required the closure of Westminster Hospital and an injection of capital to transfer resources between the two hospitals. The possibility of retaining services at Charing Cross and Westminster had a number of advantages and disadvantages, similar to those outlined for the second option. The fourth option of retaining services at Charing Cross and creating a new hospital in Riverside East had a certain amount of support from the medical profession. However, the building of a new hospital was financially precarious, delaying revenue savings until the mid-1990s. The final option of retaining Westminster and St Stephen's Hospitals and closing Charing Cross was unlikely. This would have led to the closure of a relatively new hospital with a developing expertise in medical technology.

The strategic framework noted that the most flexible option in the short term was to retain all three existing district general hospitals. Managers, therefore, were saved from making an early commitment to a single course of action. By the same token, a policy strategy of this kind was not sustainable because of the decline in revenue support. For long-term viability, considerable reductions in priority acute services were needed. Such a move specifically entailed the retention of two main hospital sites – most probably Charing Cross and one site in Riverside East. The most viable option gaining support among managers was to place this new hospital on the St Stephen's site.

7.3.3 The bargaining process

Any major restructuring had to be sanctioned and approved by the health minister. As such, senior management took informal advice from the Department of Health (hereafter, DoH) about the possibilities of closing Westminster and the concomitant development of a new hospital. The minister intimated that the proposal for a new site would be politically acceptable providing it was supported by key elements of Riverside's constituency: clinical staff of Westminster Hospital, local MPs and members of the district health authority (Patton and Bach, 1990: 52). The question here concerns how the central policy actors – the general manager and senior managerial staff – would gain the consent of these groups when there was a likely conflict of interest. As Barrett and Hill (1984: 226) argue, there are situations where compliance is achieved through the application of hierarchical authority.

Weber, in his analysis of organizations, maintained that in modern bureaucracies compliance to authority is institutionalized due to the prevalence of rational and highly centralized forms of administration. There is an 'imperative of coordination, a situation where there is a high likelihood that orders will be obeyed regardless of their content' (Swingewood, 1991: 190). Weber's thesis on bureaucratic authority has been subject to critical examination for providing a mechanical, rule-bound portrayal of human behaviour and decision-making within organizations. These arguments relegate human action to a mere adjunct of bureaucratic authority. This is problematic, especially in terms of policy-making. There are individuals and groups operating within public sector organizations who occupy positions of autonomy and, as such, cannot be subject to direct authority from above. Dunsire (1978: 229) notes:

> If an office-holder is essentially autonomous, the custodian of specialised knowledge, entitled to be consulted and to be listened to … what is left of his subordinate status? How can he be autonomous and subject to authority?

Barrett and Hill argue that the implementation of policy relies on mechanisms other than those based around formal authority. It is notable that bargaining and negotiation often feature in the policy process – characteristics which often lead to modifications and changes in the original policy. What became evident was the way management relied upon bargaining and negotiation to win the support and compliance of key constituencies within Riverside. Before this process of bargaining is detailed, brief consideration is given to the nature of bargaining in the policy process and its role in interorganizational relations.

A number of writers in the policy field have provided explanatory frameworks for the way bargaining operates. A variety of studies have focused on the mechanisms involved in the process and the conditions under which bargaining takes place. From this work, two opposing perspectives have emerged. The first conceptualizes bargaining as, what is termed, a *positive sum process*. Pressman and Wildavsky (1973), who are associated with this perspective, maintain that consensus is central to the way bargaining and negotiation proceed in policy settings: 'Bargaining must take place to reconcile the differences, with the result that the policy may be modified, even to the point of compromising its original purpose. Coordination in this sense is another word for consent' (ibid. 134). Here bargaining largely depends upon shared perceptions of mutual dependence. As a result, the exchange involved in bargaining means that all parties are due to gain, rather than one group succeeding at the expense of others. Pressman and Wildavsky's positive sum conception of bargaining portrays interorganizational relations as functionally dependent; the possibility of power and conflict entering this relation is given less consideration.

The issue of power has been redressed by those who argue that bargaining fundamentally revolves around conflict between opposing sets of interests. When consensus over goals and objectives breaks down between autonomous groups and individuals, the ensuing struggle takes place through negotiation. Hence, bargaining becomes a means of achieving certain goals or a means towards attaining control. Bardach (1977: 231), who is associated with this zero sum view of the bargaining process, observes: 'Negotiations ... are a form of future-testing; but they are also a form of future-controlling ... the negotiators attempt to control actions that will take place in the future.'

Barrett and Hill (1984) argue that both perspectives are useful, although as models in their own right they are ultimately flawed in their observations on bargaining activity. The positive sum or exchange theory is useful in those situations where there is mutual acknowledgement by groups or individuals that their objectives can be furthered through bargaining. This perspective has little utility in those situations where relations between interest groups are in conflict over certain goals. The bargaining process is linked to a struggle for control, influence or autonomy – this is a zero sum game (ibid. 230–1). Assessments of the situation in Northern Ireland – an internecine war between two sections of society divided along sectarian lines – is often couched using such terms. However, as Bacharach and Lawler (1980) note, within the zero sum perspective there is in effect very little room for negotiation, compromise or flexibility. The complexity of bargaining situations in organizational contexts is such that bargaining according to these authors is more ambivalent, or to use their term involves 'mixed motive':

> A mixed motive situation encompasses elements from both positive-sum and zero-sum situations. In other words, parties are simultaneously confronted with incentives to cooperate and incentives to compete. Such situations encompass greater complexity and uncertainty than either positive-sum or zero-sum situations. (ibid. 107)

This conception of bargaining as a mixed motive situation, involving both negotiation and struggle over control, is a prominent feature of the health service. Ham (1981) in a study of Leeds Regional Health Board makes the following observation. Several different individuals and interest groups were involved in policy-making, but none of these factions had the influence to control the others. This led to bargaining in a system of bureaucratic politics, which led to only incremental changes being made (ibid. 197). Similarly in Riverside, there were a number of interest groups which would be affected by the proposed restructuring. District managers had to negotiate the support of various stakeholders affected by these changes. One senior official observed the following about this process of engineering agreement:

> Over the years I constructed a very clear view about how change is determined in the health service ... But in those days, putting it very crudely, I pictured it as a circle with management in the middle. Around the outside were constituent interests: DoH, Region, Authority, doctors, MPs, local authorities, community groups, the establishment. (*Fieldwork Interview*, Senior Riverside Official, 26 June 1995)

The process of bargaining should be examined in terms of a political and social context where asymmetries of power exist. Not all the groups mentioned above were of equal importance. Hence, the process of bargaining very much centred on certain influential groups: the Riverside District Health Authority, the local Conservative MPs, Kensington and Chelsea local authority and the Westminster Hospital's clinicians. Indeed, the DoH made it clear to

Riverside DHA managers that ministerial approval for the scheme would not be forthcoming unless they managed to gain the backing of these groups.

Riverside's management team had to mobilize this support within a given timetable. The team was scheduled to release a consultation document on its final proposals at the beginning of 1988. Thus senior managers worked throughout 1987 trying to develop the backing of both Westminster medical staff and district health authority members. Mixed motives were very much in evidence in the bargaining process. The health authority managers used resources at their disposal and control of the overall planned strategy as a bargaining device to elicit the agreement of these two vital groups. At the same, these groups, which to a certain extent opposed some aspects of the restructuring programme, were in a position to withhold full support until health authority managers provided definite concessions.

The situation at the district health authority was complicated by the political complexion of its membership. The merger to form Riverside brought in a number of Labour councillors from Hammersmith and Fulham who were opposed to hospital closures. While Conservative councillors from Kensington were supportive, there were several other members who were uncommitted. As such, there was not a clear majority in favour of a new teaching hospital at St Stephen's. Members of the district health authority wanted smaller community-based medical units rather than a large centralized hospital. An important part of the management strategy to win over members came in its plan to use £5 million, generated by the land sales of older hospitals marked for closure, for community care schemes. One of these programmes was the building of five homes for the elderly to replace St Mary Abbot's Hospital, which provided long-term care for the elderly and the mentally ill. The second project involved the building of a primary health care centre south of Westminster. This ancillary development, according to one senior official involved, became an important bargaining tool:

> But I can't deny that in looking at the other changes – building five homes for the elderly, a south Westminster primary health care centre – all that undoubtedly was the means of persuading the majority on the Authority to vote for the scheme, because ... they could not have those community-based services unless they voted

for the whole package – which included a brand new teaching hospital. (*Fieldwork Interview*, Senior Riverside Official, 26 June 1995)

When Riverside District Health Authority finally met to vote on the final proposals in May 1988, 13 voted in favour and 3 against.

The clinicians at Westminster Hospital were a distinctly powerful group because of the hospital's close links with the House of Commons. Indeed, many MPs relied on the medical services provided at the Westminster Hospital. Consultants there also treated members of the Royal family. Hence, the Westminster doctors constituted a very powerful lobby, and this was why DoH ministers insisted that their support for Riverside plans was necessary before political backing was forthcoming. In a 1986 paper published by Riverside District Health Authority, there was intimation of what would be required to win over Westminster medical staff to the idea of closing their hospital: 'Many medical staff ... are susceptible to inducements to accept the closure of Westminster Hospital. The most obvious and effective would be the offer of a new hospital at either St Mary Abbot's or Brompton' (quoted in Paton and Bach, 1990: 48).

However, during a period of informal consultation on the St Stephen's feasibility study which followed the district health authority meeting in May 1987, problems emerged. It was made clear that the offer of a new hospital in the form of a refurbished St Stephen's Hospital was not entirely acceptable to Westminster medical staff. For these doctors, the plan did not provide what they saw as a proper teaching hospital. Nevertheless, medical staff, together with the district medical committee and the Westminster Medical School, accepted the principle of bringing hospital services under a single site; problems arose over the proposed academic and medical facilities that would be available in the new hospital. At this point, the district health authority felt there was sufficient support to produce a revised functional proposal for the new hospital which would form the basis of a consultation document. Senior managers in collaboration with the region and external surveyors, prepared a report late in 1987. The report was based on a detailed examination of the St Stephen's site in view of the functional requirements outlined by medical staff. The report showed that it was not really possible to fit all the necessary medical services and specialities required by medical staff onto a refurbished St Stephen's site (Paton and Bach, 1990: 56–7).

Consequently, at the end of 1987 managers decided to reverse their original plans to refurbish St Stephen's. Instead, they pursued a plan that would form the central part of the consultation document for the new year. The reformulated strategy would entail the total demolition of the St Stephen's site in order to build a brand new hospital. Managers and the authority chairman in their informal deliberations with Westminster medical staff offered the prospect of a new hospital on the St Stephen's site. This generally proved more acceptable to the clinicians. Because of their influence and authority, senior Westminster medical staff were able to demand that the new hospital should be called the Westminster and Chelsea Hospital, even though it was to be built on the old St Stephen's site. (For various logistical reasons, the original name of the hospital was changed to the Chelsea and Westminster Hospital.) Although doctors from St Stephen's opposed these plans, they enjoyed less status and kudos than their counterparts at Westminster. Much of this had to do with fact that St Stephen's was a community-based hospital, with limited teaching facilities. While the opposition of St Stephen's was disconcerting to Riverside management, it was not as entirely problematic as it would have been if Westminster doctors had come out in open revolt against the plans.

7.4 From consultation to the building of a new hospital

Once managers had completed their negotiations, and secured the consent of key constituencies, a formal consultation exercise was organized. A consultation document was made available for public scrutiny at the beginning of February 1988. The document provided details of a major capital project. Such plans had already been thrashed out and established, as demonstrated, during informal discussions between managers and key groups. Thus it outlined a plan for the construction of a 665-bed capacity teaching hospital on the existing St Stephen's Hospital site, and the development of complementary health centres south of Westminster (Riverside DHA, 1988: 38). It was envisaged that the development of a new hospital would allow the existing sites of Westminster Hospital and Westminster Children's Hospital to be sold. In addition, sites at St Mary Abbot's Hospital and West London Hospital could be put on the market following the removal of services. The capital costs for this large-scale reorganization were to be financed by the sale of these old hospital sites. The document noted that once built, the new hospital, it was presumed, could net revenue savings of around £15 million (Riverside DHA, 1988: 52).

The consultation phase was planned to last for three months. Like the strategy and consensus-building process, it was headed by district authority managers. Their role was to inform various effected parties about the plans. This included opponents of the re-organization. Such consultation was regarded as a sham by campaigners because the real decisions had largely been made and deals had been struck (*Fieldwork Interview*, Trade Union Official, 22 June 1995).

Even so, a number of campaigns were organized by various groups against the Westminster and Chelsea scheme. The Riverside Community Health Council (hereafter, Riverside CHC) – a body responsible for representing the views of residents and health service users – started its own consultation exercise at the beginning of February 1988. In the light of these findings, Riverside CHC decided in May 1988 to oppose the new hospital development (Riverside CHC, 1988: 2–3). Although the general manager of Riverside attended various CHC meetings, this was not an influential interest group. Unlike the doctors of Westminster and members of the district health authority, Riverside CHC, in the words of a senior manager, did not have 'vetoes in the eyes of the Secretary of State' (*Fieldwork Interview*, Senior Riverside Official, 26 June 1995).

A potentially more influential group of opponents came in the form of the Westminster Hospitals Development Fund. It was led by a respected doctor, solicitor and members of the House of Lords (*Fieldwork Interview*, Senior Riverside Official, 26 June 1995). This group did not make a significant impact. It focused mainly on Westminster Hospital and thus failed to develop alliances with doctors from other hospitals.

By June 1988, both the region and the district health authority had sanctioned the proposal. The planning committee of Kensington and Chelsea Borough Council later in the year approved the plans for a new hospital, with some adjustments to the layout. Having gained local authorization, and the support of key constituent groups, the final decision of the Secretary of State was a formality. On the 22 December 1988, a Parliamentary statement and DoH press release gave ministerial and Treasury approval for the scheme (DoH, 1988).

The above analysis has outlined the importance of local policy agents – in this case, district authority managers – in the policy process. According to centralized conceptions, government makes policy, with local agencies play a peripheral role in the whole process. Clearly, this one case study has shown that local policy agents are not passive implementers of central plans. Nor are they problematic elements in the policy chain of command from central to local centres. This case study has demonstrated the highly influential role which may be exercised by organizations and agents operating beyond the confines of central government. These local operators figured centrally throughout those phases in which the policy of reorganization emerged and developed. They were also responsible for modifying the policy in the light of negotiations.

Central government during these proceedings, though, was not redundant. It was alluded to earlier that central intervention had set the financial structure for health authorities such as Riverside. In addition, the advice of ministers during these three phases was courted to ensure that the emerging plans were acceptable to the government. Nevertheless, the main responsibility for developing this policy presided with the district authority and key actors – managers in the main. In terms of putting these plans into action, as will be shown in the next section, local bodies and key managerial staff again assumed the lead.

7.5   The construction phase

The management contract for starting work on St Stephen's was let in May 1989, with operations scheduled to last for 37 months. In the past, similar construction projects in the NHS had taken between seven and ten years. To achieve this rapid timetable, managers planned to use fast-track construction – the first time such a method had been used in the NHS (Ciorra, 1993: 27). The fast-track programme for the Westminster and Chelsea meant constructing the building in a single phase, rather than in sections. This was achieved principally by using prefabrication and a steel frame, allowing the brickwork and the construction of internal and mechanical services to take place simultaneously (Committee of Public Accounts, 1992: 11).

For some participants, this method held major advantages: once it had started, the pace of construction was such that it was difficult for politicians to reverse the planned development. Subsequent events reveal how germane this actually proved to be. In 1991, the then Health Secretary, William Waldegrave, overruled proposals to rebuild UCL and redevelop St Mary's Hospital. Immediately after the decision was taken, the Tomlinson inquiry into London's health service was established, further delaying plans for redevelopments being considered in London (James, 1994: 24–5). The Riverside project was not affected as work was already under way. A senior doctor, and a former member of the health authority, noted:

> The whole thing was done at one sitting ... If you go to most other hospitals, Charing Cross, George's, which have been built recently they have different stages, so that at any stage you could stop. Once they started the Chelsea and Westminster Hospital there was nothing they could do other than stop it completely or finish it ... That was a major advantage. (*Fieldwork Interview*, Senior Consultant, 26 June 1995)

Riverside's managers, as revealed by the consultation document, had a well-defined and costed plan of action. However, policies do not proceed in a rational and purposeful manner from planning through to implementation (Ham and Hill, 1993: 82). Managers in Riverside had to face numerous difficulties during the operational phase. In such circumstances, the autonomy granted to local policy actors can hold advantages for governments in so far as it allows the centre to be absolved from direct blame; the executive can easily distance itself from the ensuing furore. Again this underlines the interdependency between institutions of government in contemporary policy-making.

The construction was planned to be completed by June 1992. However, it was reported to the Committee of Public Accounts in February 1993 that the construction had come up against several delays. The hospital, as a result, was expected to be fully operational by the later date of April 1993. The management executive reported in its evidence before the committee that the delay was due to the sheer complexity of the scheme, involving interlocking subcontracts running simultaneously (Committee of Public Accounts, 1993: p. ix). There were also problems over management. The project development manager had in November 1990 been appointed to another post in the NHS. To ensure continuity, the manager continued to work on the Westminster and Chelsea project on a part-time basis. Although the manager was reappointed full-time to the project in 1991, the original decision was criticized by the committee.

As fast-track was an expensive method, these delays meant that the cost of the hospital spiralled from an original estimate of £109 million to £236 million (Committee of Public Accounts, 1993: 1). Additional financial problems emerged over the sale of the old hospitals' sites. Treasury approval of the scheme had been given on the understanding that total costs were to be funded by the sale of four hospital sites – St Mary Abbot's, Westminster, Westminster Children's Hospital and West London Hospitals. From these sales the district was to receive £143 million. Due to the slump in the London property market, only one site (St Mary Abbot's) was purchased, for £47 million, leaving an unanticipated shortfall of nearly £100 million (ibid.: x).

Cumulatively, these financial setbacks had major repercussions for health projects outside London. Three hundred health service projects in north and west London, Hertfordshire and Bedfordshire had to be deferred as a result of the escalating costs in building the new Westminster. Much of the region's budget was directed to maintaining the building programme at the Chelsea and Westminster (*Guardian*, 1992a). Moreover, it was reported that health authorities across England and Wales had to divert £56 million from new hospital and community care programmes in both countries (*Guardian*, 1992b). In effect, this meant a complete reversal of the RAWP strategy of reallocating resources away from acute facilities in inner London. In fact, there was a distinct shift in the RAWP strategy in 1988, in that the NHS management executive recommended a £70 million move away from the Midlands and the north and to the south (Moore, 1988: 846).

Nevertheless, once these predicaments emerged, it was inconceivable to reverse the building of the hospital as work was under way by then. Eventually, the new 580-bed district general hospital, renamed the Chelsea and Westminster, was formerly opened by the Queen in May 1993.

7.6   Conclusion

This chapter has sought to explore the relationship between central intervention and policy action by local territorial agencies. To examine some of these issues, a case analysis has been used of the reorganization programme that took place in the Riverside Health Authority between 1985 and 1993. Several conclusions and observations have been reached:

1.   Centralized theories are rejected for minimizing the role of local policy institutions outside central government. At the same time, analysts should not discount the influence of central government intervention on the behaviour and decisions of policy actors in the public sector. The case study examined how new methods of resource allocation established by central government and public sector reforms made possible the reorganization within Riverside.

2.   Events in Riverside reveal how central government and the regional health authority left crucial policy decisions to agents working on the ground – principally, following the Griffiths-inspired reforms, health authority managers, especially the general manager. The policy process as illustrated by the Riverside case study is an outcome of complex interdependencies between different government structures and actors. Scharpf (1978: 347) notes: 'Policy formation and policy implementation are inevitably the result of interactions among a plurality of separate actors with separate interests, goals and strategies.'

3.   Locally based institutions and actors are seen as better equipped to make crucial policy decisions because of their familiarization with, and their proximity to, the proposed area of intervention. To develop consensus in Riverside, it was shown that managers adopted a clear strategic plan and bargained with various groups, using the resources and decision-making powers at their disposal as devices in this 'game'.

4.   Analysts should not subscribe to general theoretical frameworks which conceptualize policy according to a limited set of variables or characteristics. In this case analysis, it was shown that policy cannot be understood solely in terms of a centralized model. Neither can the policy process be fully understood by recourse to theories which stress local policy action while over-looking the significance of central intervention.

5. It is essential to understand the interdependencies which exist between central intervention and local policy action. In the course of policy analysis, there will be occasions when it is more appropriate to focus on either central or local interven-tion. For instance, the second part of the analysis focused more on the activities of peripheral institutions. Even here, local policy actors were careful to consult the views of ministers in central government, as they ultimately had to sanction the final proposals.

STUDY GUIDE

Chronology of events in the Chelsea and Westminster Hospital scheme

1968:   Lord Todd's Royal Commission on medical education recommended that the 12 London teaching hospitals should be brought together under six groups. These proposals were rejected by the London medical schools.

1976:   In this year the Resource Allocation Working Party (RAWP) attempted to produce a formula, whereby, health resources would be evenly distributed throughout the country so that people could enjoy equal access to health care. The examination showed that London was receiving a greater proportion of resources than other regions.

1979:   The Conservative Party is elected to government with a New Right agenda to restrict public spending, which would entail a reductions in the pro-vision of government funds to the National Health Service (NHS).

1980:   Pressures on London University finances leads Lord Annan, Vice Chancellor of London University, to establish a working party under Lord Flowers. When this working party reported back in 1980 it argued that it was necessary for larger medical schools to be formed in order to achieve financial viability.

1982:   In this year the District Management Team at Victoria Health Authority attempted to examine the strategic options for the district over the next decade. The resource situation for Victoria, it was concluded, would con-tract and service provision would switch from hospital services to community-based care.

1983: The Victoria Health Authority publishes a strategic framework document for the future entitled *Evaluation of Health Services in Victoria*. The document examined existing health services, and the means by which to identify future strategic options. A later volume of this document outlined options for reducing medical services in view of resource constrictions in the district. Three plans were put forward: a considerable reduction in the number of beds; relocation of Westminster Children's Hospital; and the closure of at least one of three major hospital sites.

1984: Following the Flowers working party of 1980, the Charing Cross and Westminster medical schools were formed, partly in order to safeguard their survival.

1984: In this year, following the 1983 NHS Management Inquiry (The Griffiths Report), general managers were appointed at health authority level. These managers were given considerable decision-making and policy-setting powers.

1985 (April): The merger between these two medical schools acted as a catalyst for the creation of Riverside District Health Authority. This new health authority was created by the merger of the former Victoria and the Hammersmith and Fulham District Health Authorities. The RAWP formula was also beginning to underline the need for reductions in resource allocations to the new Riverside DHA.

1985: Riverside managers began working with researchers from the King's Fund College to review medical services and establish a plan of action for the future. The experts from the King's Fund introduced managers to the idea of multiscenario planning. A planning team was subsequently formed, which included a member from the King's Fund, to study different strategic options for restructuring health services in Riverside.

1985 (October): The North-West Thames Regional Health Authority publishes its 10-year strategy up until 1994. The region anticipated major changes in the provision of health services to meet national policy objectives. As part of the rationalization plan, Riverside – the largest district in the North-West Thames Region – was expected to deliver savings of around £26 million by 1994, and a reduction in hospital beds from 960 to around 625, which was later increased to 736 beds. This would inevitably involve a major reduction of services in Riverside. Much of this reduction would focus on the three largest hospitals in the District – Charing Cross, Westminster and St Stephen's Hospitals – all of which were teaching centres. As Charing

Cross was a new hospital, speculation focused mainly on the future of Westminster and St Stephen's.

1986 (January): A meeting of the Riverside District Health Authority discussed what should be done with Westminster and St Stephen's Hospitals. The authority failed to make a final decision, but it was more in favour of retaining St Stephen's.

1986: The planning group, having completed its study of the alternative options for Riverside, published a strategic document which outlined five main policy options surrounding the future of Westminster, Charing Cross and St Stephen's Hospitals. The strategic document was then made available for informal discussion. The DoH made it clear that any plan involving the closure of Westminster would require the support of MPs in the area, members from the district health authority, and Westminster medical staff. At the same time, the DoH recommended that a feasibility study should be carried out, looking into the possibility of building a new hospital by refurbishing the St Stephen's site.

1987 (April): A study was carried out by regional and district officers into the possibility of refurbishing St Stephen's to develop a new hospital. The view was taken that by building a new hospital this would allow other hospitals to be closed and then sold. Part of the money from these sales would be used to construct this new hospital and to build long-term care facilities south of Westminster. In view of the criticisms levelled at the plan by Westminster doctors, regional managers and external surveyors undertook another study of St Stephen's. The study showed that the existing St Stephen's site was not big enough to fit all the specialities required by a major teaching hospital. Hence, managers eventually reached the conclusion that they would have to demolish the St Stephen's site and construct a new hospital from scratch.

1988 (February): The consultation plan for the closure of both St Stephen's and Westminster Hospitals, as well as three smaller hospitals in Riverside, and the construction of a new hospital – to be called the Westminster and Chelsea Hospital (later renamed the Chelsea and Westminster Hospital) – was published for a period of public consultation, lasting three months. As part of the plan, a 665-bed teaching hospital on the old St Stephen's site, would be constructed, together with five homes for the elderly and a primary health care centre in the south Westminster area.

1988: Throughout this year various groups opposed to the planned closure of Westminster and the building of a new hospital emerge. The opposition groups include the likes of CANDOR, Riverside CHC, and the Westminster Hospitals Development Fund.

1988 (May–June):   Regional and district authorities hold separate meetings and formally sanction the Westminster and Chelsea scheme.

1988 (December):   The Secretary of State for Health, in a written answer to the House of Commons and in a DoH press release, confirms that the Westminster and Chelsea scheme has received ministry and Treasury approval.

1989 (May):   The management contract was let, with work scheduled to last for 37 months. The hospital, it was planned, would be complete by June 1992.

1991 (April):   Following the 1989 White Paper, *Working for Patients*, the government introduces the internal market to structure and control the allocation of health funding. Within the internal market, the new Chelsea and Westminster found itself at a disadvantage because the maintenance costs were very high.

1993 (May):   After a number of delays due to various construction and planning problems, the new Chelsea and Westminster hospital is finally opened at a cost of £236 million, which went far above the original projected cost of £109 million.

A reading schedule

There are several useful books, articles and chapters to recommend on the subject of central government contribution to policy making. For a good summary, check Ham and Hill (1993: chapter 6). Ferlie *et al.* (1996) examine how a range of different public services and institutions have been transformed by central reforms. Hogwood and Gunn (1984) put forward top-down prescriptions for overcoming impediments associated with the implementation of policy.

A good introduction to the field on intergovernmental relations is provided by Parsons (1995: in section 3.6) and Ham and Hill (1993: chapter 10). Articles by Benson (1975, 1977) provide a radical approach to the study of interorganizational networks. Both articles are full of useful insights. Hanf and Scharpf's (1978) collection of edited articles examine the complexity of interorganizational relations and the implications for policy-making. Rhodes (1992) provides a good theoretical overview of the various positions on

▶▶

▶▶

intergovernmental relations. Barrett and Hill (1984) summarize the various perspectives on bargaining in the intergovernmental network. Ham (1981) is an informative case study of health politics at the local level. Pettigrew *et al.* (1992) is a very authoritative study of organizational change and interorganizational relations within the health service; this study is useful as it employs empirical research.

Issues for revision and further consideration

Having studied this case study you should be familiar with several key concepts relevant to policy analysis. These are as follows: intergovernmental analysis (section 7.1); centralized structures and policy-making (7.2); general management (7.2.2); territorial/peripheral organizations (7.3); positive sum bargaining (7.3.2); zero sum bargaining (7.3.3).

▶   Why is it still important for policy analysts to consider the influence of central government intervention?

▶   Explain the advantages to central government in giving local territorial institutions autonomy over policy-making?

▶   Why are local policy actors relied upon by central administrations?

▶   Why did matters progress in Riverside, whereas the neighbouring authority of Bloomsbury was less dynamic? What does this demonstrate about local institutions?

▶   What does the bargaining process in Riverside show about relations of power in intergovernmental networks?

▶   To what extent do the public sector reforms of the 1980s in such areas as the health service show the importance of central intervention?

8

The emergence and implementation of policy: the Tomlinson reorganization of London's health service

8.1 Introduction

Historically, there has been a deep-seated structural imbalance in London's health service. The capital has a large number of teaching hospitals, seemingly disproportionate to the size of population, providing expensive and complex acute treatments. At the same time, London's community and primary care facilities are less well developed. There is nothing particularly new about this situation, of course. The conflicting demands of maintaining acute provision for the purposes of medical education and research, while providing facilities for the local populace, have rankled policy-makers since the nineteenth century.

The mid-1970s, though, proved a significant watershed for London's health service. It was in this period that governments and relevant authorities began to step up their efforts in addressing the various anomalies within London's health system. A number of significant developments emerged from these initial efforts. However, these were difficult to coordinate, as health services in London were governed by four separate regional bodies. Ironically, it was not until the early 1990s with creation of the internal market that planned reorganization across London was realized. This attempt to engender strategic change throughout the London region centred on the establishment of the Tomlinson inquiry.

In this chapter we examine the review embarked upon by the Tomlinson inquiry to illustrate key features of the policy process.

This case study, as with the case study in Chapter 9, is concerned with stages or phases of the policy process. Specifically, the study of the Tomlinson review focuses on the emergence, formation and eventual implementation of policy. Organizational theory and research is used to demonstrate that the emergence of this policy issue was not a chance event: it was linked to certain organizational factors that often accompany restructuring in both the private and public sector. Exploring this issue is the task of the first part of the chapter.

The second part of the chapter traces the recommendations made by Tomlinson and the subsequent attempts to implement the inquiry's pan-London strategy for restructuring health services. This has proven to be an ongoing process. As such, the analysis focuses on the first two years following the publication of the Tomlinson report. Developments that took place within this relatively short period are highly informative of the problematic dynamics that underpin the implementation of policy. The Tomlinson inquiry presented a clear and unequivocal set of guidelines for strategic change. But in reality, as events following the Tomlinson inquiry showed, strategic policy change is the outcome 'of an uncertain, emergent and iterative process' (Pettigrew *et al.*, 1992: 273).

8.2   The Tomlinson inquiry as strategic change

The setting up in 1991 of an inquiry into London's health system was not a unique event. Twenty separate public reviews of the capital's health institutions had already been conducted between the nineteenth century and the early 1980s (Rivett, 1986: 349–63). However, the inquiry carried out under the auspices of Sir Bernard Tomlinson merits distinction from its forebears. According to James (1994: 25), the Tomlinson inquiry was 'the most fundamental and far reaching of all the myriad attempts that there have been over the last century to reform the provision of health care in London'. The terms of reference set for the inquiry team by the Health and Education Secretaries speak for themselves. They requested a year-long investigation into health care within London, focusing particularly on the balance between primary and acute health services. London's position as a prominent centre of medical education gave the investigation an added dimension: the team would assess, and pronounce upon, the organization of undergraduate medical education, postgraduate medical training and scientific research related to medicine.

What both Secretaries of State desired was a blueprint for re-organizing health institutions throughout London. The envisaged changes were to be neither piecemeal nor ad hoc. In effect, Tomlinson was being asked to formulate a programme of what organizational theorists have termed 'strategic change'. Ferlie *et al.* (1996: 91) provide the following definition: 'Strategic change ... is seen as effecting major subsystems and producing outcomes which impact across many parts of an organization. The timescale of strategic change is seen to be longer'.

The question that needs to be addressed now concerns the reasons why executives, managers or public administrators embark on change of this magnitude. Clearly, decisions are not taken lightly, as strategic restructuring is potentially disruptive and costly in political terms. Addressing these points will go some way towards understanding how issues emerge and are formed into formal policies.

8.3   The emergence of policy: the force of external pressures

Organizational research has notably examined the process of strategic change in both private and public sector institutions. Although distinctions should be made, there are commonalities across these organizational forms. One generic link are those factors which induce strategic change in organizations spanning the public–private divide. According to Pettigrew (1985: 438), such changes are triggered by pressures emanating from the external environment. The outer environment refers to the national economic, political and social context. It also includes the actions and policies followed by central government or the regional agencies of central Whitehall departments (Pettigrew *et al.*, 1992: 7).

Pettigrew's observation about the relationship between external movements and strategic change is not purely theoretical. Meyer's (1982) study of organizational adaptation by a group of voluntary hospitals located in San Francisco establishes empirical support for this claim. In 1975, the hospitals instigated a series of organizational changes. According to Meyer, this policy was brought about by a severe environmental jolt in the form of industrial action by doctors.

The strike left the hospitals in a financially precarious position: 'only 40 per cent of the hospital beds in the Bay Area had been occupied on an average day in 1974. Yet hospitals had acquired these beds by incurring debts that left many in tenuous financial positions' (ibid. 515).

The outer context not only galvanizes adjustments within single, independent organizational units like the hospitals in Meyer's research. The outer context can also effect complex organizational configurations of considerable magnitude. The process of organizational change in multinational corporations confirms the point. Pettigrew, for instance, studied the commercial vicissitudes experienced by Imperial Chemicals Industries (hereafter, ICI) over a 25-year period, between 1958 and 1983. ICI is a vast commercial enterprise, with diverse interests in petrochemical, plastics, paints and agricultural products. The commercial development of this multinational, in the said period, was characterized by periodic phases of intense organizational change. These phases according to Pettigrew (1985: 453) were 'precipitated by ... economic and business-related environmental disturbance'. For example, one restructuring phase in 1958 was triggered by a recession in America. Faced with dwindling markets at home, US companies searched Western Europe for new opportunities, which intensified competition for ICI. In response, the company introduced new commercial and organizational policies. These involved structural changes to prepare the business for competition and new commercial opportunities.

Similar patterns of restructuring following external movements have emerged in London's health system. The capital's health service in essence, like ICI, is an extensive organizational conglomeration – a composite body of assorted medical institutions and levels of administration within the London region. Prior to Tomlinson, this disparate organizational entity was punctuated by periods of dramatic reorganization. These phases, like the process of strategic change in ICI, were prompted by external jolts. With London's health service, the environmental jolt came through central government reforms of procedures and mechanisms for allocating resources.

A considerable phase of reorganization came about as a consequence of a new funding formula for the health regions. Introduced in 1977, the Resource Allocation Working Party, or RAWP as it became known, based its funding allocations on the mortality rates and demographic features of regions. Previously, funding very much followed patterns established by historical precedence; the outcome was that prosperous areas such as London tended to benefit more than other needy regions, which were left to relative neglect. Under the new RAWP system, London's hospitals, over time, were poised to face significant reductions in support. The formula established by RAWP began to exert considerable pressures in the early 1980s (see Chapter 7).

Medical education became a prime target for restructuring. After a series of deliberations, 8 of London's 12 medical schools were merged in 1981. These mergers led to the reconfiguration of district health authorities. A joint venture between Charing Cross and Westminster Medical Schools in 1984 was the catalyst, in the following year, for merging Victoria and Hammersmith and Fulham Health Districts. As shown in Chapter 7, this led to the creation of the Riverside District Health Authority, containing three teaching hospitals. In view of projected falls in financial support following the RAWP exercise, this situation was unsustainable and Riverside promptly developed an agenda for the retrenchment of acute services. Mergers of other health districts, such as those that formed Bloomsbury and Paddington and North Kensington, also took place on a service-cutting mandate.

8.3.1   The internal market and emergence of Tomlinson

Significant attempts to restructure acute services were made by some London health authorities as a result of the external jolt administered by the RAWP system. However, restructuring proceeded gradually from district to district, with some health authorities achieving greater change than others. Planned reorganization across London was hampered by the existence of four regional health authorities within the capital. It was not until the end of the decade that a planned reorganization across regional and district boundaries in the capital was contemplated by policymakers. Again, the catalyst for change came through an external development – a set of new funding mechanisms outlined in the 1989 White Paper, *Working for Patients*. The proposed reforms were more far-reaching than anything the RAWP system had to offer.

Central to the proposed reforms was the creation of an internal market for the health service. In the internal market, regional and district health authorities would receive funding weighted by demo-graphic characteristics – size, age, and morbidity – of their resident populations. The providers in the new system would be mainly dis-trict hospitals, which could apply for self-governing status. Under the previous arrangement, districts gained automatic funding alloca-tions from their local regions. The 1989 White Paper proposed to empower regional and district health authorities to 'shop around' for cost-effective health care. In addition to these reforms, the docu-ment also suggested that general practitioners with more than 11,000 patients (then changed to 7,000) could apply to become players within the internal market as independent fundholders. As managers of their own budgets, general practitioners (hereafter, GPs) could purchase certain non-emergency services for their patients from provider units.

Within the untested confines of ministerial papers and legisla-tive documents, the internal market seemed an ideal mechanism for achieving the most prized shibboleths of modern Conservatism – cost effectiveness and sensitivity towards the consumers of services. The a priori judgement of legislators was that the internal market would improve the health service. For policy-makers involved, the market would create an incentive to increase efficiency and service standards as providers vied for custom from purchasers. In practice, matters proved rather different.

The internal market formally came into operation in April 1991, following the NHS and Community Care Act of 1990. It was soon evident to ministers that this 'money follows the patient' mechanism could result in wholesale and indiscriminate hospital closures (Baggott, 1994). Nowhere, as the government was to find out, was this a more distinct and real possibility than in London. Here, com-petition, due to the surplus institutions and the high cost of medical treatment, could disrupt and deplete health services. Moreover, evi-dence showed that London hospitals acted as major exporters of care, treating on a yearly basis 80,000 patients living outside the Thames health authorities. It seemed unlikely that these patient flows could be sustained within the internal market. As a conse-quence of the 1990 Act, district health authorities were under pressure to seek cheaper providers of health care. This often meant that local units, rather than the traditionally more expensive care centres found across London, would be used (Sheldon, 1992).

The market had an immediate effect, inducing pressures on

London's hospital services. One of the first self-governing trust hospitals, Guy's in south London, was saddled with an £800,000 trading deficit only a few months after the internal market began operating (Brindle, 1991). In December 1991, discussions were under way at the North West Thames Regional Authority on cost-cutting measures – ward closures, job losses and a freeze on recruitment – to balance an end-of-year deficit of £4.9 million. The deficit was partly due to the failure of provider units to generate the necessary income from GP fundholders and extra-contractual referrals (Limb, 1991). Unit managers from University College and Middlesex Hospitals estimated in 1991 a reduction of 15–20 per cent in clinical activity from more distant purchasing authorities. But confidential figures disclosed to the *Health Service Journal* showed that activity had dropped alarmingly by 71 per cent, plunging the hospital group into financial crisis (Butler, 1992).

Such was the devastating efficiency of the internal market, that the government was forced to cushion its impact in London. Two measures were taken. First, the introduction of a fully weighted capitation scheme was delayed. The Thames regional authorities, most of which were in line to gain smaller allocations under the capitation system, gained a minimum funding increase of 4 per cent (Sheldon, 1991: 3).

Second, and most notably, the government established an inquiry into health care in London. It was the then Health Secretary, William Waldegrave, who announced the inquiry at the Conservative Party's annual conference on 10 October 1991. Sir Bernard Tomlinson, a Newcastle University pathologist and a recently retired chairman of the Northern Regional Health Authority, was named as the chairman of the inquiry team. Tomlinson's panel included four other experts, a mixture of medical representatives and academics, in the field of health care. Tomlinson offered experience in both medicine and administration. There was also the added factor that he was seen as a 'neutral chairman', having spent most of his professional career outside London (see Glasman and Sheldon, 1991: 4).

The decision to launch the Tomlinson-led review effectively marked a significant reversal in policy. Rather than allow the market to do its work by closing 'inefficient' hospitals, the government opted for planned rationalization (Baggott, 1994: 186). This, it could be argued, was an unintended consequence of establishing the internal market. Similar endeavours to plan rationalization across London in the past lacked coordination, with restructuring taking place within specific districts. It was a testament to the external impact and pressure wrought by the internal market that policy-makers were forced to consider planned intervention throughout the capital. The Tomlinson inquiry, according to Mintzberg's (1978: 945) formulation, was an *emergent* strategy. The planned policy strategy that Tomlinson was asked to produce was never intended at the outset of the government's 1990 health reforms. Once the unintended effects of the internal market became apparent, a policy of strategic change began to emerge.

This background outline to the Tomlinson inquiry, together with the earlier summaries of research into organizational change, has pursued a specific thesis. The argument is that policy issues, such as those involving strategic reorganization, often emerge as a result of external forces. This analytical focus was pursued in order to understand the structural factors which led to the Tomlinson inquiry. However, a caveat should be added. Solely focusing on the role of external forces produces a deterministic conception of organizational change. This excludes the possibility of deliberate conscious action and agency in responding to environmental jolts. The impression given is of decision-makers and agents being steered and controlled by external forces over which they have no control. This case study intends to avoid the pitfall of external determinism.

There are analysts who concede that external forces alone cannot force change. For these writers, the relationship between strategic change and environmental pressure does not follow a strict causal sequence. The agents that inhabit institutions, and the deliberate choices that they make in the face of external pressures should also be considered. Hence, external pressures can create a sense of urgency for addressing a particular issue of public concern. The momentum for developing the policy is inherently dependent upon the perceptions and actions of agents within organizations. Pettigrew (1985: 453) notes with regard to ICI:

> Behind the periodic strategic reorientations in ICI are not just economic and business events, but also processes of managerial perception, choice, and action influenced by and influencing perceptions of the operating environment of the firm, and its structure, culture and systems of power and control.

Pettigrew's observations, though specific to ICI, are relevant to the Tomlinson affair. The importance of action becomes increasingly evident as medical institutions attempted to implement the proposals made by Tomlinson.

8.4 The formation of policy: Tomlinson's a priori recommendations

The year-long Tomlinson inquiry utilized three main sources of evidence: first, the inquiry team interviewed over 1,000 individuals, and received over 127 written submissions; second, the team examined the purchasing plans of health authorities both in and outside London; and third, past reports and inquiries into London's hospitals were consulted.

The end result of this inquiry was a radical set of proposals for major strategic restructuring in London's health service. The report had very little to say about the dynamics of realizing such a strategy. In Mintzberg's (1978: 945) words, the Tomlinson report in effect produced a set of 'a priori guidelines to decision-making'.

The Tomlinson report was released for public consumption on 23 October 1992. Hard statistical data were sparingly used, as the report offered more strategic advice than a systematic analysis of health care in London. Nevertheless, the report furnished empirical data on the current state of, and the future demand for, health services to support key recommendations (Tomlinson, 1992: 2). Using research by the King's Fund, it was concluded that London enjoyed a higher level of health service funds and hospital provision than other areas in the country. Spending on hospital services per resident within inner London is 20 per cent greater than the average for England (ibid. 21). Yet, access to community care in the capital is extremely poor (ibid. 8–9). This anomalous situation has come about because health resources in the capital have traditionally been dominated by the requirements of teaching hospitals, which prioritize acute care. At the same time, the report noted that between 2,000 and 7,000 hospital beds will become surplus by the end of the century. The fault for this lies with the internal market. Its operation, the report argued, is likely to reduce patient flows from outside London and lead to a concomitant increase in purchasers using local services (ibid. 4).

Tomlinson maintained that there is an overwhelming case for

transforming the dominant pattern of health care in London. Accordingly, the report recommended that a special Implementation Group should manage and oversee this much needed phase of restructuring. Central to this reorganization, the inquiry team suggested, should be a reduction of 2,500 in the number of acute beds. This would be achieved by closing entire hospital sites. And, in what is the most contentious and emotive part of the report, it specifically recommended the closure of several hospitals – ten altogether (Tomlinson, 1992: 31–8).

The decision to put forward these hospitals for closure was based on an analysis of the size of their local populations, the condition of buildings and the internal market's impact on patient flows for these institutions (ibid. 29). Using this information, the report assessed the relative vulnerability of different teaching hospitals. Controversially, the report recommended the closure of such internationally famous teaching hospitals as St Bartholomew's and Middlesex. St Bartholomew's was seen as particularly vulnerable to closure, especially in the context of the internal market: 52 per cent of its patients are non-local residents, and it possesses the highest capital charges. In addition, such is the age of St Bartholomew's estate, predominantly listed in status, that the scope for new developments is limited.

As part of the restructuring of acute care, the Tomlinson inquiry also pronounced upon medical education. The report outlined a programme where eight of the nine medical colleges would merge into four faculties of medicine within Imperial College, King's College, University College and Queen Mary and Westfield College. These schools would have a higher undergraduate intake. As such, Tomlinson argued that, in order to manage teaching efficiently, there should be a reduction of 150 in the annual intake of medical students to London (ibid. 51).

The Tomlinson report did not focus solely on the rationalization of acute services. Several recommendations were made over expanding community and primary care facilities in London. In comparison with the rest of England, the indigenous population of London has poorer access to, and a lower provision of, health screening by primary care services. Forty-six per cent of general practices in London are below minimum standards, compared with a 7 per cent average for England. This is evident in the fact that London practices have larger patient lists and employ fewer staff when compared to their counterparts in other cities (ibid. 9).

A programme for improving community and primary health services was put forward. This entailed a £140 million cash injection 'over several years' to either improve existing GP premises or build new practices. A further £2 million was suggested for constructing four community care units. In addition, the inquiry advocated the idea of designating parts of London as 'primary care development zones'. Here, general practitioners could be released from national contract terms and given specific contracts shaped by local health care needs (ibid. 12).

The Tomlinson recommendations amounted to an overarching policy plan for strategic restructuring of London's health services. But it has already been observed that the plan of action provided a set of a priori guidelines. The Health Secretary, Virginia Bottomley, confirmed this in her statement about the report to the House of Commons. She commented that, while the government welcomed Bernard Tomlinson's conclusions, the 'report is advice to the Government, not Government policy' (Parliamentary Debates, 1992: 696). Nevertheless, she outlined in her statement that some of the recommendations would be acted upon immediately. For instance, a London Implementation Group was formed straight away to carry forward the work of the Tomlinson report. Even so, the Health Secretary maintained that a period of consultation should pass before the government would enact any of Tomlinson's recommendations. The first step in all of this was the publication of a formal response to Tomlinson.

8.5   From inquiry to realizing an intended strategy for change

The government's official response to the Tomlinson inquiry, *Making London Better* (DoH, 1993), was published in February 1993. If Tomlinson constituted a set of guidelines for action, *Making London Better* presented a strategy for implementing the planned changes.

The report, like Tomlinson, concurred with estimates that there would be 15–20 per cent fewer acute beds in the capital over a five-year period (DoH, 1993: 8). To cope with these developments, major changes to service provision, the document maintained, were required in London. The Tomlinson review wholly informed the government's conclusions: 96 of the 106 recommendations made by the original inquiry were included in *Making London Better* (Health

Committee, 1993, p. 25). Rationalization, involving the concentration of services on fewer sites, was high on the agenda. The merger of Guy's and St Thomas's Hospital on a single site was endorsed, although this like the other mergers would be subject to consultation. Plans were also sanctioned for bringing University College and Middlesex Hospital onto a single site in the west end. (Momentum was injected by the fact that these mergers had already been agreed by the various institutions.) Controversially, it proposed the closure of St Bartholomew's accident and emergency department. In the long-term this would result either in closure for the whole site, a merger with the Royal London or retention of the hospital as a smaller specialist unit.

In terms of medical education, the government endorsed Tomlinson's recommendations for eight medical schools to be merged into four separate institutions. Half of these joint ventures had already agreed terms by the time *Making London Better* was published. There were also related plans for improving the cost effectiveness of London's eight postgraduate hospitals or special health authorities. Rather than being directly funded from the centre, the government envisaged that these specialist services would have to compete for custom within the internal market. A plan of action for bolstering community and primary health services in London, as Tomlinson had recommended, was also included. Primary health care services, provided through GPs, nurses and other health workers/professionals operating in localities, were in line for support to improve facilities and staffing levels.

Events following *Making London Better* exemplified the government's determination to implement the Tomlinson-inspired plan for London. There was little procrastination in forming, as Tomlinson had advised, a London Implementation Group. This operational body was established for an initial period of three years up to March 1996. The body was filled with central appointees, mainly Department of Health officials. Its role was to be a facilitator, working through existing agencies (regional health authorities, local purchasers and providers) and research bodies to oversee the realization of the government's designated strategy.

Setting-up the London Implementation Group was an unequivocal statement of intent on the government's part. But enacting strategies is not a clear-cut or straightforward matter. With reference to Tomlinson, one health commentator noted, 'she [the Health

Secretary] needs to remember that devising strategies is easy; implementing them is hard. She has given a lot of commitment to the strategy; she now needs to give as much to the process of change and to ensuring that the public understands it' (Smith, 1993: 535).

These Tomlinson-inspired plans encountered particular difficulties as time progressed. The rationalization of tertiary specialties in the capital is a case in point. Part of the Implementation Group's remit, *inter alia*, involved the setting-up of six independent review teams to examine the duplication of specialist services across London. Their findings, published in the summer of 1993, confirmed that a number of hospitals earmarked for closure should be wound up. While the Implementation Group had completed the reviews, it was patently less clear who would be responsible for rationalizing these specialist services. This only confused proceedings and generally stalled progress towards reorganization.

The development of primary and community care services proved equally problematic. Resources were made available for specially appointed bodies to bolster community and primary health care services. Over time, improvements in this area proved worryingly slow. The difficulties were such that the London Implementation Group was abolished prematurely in March 1995. This took place a year before it was officially planned to be disbanded. Clearly, operationalizing planned strategies is more problematic than portrayed in policy documents like the Tomlinson report and its forebear, *Making London Better*:

> Planning theory postulates that the strategy-maker 'formulates' from on high while the subordinates 'implement' lower down. Unfortunately, however, this neat dichotomy is based on two assumptions which often prove false: that the formulator is fully informed ... and that the environment is sufficiently stable, or at least predictable, to ensure that there will be no need for *re*formulation during implementation. (Mintzberg, 1978: 946)

Mintzberg offers a glimpse over why there is often a lack of congruency between the formal policy and its operationalization. But work on this area has shown that there are diffuse, often complex reasons for this lack of 'fit'. During the 1970s, a series of studies, mainly American-based, were carried out into the implementation process (see for instance Bardach (1977) and section 2.4 from Chapter 2 in this text). Such research gave prime consideration to the question of policy failure. Below we consider these models and ensuing debates that emerged out of this formative analysis.

8.6 The implementation phase

8.6.1 A theoretical framework

One of the most influential studies to emerge from this research of the implementation process was carried out by Pressman and Wildavsky (1973). The authors studied the implementation of an economic development programme in California. They note that effective implementation is based on the ability of the central administration, which had set the policy, to coordinate and control the implementation phase. As Pressman and Wildavsky found, this was not evident in the strategies pursued by the Oakland Economic Development Administration. This early salvo in the implementation debate was highly influential and established the parameters for what became generically known as 'top-down' explanations.

Advocates of the top-down or rational control model perceive implementation in terms of an administrative process. The development of policy follows a hierarchical chain. Elected politicians in central government, or other executive agencies, set and formulate policy. Civil servants and officials, either within central or local administrative bodies, are then responsible for implementing these strategies and programmes set by the centre. Hogwood and Gunn (1993), who have carried the top-down flame in Britain, argue that it is the devolution of responsibilities for implementation down from politicians to administrators which causes difficulties. The administrative level of this hierarchical chain has the scope for independent action. It is this relative independence, according to top-down theoreticians, which undermines 'perfect implementation', limiting 'centrally imposed objectives, co-ordination, and demands for compliance' (ibid. 245).

From a top-down perspective, the difficulty with regard to implementing Tomlinson was not due to the government's strategy. Rather, it was down to the way administrators carried it forward. There was a distinct inability on the part of health officials, in such bodies as the London Implementation Group, to steer through the necessary changes.

Top-down theoreticians such as Hogwood and Gunn argue that the central bureaucracy, should seek to minimize the level and extent of dependency with implementing agencies. The less complex the series of linkages with administrative, implementing agencies, the more likely that compliance will be achieved.

This formula seems to offer an enticing analysis for policy failure and a clear prescription for improving matters. Significantly, though, it overlooks the fact that policy-makers are confronted by issues which tend to vary in terms of their complexity and form. For some analysts, barriers to policy implementation do not necessarily derive from a lack of compliance on the ground. The main variable shaping implementation concerns the type of policy. The aim of policy analysis is to elucidate the relationship between policy type and the factors which may influence its implementation. Ripley and Franklin (1982: 69) devised the following fourfold classification of policy types: distributive, competitive regulatory, protective regulatory and redistributive policies. Redistributive policies are regarded by the authors as the most difficult to implement, and distributive the least troublesome; regulatory policy categories occupy an intermediate position of relative difficulty. Redistributive policies face severe barriers because of their controversial objectives and the concomitant political manoeuvring and bargaining that takes place between affected interest groups (ibid. 83–4). Grindle (1980) makes a similar point in relation to policy implementation in the context of Third World politics. It is acknowledged that, when policies involve conflicting interests, long-term changes, wide-ranging behavioural adaptation and complex networks of different agents, problems will emerge over implementation.

The Tomlinson-inspired strategy to reorganize London's health service comes under this problematic category. The plan involved a significant restructuring across the capital. A number of influential constituencies were effected by these proposals; and thus the possibility for straightforward implementation, as we have seen, was a remote ideal.

The type and content of policy can undoubtedly affect its implementation. But this variable alone cannot explain the various difficulties that arise when a policy is being enacted. The execution of policy can be fundamentally influenced by other factors, including relations within and between organizations and the agents that operate in these settings. Grindle(1980: 33–4) notes 'that the content of public programs can be considerably affected during their execution due to the nature of political participation, demand making, and bureaucratic response'. Of the factors identified above, a growing corpus of work in this period concentrated on the activities and interactions of officials responsible for implementing policy. These studies articulated what became known as the bottom-up model (see section 2.6 from Chapter 2).

As suggested by its title, this model was proffered as a countervailing thesis to the top-down approach. In contrast to the top-down framework, the likes of Hjern and Porter (1981) and Lipsky (1980) argue that policy is not the sole preserve of the political centre. Policy can be assembled and developed by those responsible for implementation. According to Lipsky (1980: 13), so-called 'street level bureaucrats' make policy in their decisions and individual actions on the ground. This ability to shape policy on the ground, as shown by Hjern and Porter's (1981: 215–16) research, allows bureaucrats to deal with local pressures and to meet local expectations. Thus a linear sequence of events involving policy formation followed by implementation has little substance in reality. The central argument of this bottom-up perspective is that policy is a dynamic phenomenon – something which is continually modified by the decisions and actions of those responsible for enacting policy.

Rational thinkers like Hogwood and Gunn (1993: 245) do concede that policy can be shaped by officials working on the ground. This is not in dispute. The main point of departure is that for Hogwood and Gunn, and other top-down theorists, these features should be minimized or controlled. Bottom-up theorists, on the other hand, maintain that these features are integral to the development and creation of policy. Minimize these features and you do away with policy.

Research on policy implementation by the School of Advanced Urban Studies at Bristol University sought to extend these arguments within a British context. In their publications, authors within the School largely echoed the criticism made by bottom-up theorists of the rational conception of policy-making. Policy implementation is conceptualized as an essentially *interactive* process (Barrett and Fudge, 1981b: 26). Here the response of officials and agents during the course of implementation can transform the goals and nature of policy. Policy is not always unequivocal or precise – the objectives of policy, against which subsequent actions will be assessed, can be ambiguous. According to this view, implementation entails a policy/action continuum, involving those responsible for implementing policy and those who will be effected. As such, it is difficult to reach a definite conclusion over whether a policy has been successfully implemented:

> At any point in time it may not be possible to say whether action is influencing policy or policy action. Hence action cannot be directly related to and evaluated against specific policy goals. Even where 'policy' appears to exist, it may not involve clear goal specification. (Barrett and Hill, 1984: 219)

Clearly, the British interactionist tradition has a certain affinity with bottom-up theory. Advocates of this interactive approach, however, have addressed certain conceptual limitations in the bottom-up approach. Like the rational framework of policy implementation, the views of theorists such as Lipsky and Hjern tended to simplify the nature of implementation by overlooking the context of the policy process. Thus Barrett and Fudge argue that analysis should not simply focus on those groups of agents involved in, and likely to be effected by, policy. In addition, analysis has to consider the structural framework in which this policy/action continuum is enacted. The structural framework is the organizational context in which policy action takes place. Notably, the policy–action perspective takes into account the asymmetrical distribution of power and influence within and between organizations.

In these organizational settings, policy actors are not mere adjuncts of the organizational hierarchy. This perspective acknowledges the multiplicity of actors engaged in the implementation process; the distinct interests of these actors and differences in terms of their access to resources and power; and the interactions between actors responsible for implementing policy and those who are effected by such processes, who endeavour to defend their own interests.

The policy–action perspective offers a significant, multidimensional view of the implementation process. It is devoid of existing assumptions about policy failures being located in caveats within the chain of hierarchical command. Neither does this perspective reduce policy to the actions and decisions of local officials responding to exigencies on the ground. What is more, this approach closely reflects the empirical evidence surrounding the complexity and politics of policy implementation.

The issue now concerns whether these ideas provide a useful

starting point for understanding developments in London's health system, post-Tomlinson. The evidence seems to suggest that they do. A similar approach to the study of organizational change and policy implementation in the health service was developed by Pettigrew and his colleagues in the Centre for Corporate Strategy and Change, at the Warwick Business School. The Centre has examined organizational change in private sector institutions (Pettigrew, 1985; Pettigrew and Whipp, 1991) but its most recent analysis has focused on the public sector – initially the health service (Pettigrew *et al.*, 1992) and latterly a wide array of public services (Ferlie *et al.*, 1996).

Analysts in the main, argue Pettigrew *et al.* (1992), concentrate on national or external barriers to policy change. They maintain that it is also imperative to consider local factors that can effect policy implementation. These researchers decline from assuming that local actors and institutions are inclined to blocking national policy. Such local factors, it is maintained, can create differential progress across organizations towards implementing a nationally established policy:

> Analysing the fine shading of the inner context of Districts has permitted us to differentiate between receptive and less receptive contexts for change, highlighting the importance of management style, strategies and tactics as well as structural, political and cultural features of particular locales. (ibid. 270)

Like the policy-action perspective propounded by Barrett and Fudge (1981a), Pettigrew and his colleagues at the Centre for Corporate Strategy stress the context of policy-making. The context, as already pointed out above, refers to features external to organizations of the health service. This includes the prevailing economic, political and social environment in which the NHS network operates. In addition, it includes the organizational structures within the health system – be this at national, regional or district level. At the same time, their approach is underpinned by a concern for action. Pettigrew *et al.* note that organizational change should take into account the agents who formulate strategies and how they manage to enact these (ibid. 269).

This framework enables analysts to consider that barriers to policy implementation can operate on different levels. The interconnection between organizations in the health service means that the operationalization of a strategy is dependent on a complex mesh of external and internal forces and various interest groups. The aim is to decipher and understand this relationship. The remainder of this chapter examines three factors that effected local receptivity in London to what the government had intended to achieve in its Tomlinson strategy. Each one will be examined in turn.

8.6.2   Conflicting evidence, contesting the policy

The guiding rationale of the Tomlinson inquiry was that changes in London's health service should be strategically planned. The inquiry team relied heavily on local knowledge to develop a planned policy of strategic change in London. As well as taking oral submissions, the team used analytical research and empirical evidence. Empirical evidence of this sort can play a major part in solidifying support and compliance behind a policy, especially when the constituencies effected are powerful professional groups. The main analytical source used by Tomlinson was a series of studies carried out by an independent health service research body, the King's Fund.

A year prior to the formation of the official inquiry, the King's Fund established a Commission for London to conduct an 18-month-long investigation. The final report published in June 1992 was the culmination of 12 separate studies. The findings provided up-to-date information on the standing of London's health service. These studies had an influential bearing on the Tomlinson team; the data produced by the King's Fund Commission were used extensively by Tomlinson, as acknowledged in the final report (Tomlinson, 1992: 2).

This programme of research concluded that there was a considerable surplus of acute hospital provision. In 1990, there were 115 hospitals, including 12 teaching hospitals, within the four Thames health authorities. Significantly, the capital's hospitals consumed a disproportionate amount of the nation's health resources. The figures showed spending on hospital provision in England for 1989–90 accounted for 58 per cent of the total national budget on hospital and community health services (HCHS) and family health services (FHS). In London this figure stood at 64 per cent. In addition, around 20 per cent of all HCHS expenditure in the same period was spent in London, although London's health districts contained only 15 per cent of the population of England (King's Fund, 1992: 45–6). These studies also confirmed that the long-standing paradox in London's health provision still persisted: despite the concentration of hospital facilities, London experienced inadequate community health provision. This is symptomatic of the fact that acute specialist services, assisting medical education and research, have dominated hospital care in London.

The report suggested a reduction in the number of acute London hospitals from 41 to 30, and a 30 per cent cut in the number of doctors. Nine London medical schools, the analysis went on to argue, should merge to form four integrated schools. It was estimated that such reorganization would cost £1.2 billion. The King's Fund recommended that the obverse of such rationalization should be a £220 million investment to develop community health premises (ibid. 86).

The evidence presented by the King's Fund seemed to confirm the long-standing structural imbalance within London's health service. Analytical evidence of this sort is vital in establishing a substantive case for a policy, and it clearly informed Tomlinson's recommendations for strategic change.

Nevertheless, the findings produced by the King's Fund and the subsequent policy strategies that emerged from the research did not go unchallenged. The main point of controversy came over the actual evidential base of the government' strategy. In one notable contribution, Professor Brian Jarman, head of primary health care at St Mary's Hospital, in April 1993, published an extensive survey of London hospital provision which was at odds with the respective conclusions of the King's Fund and Tomlinson reports. Jarman examined the provision of both acute beds and long-stay hospital beds for the elderly and mentally ill. This contrasted with Tomlinson who based his calculations on acute bed provision. As such, Jarman found that over the past 10 years in London, acute beds have closed at twice the national rate. Comparable figures show that in other deprived metropolitan centres (Manchester, Birmingham, Wolverhampton and Liverpool) in 1992–93 there was on average 60 per cent greater bed provision than the national figure, compared with 11 per cent for London. Jarman (1994: 22) concludes: 'It is clear that by comparison with other large cities, which also have bad health and poor social conditions, London has fewer beds available per head of population.'

The Health Secretary revealed in her evidence to the Health Select Committee that while Jarman's figures were available to Tomlinson, the inquiry team preferred to consult alternative sources, such as the King's Fund. The DoH's action demonstrated that empirical evidence is not always clear-cut; it may be slanted in a certain fashion in order to support particular arguments. Indeed, the Department of Health employed private consultancy firms – namely, Touche Ross, Ernst and Young, and Coopers and Lybrand – to support policy decisions based on the Tomlinson inquiry. This backfired because opponents of the changes similarly brought in private consultants to draw up detailed evidence to support cases against closure (Anderson, 1992).

Subsequent figures produced by DoH on per capita spending in major cities also seemed to support Jarman's analysis. As disclosed in a written answer from the then health minister, Brian Mawhinney, total health spending per head in London came at £584 compared to £791 in Manchester, and £649 in Newcastle (Parliamentary Debates, 1994: 72–3).

The DoH's empirical analysis of London's health service, based on the Tomlinson inquiry, was further undermined by a later report published by the King's Fund in 1994. The original report produced by the King's Fund in 1992 was used extensively by Tomlinson, but the later report disclaimed some of the earlier findings. Using more up-to-date evidence, the report argued that hospital bed provision in London had declined rapidly since 1982. Thus, rather than being over provided in terms of acute beds, the number of hospital beds in the capital per person is comparable to other large cities. The report concluded that London has to spend more on health because social problems and deprivation are severe in the capital (Phillips, 1994).

For politicians and officials, controversy over Tomlinson's report began to undermine the overarching strategic plan for London. Brunsson (1982: 41) notes that incoherence at the level of ideas can effect change: 'Ideological inconsistencies increase uncertainty and make it extremely difficult to marshall commitments for organizational actions.' Pettigrew *et al.*'s (1992) research of psychiatric hospital closures confirms Brunsson's assessment. Their research showed that the rationalization of psychiatric services by St Helens and Knowsley and Preston DHAs was beset by confusion over reorganization plans. This destabilized the progress required to achieve the necessary changes in services. One source of confusion was the lack of evidence presented over the future configuration of staffing levels. Confusion and dissension over the analytical basis of the strategy meant that the rationalization of psychiatric hospitals fell into inertia.

The conflicting voices and evidence in the London reforms similarly had a destabilizing effect. The fact that alternative sources showed that London had fewer acute beds than was needed placed significant question marks over the government's desired policy for change. The Secretary of State for Health at the time, Virginia Bottomley, faced stern questioning by members of the Health Committee in March 1994 over this conflicting evidence. The government was criticized for partial use of the available evidence in order to support its calls for rationalization of acute care in London. Although these claims were denied, the controversy caused by Jarman's conflicting findings, together with backtracking by the King's Fund on its original research, undermined the implementation of Tomlinson's policy.

8.6.3   The structural incoherence of the internal market

Conflicting views over the veracity of data concerning acute provision leant a significant fillip to opponents of the governments plans. However, this controversy in and of itself was not a sufficient impediment. The organizational structure of London's health system should also be considered. Research by Pettigrew and Whipp (1992: 261–2) of private industry found a positive correlation between organizational incoherence and barriers to policy or strategic implementation. Such links between structural incoherence and policy implementation have been uncovered in the public sector. The health service is a prime example:

> The NHS is an extremely large and complex organization. It is also an extraordinarily segmented and incoherent series of interlocking systems and groups divided on every conceivable axis: political and managerial; professional and managerial; professional and professional; Regional District and Unit levels of management; and, of course, geography and care group. (Pettigrew *et al.*, 1992: 291)

Similar observations apply to the capital's health system. Certain health authorities, though, have been plagued in the past by greater organizational incoherence than others within the four Thames regions. However, the level and nature of organizational complexity underwent substantive transformation under the internal market.

The impact of the internal market, as already shown, led the government to establish the Tomlinson inquiry. This was done to avoid unplanned hospital closures across London. The full introduction of the internal market, in the short term, was also delayed to avoid a collapse of health services in the capital. Eventually, ministers were determined, once they had managed to avert crisis in London, to establish a fully operational internal market in London. All this injected a degree of uncertainty and organizational incoherence which was ubiquitous across the Thames regions. This created barriers in terms of rationalizing services.

Planning in London was historically difficult to achieve because the capital was composed of numerous health authorities which in turn were overseen, at the regional level, by four different bodies. The Tomlinson review, as already noted, attempted to overcome this by outlining a framework for strategic change across the various health and regional authority boundaries in London. The internal market, however, introduced strategic uncertainty and further organizational fragmentation. The main issue was that the government attempted to plan reorganization within London, while insisting that strategic provision of health care should be left to the internal market. The DoH's (1993: 3) *Making London Better* document noted: 'The Government can set the framework for change. But change must be driven locally and, above all, by patients' needs. The operation of the NHS internal market will determine the precise patterns of health care in London in the future.'

The architect of London's reorganization, Sir Bernard Tomlinson, argued, following the publication of his report, that planned closure and the freedom of the market could not be reconciled (Mihill and Brindle, 1993). Tomlinson did acknowledge before the Parliamentary Health Committee that the market has contributed to an improvement in services. Yet he also explained that the operation of the market in London's reorganization was unsustainable:

> We think that the danger in the indiscriminate reduction of hospitals in London is so great, if the market is allowed to operate as it does, that we believe the process of reduction of hospitals, and with it of course the improvement in primary care, has to be a ... firmly managed process. (Health Committee, 1992: 2)

As was predicted by Tomlinson and other commentators (*Guardian*, 1993), the internal market soon after its introduction in

April 1991 rebounded on the government's plans for London. In July 1993, four months after the publication of *Making London Better*, the government's overhaul of London's hospitals was thrown into doubt by the purchasing decisions of Camden and Islington health authority. The policies of this health authority threatened a group of hospitals that were supposed to remain open under the government's plans. The authority revealed it was intending to transfer its contracts for treating local people away from the University College and Middlesex hospital group. Loss of this contract, worth £20 million, would have resulted in the closure of the group's accident and emergency facilities, and eventually the hospitals. This accident and emergency department was of strategic importance to central London: it served a significant resident population and a heavy concentration of visitors. Consequently, the Health Secretary announced on 16 December 1993 that she was intervening to prevent Camden and Islington Health Authority from switching contracts. Moreover, additional funding was also put aside for the University College group.

The University College dilemma underlined how the government's avowed support of the internal market proved untenable. While insisting that purchasing of health care should be left to the market, it was prepared to intervene directly when the market began to take effect. Similar interventions to prevent hasty, unplanned dismantling of hospitals, even those outlined for closure under Tomlinson, took place throughout the 1994–95 period. For example, Guy's was due to transfer acute in-patient and emergency facilities to St Thomas's. But in April 1995, the Health Secretary revealed that Guy's Hospital would retain its accident and emergency service until alternative facilities were in place. These services were not due to be in operation before the end of 1998, thereby delaying the rationalization of Guy's Hospital (Parliamentary Debates, 1995: 1044).

Tomlinson's rationalization plans for acute services encountered further difficulties because of the implementation mechanisms that were in place. An illustration was provided by developments following the reports of the six specialty review teams. The teams put together plans for rationalizing tertiary specialties in the capital. From their plans, nine hospitals appeared threatened, including some not even earmarked for closure by Tomlinson. For instance, the cancer specialty review recommended the closure of the Royal Marsden site in Fulham (Dillner, 1993).

The government made it clear that the specialist reviews were advice and not definite, final policy decisions. But this did not alleviate the problem over implementation. While the London Implementation Group coordinated the specialty review studies, it was unclear who would be responsible for rationalizing specialist services. According to James (1994: 33) this was one of the inherent difficulties in attempting to implement Tomlinson:

> Are the purchasing District Health Authorities and GP Fundholders to decide whether to implement the Specialty Review recommendations or not? . . . But it is not easy for them to find a way in which to operate at a strategic level on a pan London basis.

Not surprisingly, it was announced in August 1994 that the London Implementation Group would be abolished prematurely in March 1995, a year before it was planned to be wound up. Another body was formed in its stead to carry forward the reorganization of London's health service. The government established a committee with representatives from the Thames regional health authorities, which had been reduced from four to two bodies in April 1994. According to some commentators, this development signalled an acceptance that a single, strategic planning body is needed to implement the sweeping changes recommended by Tomlinson (Eaton, 1994).

In addition to confusing the implementation process, the internal market hampered those engaged in rationalization plans. This had made it easier for campaigners to slow down or halt acute closure programme. Two separate reports published in November 1994, one by the Institute of Health Services Management and the other by the South Thames Regional Health Authority, found that the internal market had curtailed major rationalization embarked upon by several authorities. Health authorities in south-west London found that the internal market tended to isolate planners. Rationalization plans in Bristol wavered not due to any division between health authority purchasers and hospital providers, as there was a level of collaboration from the outset. Instead, the main problems stemmed from relations between hospitals; these institutions were pitted as rivals by the internal market (Brindle, 1994).

8.6.4   Inconsistent and inadequate external pressures

Earlier in this chapter a number of studies and theoretical perspectives were drawn upon to understand the sociological basis of strategic change. These showed that intense environmental pressures can lead to major periods of restructuring in both private and public sector institutions. At various junctures it was shown that external impositions in the form of financial pressures induced periods of reorganization in London's health service. This view, as pointed out earlier, requires certain qualifications. As Pettigrew *et al.* (1992: 280) note: 'The picture in the NHS is more complex, as in some instances excessive pressure can deflect or drain energy out of the system.' The same could be said concerning the implementation of the Tomlinson strategy for London. Here, certain aspects of the Tomlinson strategy were hindered by inconsistent constraints from without. Recommendations concerning primary and community health services provide a revealing example.

As the Tomlinson report made clear, the reorganization of London's health service not only involved rationalization, but also a positive effort to bolster community health services. The government acknowledged that the internal market would enforce rationalization before alternative primary facilities were in place. Hence, it proposed early investment in these alternative services and continued transitional funding for struggling hospitals. This strategy was to be carried forward by the London Initiative Zone (hereafter, LIZ), made up of representatives from 12 Family Health Service Authorities (FHSAs). The role of LIZ was to concentrate resources in those areas of the capital where primary care facilities proved unsatisfactory.

It was understandable that difficulties emerged over the rationalization of acute services, involving as it did the closure of hospital sites. However, the development of primary and community care services proved equally problematic. The government provided £170 million for the London Initiative Zone to fund new GP surgeries. A further £40 million was made available for investing in community health services throughout 1993, doubled to £85 million in 1994. A further £7.5 million was made available for voluntary projects over three years.

Despite this investment, there were 2 per cent fewer GPs in 1993 than there were in 1990, 5 per cent fewer health visitors and

11 per cent fewer district nurses; these figures were not contested by the Health Secretary when they were presented to her at the Health Committee (Health Committee, 1994: 11). In addition, the primary care development programme in the North Thames Region was running at a 28 per cent underspend (Snell, 1995: 22).

Opinions expressed by a senior health spokesperson and health officials from London suggests that there were a variety of reasons for the limited progress. One significant factor was the type of influence exerted by central government on health authorities and other relevant bodies in London. The external pressures applied by government impacted detrimentally on the development of community health services in two respects. First, health officials were pressurized into delivering extensive changes in a short period of time. Second, the pressure for change, at the same time, was inconsistent.

Taking the first point, politicians in the DoH expected a great deal to be achieved in a short space of time. For some officials, the political demand for rapid results was such that some finances, initially, were used ineffectually. The system of bidding for LIZ funds was ad hoc. In the early stages, it was reputed that some agencies were afforded very little time in making bids for LIZ resources. As such, little forethought went into some of the plans for developing primary health services. A spokesperson for the North Thames Regional Health Authority acknowledged these difficulties:

> When the whole LIZ programme was fired off by Brian Mawhinney it took people by surprise and you had to be up and running very quickly. In many cases the mechanisms were not in place to successfully spend the money and that has contributed to the underspend we have at the moment. (cited in Snell, 1995: 23)

The second point was that pressure from the government was inconsistent. Initially, after applying intense pressure to achieve immediate, and often unrealistic results, momentum from the government began to wane. One official from the Community Health Trust in Wandsworth noted that once the London Implementation Group was disbanded, much of the commitment for developing primary services rescinded (ibid. 24). For this official, the political will to redevelop community services in the long term is severely lacking.

The lack of appropriate external mechanisms for improving primary services has effectively overloaded the system:

Three separate agendas have had to be dealt with at the same time. Basic services have had to be dealt with at the same time. Basic services have had to be brought up to scratch and services have had to be developed for groups like homeless people ... and, on top of all this, care is supposed to move out of hospitals into the community. (ibid. 24)

8.7 Concluding remarks

This chapter has examined the route by which policies emerge and are subsequently implemented. The government's policy for strategic change in the capital's health service has formed the case study through which this analysis has been pursued. The main issues emerging from this case study are summarized as follows:

1. It was found that major strategic restructuring of organizations, as envisaged by Tomlinson, follows a familiar pattern according to organizational theorists. It is argued that environmental jolts, external to organizations, can lead to the reshaping of organizations. In London's health service, external pressures emerged from the government's establishment of the internal market. The purchaser–provider split had the effect of jeopardizing a number of hospitals in the capital. The government responded by forming the Tomlinson inquiry – in effect it attempted to plan changes within the capital. Such explanations may be used to explain the way many policy issues emerge in the first place.

2. Tomlinson's recommendations, adopted practically wholesale by the government, was an idealized policy for strategic change. The dynamics of implementation, though, are more problematic than portrayed by officials in policy documents. Events post-Tomlinson provide confirmation of this point.

3. In the above, it was argued that the implementation process is best examined using the more sociologically based insights of policy–action and contemporary organizational theory. The policy–action perspective is particulary strong on the role of actors in negotiation over policy and the influence of asymmetrical relations of power in the policy process. These frameworks, particularly organizational theory, also take into account the constraints of structures, whether external or internal, on policy implementation. These models seem to acknowledge the importance of links between agency and structure in the policy process.

4. Using the insights of organizational research, which empha-sized the importance of local impediments to the implementation of policy, three factors were influential during the operational phase of the government's plans to reorganise health services in London. First, the research has shown that actual research evi-dence does play a vital part in cultivating support for, and compliance of those effected constituencies, behind a specific policy. This can be jeopardized, as in the above case study, when doubts arise over the accuracy of the evidence being presented. Second, policy implementation can be affected by the cogency and togetherness of the interorganizational structure of local net-works. The health system in London is a complex entity with many distinct levels. Greater uncertainty and incoherence was introduced as a result of the internal market. This impeded plans for rationalization. Such were the difficulties that the government was forced to assume a more interventionist, planning role in London. This went against its initial *laissez faire* strategy of leaving the internal market to do its business. Third, inappropriate exter-nal pressure by central government, through financial mechanism, may galvanize institutional reshaping. But if this external pressure is too intense or inconsistent, as demonstrated by the government's attempts to develop primary health services in London, they can hinder the implementation process.

5. These developments only confirm what action and organiz-ational sociologists have shown in their research on the implementation process: that policies, even when formally set out in documents, can be rearranged and redefined once they are oper-ationalized on the ground. This was not just down to local agencies within the capital's health service. Interestingly, the restructuring of London's health service demonstrated that central government also contributed to the gradual redefinition of official policy.

STUDY GUIDE

Chronology of events surrounding the Tomlinson inquiry and the subsequent reorganization of London's health service

April 1991: The internal market comes into operation in the NHS. This new regime establishes purchaser–provider splits in London's health service. In view of the high costs of medical care in the capital, medical services are under threat of indiscriminate closure. The flagship trust hospital, Guy's in south London, runs up an early deficit in the new competitive market for health care.

June 1991:   The Secretary of State for Health, William Waldegrave, junior ministers and Health Department civil servants meet officials from the North-West Thames and North-East Thames Regional Health Authorities. A presentation is made by the officials about the prospects of funding hospital building programmes in London. According to one commentator, this meeting 'was to have unforseen repercussions for the whole of the Health Service in London' (James, 1994: 24).

10 October 1991:   During his keynote speech at the Conservative Party's annual conference, the Health Secretary, William Waldegrave, announces a commission of inquiry on health provision in the capital. The planned inquiry was placed under the auspices of Sir Bernard Tomlinson, a former pathologist and chairman of the Northern Regional Health Authority.

October–December 1991:   Thames health authorities and hospital units faced budget deficits as they fail to win the necessary number of contracts in the internal market system. The government, in response, delayed the introduction of full weighted capitation and the Thames regional health authorities received extra funding to cushion the impact of the internal market.

April 1992:   Following the Conservative general election victory, Virginia Bottomley is installed as the new Health Secretary. She makes clear her determination to press on with health service reforms, including a planned reorganization of London hospitals when the Tomlinson inquiry publishes its results later in the year.

June 1992:   The King's Fund Commission for London published a report on London's health service, *London Health Care 2010*. The report is the culmination of earlier studies on London's acute services and medical teaching and training. The findings contained in the report are particularly influential.

August 1992:   A report by North-West Thames Regional Health Authority confirmed that 2,000 beds could be closed in a planned reorganization of health services for north-west London. The report argued that the Charing Cross teaching hospital should close its accident and emergency department.

10 September 1992:   It is confirmed by the British Medical Association that it will not resist any closures of London hospitals resulting from the Tomlinson inquiry.

September 1992: Chiefs of the UCH/Middlesex group recommend that the Middlesex Hospital should be closed in order to save its sister hospital, University College. This was the first London teaching hospital named for closure as a result of the internal market. The planned closure was also viewed to be a response to speculation that the Tomlinson inquiry will recommend closing both hospitals.

15 October 1992: The Tomlison committee submits its report to ministers. It is rumoured that the hospitals most at risk of closure or enforced merger are Charing Cross, Guy's or St Thomas's, St Bartholomew's and the University College and Middlesex group. On the same day, Labour's health spokesman, David Blunkett, issued a statement which confirms that the Labour Party will conditionally support moves to rationalize London's hospital services.

23 October 1992: The Tomlinson inquiry into London's health services and hospitals is published. Altogether, it makes 106 recommendations concerning the restructuring of health services in the capital.

9 November 1992: A report published by York University's centre for health economics raises doubts about the government's ability to fund the Tomlinson programme for hospital closures while simultaneously boosting community and family doctor services in the capital. The report argues that this programme will be difficult to implement because the national health expenditure budget faced a tight squeeze.

2 December 1992: Peers debate the Tomlinson report on the future of health care in London. A number of objections are raised about the proposed hospital closures. St Bartholomew's was particularly singled out.

8 December 1992: In the Department of Health budgets for 1993–4, it was announced that ministers would set aside millions of pounds to act upon the Tomlinson proposals. Despite the introduction of weighted capitation, which was introduced to distribute resources from London to outer population centres, London and the south-east would receive £59 million to assist the health service in the capital.

16 December 1992: The head of the inquiry on London's health services, Sir Bernard Tomlinson, accompanied by other members of the inquiry team, present evidence before the Health Committee on their findings.

2 February 1993:   The Labour party published a report which is highly critical of the Tomlinson inquiry, although it concedes that the party is committed to the long-term reorganization of the health service in London. The report calls for the suspension of the internal market and for social deprivation to be taken into account before cuts are made.

16 February 1993:   The government published a report, *Making London Better*, setting out how the Tomlinson recommendations will be implemented. As part of this process, the London Implementation Group is formally established to take forward the work outlined by the government. Key decisions are still subject to consultation.

2 March 1993:   The Health Secretary and the health minister, Brian Mawhinney, together with two senior officials, give evidence on London's health service before the Parliamentary Health Committee.

April 1993:   Professor Brian Jarman published a report in the *British Medical Journal* which outlined the findings of an extensive survey of London's hospital provision. The conclusions of Jarman's research were in sharp contrast to those produced by the Tomlinson report. This has significant repercussions. The reason for this is that Tomlinson was used as the basis of the government's planned reform of the health service in London.

23 June 1993:   Six teams of experts publish their conclusions on specialist services in the capital. The teams were established by the London Implementation Group to further explore the main recommendations of the Tomlinson report. The six specialist review teams in their findings called for the rationalization of 'tertiary' specialities in and around the capital.

12 July 1993:   A report for the Department of Health is published that reviews the work of Special Health Authorities, which enjoy protected funding due to their research activities. The report concluded that several leading research hospitals, which come under the protected animus of Specialist Health Authorities, are carrying out indifferent work of little importance to the health service. This added further credence to those arguing for hospital closures in London.

14 July 1993:   Members of the London Implementation Group present evidence to the Parliamentary Health Committee.

July 1993:   It is announced by Camden and Islington Health Authority that it wishes to take contracts away from the University College London group, seeking cheaper treatment outside the capital. Without these contracts, the future of the UCL group was in doubt.

1 September 1993:   Speaking at the annual general meeting of the British Association for the Advancement of Science, Sir Bernard Tomlinson argues that the government should assist those hospitals which are being threatened financially by the internal market yet are not scheduled for closure, such as the UCL group. He warns it will be disastrous if other hospitals in the country were allowed to be closed by the internal market.

September 1993:   St Bartholomew's discontinues its campaign for independent status by agreeing to merge with the Royal London and London Chest hospitals.

16 December 1993:   The Health secretary intervened to avoid the internal market from closing University College Hospital. She confirmed in a Commons written answer that Camden and Islington Health Authority will not be allowed to continue with plans to switch contracts worth £20 million form University College Hospital. This allows UCL to continue as a major centre for research and training with its own accident and emergency department.

21 December 1993:   In this month, the North-West Thames Regional Health Authority proposed to merge Great Ormond Street Children's hospital with University College Hospital.

February 1994:   In this month, the Health Secretary updated the Commons on changes to the health service in London. The statement revealed that for the following year the government will double new investment in London's primary and community care to £85 million. In addition, the Health Secretary outlined a number of developments on hospital mergers and the current status of applications for trust status. The application of Hammersmith, Charing Cross and Queen Charlotte's to become a joint trust will be decided after public consultation ends in March. It is also revealed that discussions are taking place over a possible merger of Charing Cross and Hammersmith Hospital on one of these two sites. Following the establishment of a single trust for Guy's and St Thomas's Hospitals, the Health Secretary announced that the government will ask the trust to transfer most of the clinical services at Guy's to St Thomas's. As a result, Guy's will be little more than a medical school, providing some day surgery and outpatient clinics.

March 1994:   Campaigners and the London boroughs of Islington and Hackney win leave to seek a judicial review of the decision to close the casualty unit of St Bartholomew's Hospital in the City.

21 March 1994:   Following a statutory public consultation which began in February, ministers decide against further planned hospital closures in west London. The Health Secretary confirmed the setting up of a hospital trust on the 1 April, combining the Hammersmith, Charing Cross, and the smaller Queen Charlotte's and Acton Hospitals. It is envisaged that the trust will eventually operate from a single site. But in the immediate future the Health Secretary confirmed that the trust will provide services from across all its sites. It is suggested that ministers have sought to avoid any more political damage over planned closures before imminent local and European elections.

April 1994:   At the beginning of this month, the first phase takes place in a major reorganization of regional health authorities in England. As part of the planned changes, the 14 regional health authorities are to be reduced to eight as the initial step in their eventual transition in 1996 into regional offices of the NHS management executive. For London, this involved a reduction from four to two regional health authorities.

25 April 1994:   A legal attempt to save St Bartholomew's fails after the High Court rules that the Health Secretary acted properly in deciding to close the hospital's casualty department.

May 1994:   Campaigners attempting to save St Bartholomew's casualty department seek leave to appeal against the High Court's decision that the Health Secretary acted legally in deciding to close the casualty unit at the hospital. The appeal was made possible after a fund-raising drive generated £97,747.

29 July 1994:   The Court of Appeal refused the London boroughs of Islington and Hackney leave to appeal against the High Court's decision to reject a judicial review challenging the Health Secretary's decision to close the casualty unit at St Bartholomew's. On the same day, managers admit that the transfer of services from St Bartholomew's to the Royal London would cost £144 million. Managers at the Royal Hospitals NHS Trust observe that the transfer should be completed quickly, preferably within six years.

September 1994:   Ministers and Department of Health officials confirm that the London Implementation Group, a body established to reorganize London's health services over a three-year period, would be dismantled prematurely in March 1995. The merger earlier in the year of the four Thames health authorities into two bodies rendered the London Implementation Group superfluous. The greater coordination afforded by the creation of two regions means that LIG's functions will be transferred to a joint committee of two Thames regional health authorities in April 1995.

1 September 1994:   The King's Fund published another report based on a collection of five studies conducted by academics at the Guy's and St Thomas's Medical Schools. While the report largely supported a general shift from acute to primary services in the capital, it is argued that alternative community services must be provided before wholesale bed closures, otherwise major problems are likely to occur in the treatment of acutely ill patients.

27 January 1995:   The scheduled closure of the accident and emergency unit at St Bartholomew's takes place.

13 March 1995:   The East London and the City Health Authority approves the closure of St Bartholomew's Hospital on condition that the site would be kept for health care purposes. The local DHA concludes that acute care should be concentrated at the Royal London and the Homerton Hospital, Hackney, while closing down St Bartholomew's and the small London Chest Hospital.

4 April 1995:   The Health Secretary, in a written answer, outlined her decision for the reorganization of health services in the south and east of London. This came following the results of four separate statutory consultation exercises carried out by health authorities over proposed changes to health care in the south and east of London, and around Barnet and Edgware. The most significant decision to emerge from the Health Secretary's reply concerned the future of Guy's and St Bartholomew's Hospitals. The Health Secretary confirmed that she accepted the proposal that acute services at Guy's should be transferred to St Thomas's, leaving Guy's to develop as a local community hospital. However, it was made clear that Guy's accident and emergency department and supporting beds would not be closed until alternative facilities were in place. As these services would realistically not be in place before the end of 1998, this gave Guy's Hospital something of a reprieve. The Health Secretary also confirmed, following the findings of the East London and the City Health Authority, that most of the services from St Bartholomew's would be transferred to the Royal London Hospital at its Whitechapel site.

April 1995:   There was uncertainty over Mrs Bottomley's position as Health

Secretary. The *Health Service Journal* (13 April 1995, p. 15) argued that Mrs Bottomley will probably move to another department in a summer Cabinet reshuffle.

10 July 1995: In the Cabinet reshuffle, Virginia Bottomley was moved to the Department of National Heritage. Stephen Dorrell became the new Health Secretary.

A reading schedule

All the best textbooks dedicate space to the question of policy formation and implementation. For a selection see Ham and Hill (1993: chapter 6), and Parsons (1995 sections 4.2 and 4.4) is a very readable and very comprehensive examination of the attempts to theorize the barriers that hinder implementation. Hill (1993 parts VI and VIII) contains relevant chapter articles; the chapters by Hjern and Porter, Hogwood and Gunn, and Sabatier cover the top-down versus bottom-up arguments. Hogwood and Gunn's (1984) text on policy systematically covers the various stages of the policy process; chapters 6 and 11, though a little dry, cover the issues of policy formation and implementation. For a completely different analysis of the policy process Barrett and Fudge's (1981a) collection of articles is useful. It would also be worth reading some of Lipsky's (1980) classic text in the original for a bottom-up analysis of implementation. For examinations of policy implementation in the health service, Pettigrew *et al.* (1992) is highly informative, providing a sociological analysis of organizational change across various areas of the health service.

Issues for revision and further consideration

Having studied this case study you should be familiar with several key concepts relevant to policy analysis. These are as follows: the outer environment (section 8.2); strategic change (8.2); policy formulation (8.3); top-down intervention (8.6.1); bottom-up theory (8.6.1); street-level bureaucrats (8.6.1); policy action (8.6.1); policy type (8.6.1) policy evidence (8.6.2); structural incoherence (8.6.3).

▶   Identify the factors that might be responsible for the emergence of a policy issue?

▶▶

▶   What are the main differences between top-down and bottom-up approaches to policy implementation? Can the two models be reconciled?

▶   Why are issues regarding power relevant to the study of implementation?

▶   Is it inevitable that policies encounter difficulties?

▶   In what ways could policy implementation be improved?

▶   How significant is the institutional context to the implementation of policy?

Chapter 9

How successful is Dutch drug control policy? A case study of the evaluation process

9.1 Introduction: evaluation and drug control policy in the Netherlands

The case studies in this part of the analysis are organized to explore features of the policy cycle. The previous chapter examined the formation and implementation of policy. Attention now turns to a phenomenon normally associated with the aftermath of implementation: that phase of the policy cycle involving evaluation. Of concern here are the procedures where analysts evaluate the impact of a policy on its intended targets – the issues or areas it sought to address.

This form of analysis should be distinguished from 'evaluation as an activity involved in the measurement of goal performance' (Parsons, 1995: 545). This type of research is less analytical in nature. It focuses on the provision of objective information about the effectiveness of ongoing policies. This may be generated by measuring the resources and effects of policies, or by assessing the performance of those administrators and institutions responsible for implementing programmes. This field of evaluative research has been colonized more by practitioners than academic researchers. Given the fact that this chapter is concerned with the post-implementation phase of the policy cycle, it is more appropriate to focus on impact evaluation. Moreover, this mode of evaluation, by its very nature, is less practical in orientation, requiring the type of analytical approach deemed necessary in the analysis of policy embraced by this text. The subject chosen for conducting this investigation is Dutch drug control policy.

There are several reasons why the Dutch drug policy is an appropriate case study for considering impact evaluation. First, Dutch policy is useful for this purpose as it amounts to an explicit and consciously planned intervention to address the social problem of drug abuse. The anticipatory nature of the Dutch stance in relation to drugs has given analysts clear and distinct criteria by which to assess the impact of the policy. The essence of what is seen as *the Dutch policy on drugs* is enshrined in the Opium Act of 1976. The Act revised the Opium Act of 1928 to introduce the significant, and nefarious, distinction between drug markets. Specifically, the Act differentiated between drugs that present an unacceptable risk – the so-called hard substances of heroin, cocaine, LSD and amphetamines – and cannabis products (hashish and marijuana). Those drugs presenting an unacceptable risk were classified as Schedule 1 and, under the Act, penalties for dealing in these substances were stiffened. On the other hand, there was a considerable decrease in penalties, partial decriminalization even, for the possession and retail of what were classified as Schedule 2 drugs – cannabis products. Underlying this legal distinction in the drug markets is the idea that cannabis presents less of a risk to the individual and society than opiates and amphetamines. The whole rationale of establishing different legal penalties for those drugs that present an unacceptable risk is this: to control their use and distribution among the general population (Ruggiero and South, 1995: 32). As a recent government document noted, 'the policy pursued in the Netherlands has always had the more modest objective of bringing or keeping the use of dangerous drugs, as a health and social problem, under control' (Ministry of Health, Welfare and Sport, 1995: 5).

The second reason for this case analysis is that the policy of establishing separate markets has now been in place for 20 years. With the passage of time, it should be possible to reach a considered and reasoned assessment of the extent to which the policy has met its objectives. It will also be possible, by looking at the policy longitudinally, to gauge how the 1976 Opium Act has shaped the subsequent responses and interventions to the issue of illicit drugs in society.

Finally, such has been the controversy surrounding the Netherlands partial legalization of cannabis that Dutch governments have been keen to justify their position on various fronts. Most notably, there has been a willingness, especially in recent years, to scrutinize and evaluate the impact of the policy across a range of areas – the drug market, patterns of drug behaviour, the incidence of drug-related deaths and diseases, the extent of drug-related crimes, trafficking and so on.

The objective for the remainder of this chapter is to assess the impact of the Dutch intervention on the drug problem. Before embarking on this substantive analysis, consideration is given to those procedures and ideas that are employed in the field of policy evaluation. These approaches are characterized by distinct methodologies and theoretical positions in relation to the policy process. In particular, quantitative-orientated positivist approaches are compared with models that adopt a qualitative position regarding evaluation. This discussion provides the framework through which a substantive examination of Dutch drug policy is conducted. The central aim is not only to appraise whether policy-makers have fulfilled their objectives. It is also to understand the degree to which government intervention through planned policy interventions can make a difference to social problems and issues.

9.2   Surveying the field of policy evaluation

The field of policy evaluation and impact studies expanded dramatically after the Second World War. American academics and institutions were at the forefront of these developments. This was to be expected as the formative contributions to policy studies came from across the Atlantic. Large-scale evaluation studies in such areas as delinquency prevention programmes and public housing schemes were conducted during the 1950s (Palfrey *et al.*, 1992: 3). The 1960s witnessed a proliferation of published material on policy evaluation, creating a major growth industry. According to Rist (1995a: p. xv) the tendency of Western governments during the postwar years to become embroiled in social problems created a ready proclivity for evaluation work. Educational failure, crime, drug abuse, urban deprivation, environmental pollution: these became some of the staple issues that drew the attention and efforts of government authorities.

In Britain, officials and ministers also made provision to include evaluative research and evidence in policy-making. The Fulton Committee in a review of the Whitehall bureaucracy and civil service in the late 1960s was a revealing development. It criticized the short-term attitude towards planning that was evident in the mandarin milieu. In response to Fulton, the government published the 1970 White Paper on the reorganization of central government. The Central Policy Review Staff (CPRS) and the Programme Analysis Review (PAR) were conspicuous products of the White Paper. These bodies were formed to provide an independent source of inquiry 'to Ministers in order for them to make more "rational" decisions and to explore in detail the efficiency of existing policies' (Palfrey *et al.*, 1992: 13). Such was the popularity of policy advice that by 1980, thirteen government departments had formed planning units.

Such were the efforts being made by governments that much of the early academic work on evaluation was concerned with practical application. Methodologically, this meant that most of the formative work on policy evaluation was dominated by quantitative forms of analysis. The American academic, James Coleman, was a notable proponent for the use of scientific-style methodologies in policy evaluation. Policy research, for Coleman, should become an applied science – the aim being to provide a framework for practical action. As a social science, the methodologies that come closest to replicating scientific research designs are statistically based. These methods are to be used in order to identify and focus on those policy variables that can be manipulated and changed. These are distinct from situational variables that may not be easily modified. The central aim of evaluation is to provide concrete results that may lead to policy changes (Kelly, 1987: 280).

For Coleman, statistical techniques, moulded on scientific models, form the appropriate research methodology for evaluating policy. The emphasis on scientific modelling is a consequence of Coleman's positivistic ontology. Here, reality is viewed as an objective phenomenon, external to the researcher, and, therefore, capable of being accurately reported by observers:

> Reality is tangible, separate from the observer, stable over time and space ... With proper designs, appropriate operational definitions, measuring instruments, and research techniques, reality could be apprehended and linked to extant theories ... Methodology would protect the researcher from political efforts to distort meaning. Operational definitions would clarify what reality actually is regardless of political intrusions. (Kelly, 1987: 280)

The positivist principle to evaluation as exemplified by Coleman is straightforward. Quantitative-based techniques provide objective data about the performance of a policy. Because behaviour in reality is seen as following a causal chain of cause and effect, these techniques are able to isolate those variables that are determined and shaped by policy. Such data are then used as the basis of evaluation, from which the policy may be manipulated to produce the desired effects (Parsons, 1995: 563).

Typical of this mode of evaluation was the use of economic techniques to assess policy options. The prime evaluative model in this respect was cost-benefit analysis. The modus operandi of the technique is to measure the outward costs of a policy against the objective benefits that will accrue. This process is repeated on the other policy options, allowing decision-makers to compare their value. The option that brings the highest aggregate benefits according to the cost-benefit analysis is the optimum course of action for policy-makers. Such techniques were first used by American legislators in the 1930s. It obtained wider usage during the 1950s and 1960s in Europe and America. Cost-benefit analysis here was applied to the field of welfare economics and to defence programmes, especially in America (Parsons, 1995: 400).

Evaluating the impact of policy was dominated by similar quantitative techniques. Much of the analysis took the form of statistical output measurements of policy programmes and government activities. Most notably, the areas of criminal justice and health services, and education were subject to this mode of evaluative analysis. The central approach here has been to use statistical indicators to measure performance according to various objective criteria. In the 1980s, these quantitative measures gained especial significance. Consecutive Conservative governments endeavoured, as part of their restructuring of the public service, to institute performance indicator regimes throughout the public sector. These were a fundamental part of the government's self-appointed task of transforming the public sector from an administrative to a managerially based organizational entity.

9.2.1   Using statistical evaluation: a critical view

Quantitative measures of the sort used in cost-benefit analysis and output studies are also prominent in the analysis and evaluation of drug policy. Authorities in the Netherlands have shown a particular willingness to research trends in drug use. This is to be expected. The separation of drug markets has differentiated the Dutch policy from the drug control practices of other countries. Officially at least, the distribution and possession of all types of drugs still remains illegal in most European states. For the Dutch, there is a need to demonstrate that qualified liberalization of soft drugs has not led to an adverse increase in the use of both soft and hard drugs.

Thus one year after the passage of the 1976 Opium Act, the first estimates of hard-drug addiction were published in the Netherlands. Figures released periodically in 1977, 1979 and 1983 showed an increase from 10,000–20,000 to 20,000–30,000 in the number of hard-drug addicts (Spruit and Zwart, 1994: 4). This figure was based on the registers of drug rehabilitation centres. The registers revealed a total of between 21,000 and 25,000 heroin addicts. These estimates have been confirmed by recent studies conducted by the Ministry of Health. The research has revealed that there around 25,000 hard-drug addicts, equivalent to 0.16 per cent of the Netherlands 15 million population (Ministry of Health, Welfare, and Sport, 1995a: 9–10). The estimates for soft-drug use are higher. There are an estimated 600,000 people in the Netherlands who regularly use cannabis, which amounts to 4.6 per cent of the total population. Significantly, there has been an increase in the number of school children using cannabis. Nationwide surveys among secondary school children found that cannabis use had increased from 4.8 per cent in 1984 to 8.0 per cent in 1988. By 1992, this total stood at 13.6 per cent.

These figures would seem to provide significant ammunition for critics of the Dutch drug control policy – and there are many. Chief among these are conservative politicians within the Netherlands and neighbouring countries such as France and Sweden. However, the point neglected by the positivist approach is that quantitative methods do not necessarily provide objective insights into the area of reality that concerns policy-makers. To assume that unequivocal conclusions can be reached about the performance of a policy simply by reading off a set of figures is questionable. Part of the reason for this is that quantitative techniques do not provide an entirely objective and neutral insight into the social world. These methodologies can easily produce data that is skewed by any number of intervening variables. Numerical techniques may give the appearance of empirical rigour, belying the partial nature of the evidence being provided. For example, one Dutch report commented that the statistical growth in hard drug addicts between the late 1970s and late 1980s may not reflect a real or actual increase at all. It may be that the increases are the result of improved methods used to calculate the number of drug addicts (Spruit and Zwart, 1994: 4).

What the statistical evaluations of drug policy also fail to convey are the hidden numbers of addicts not included in official figures. There are always likely to be hidden numbers that fail to be detected: 'Because of the illegal nature of drug use, statistics on it depend on estimates compiled on the basis of information from the police and care agencies, among others. However, there is an unknown "dark number" of drug users who have no contact with any official body' (Ministry of Health, Welfare and Sport, 1995a: 8). In addition, problematic groups tend to be unrepresented in surveys where sample populations are used.

The positivist approach is further undermined by the fact that the process of evaluation is invariably a highly political matter. In this respect, personal values and ideologies are likely to come into effect when evaluating a policy in terms of its overall impact. Positivism assumes that personal views and the political context will not influence the evaluations made by analysts. The singular nature of reality means that independent, objective assessments are possible. But as Parsons (1995: 602) writes: 'Analysis of the effects of government policies may ... be said to be contingent on "where you sit" '.

Palumbo and Hallett's (1995) study of policy implementation in the state of Arizona is a case in point. The authors demonstrated the highly politicized nature of evaluating two new state-run penal initiatives: the first concerned two juvenile detention programmes for women – one being public and the other private – and the second an electronic monitoring system. A positivist approach would presume a consensus model of evaluation. The argument propounded is that analysts will eventually reach similar results when evaluating a policy programme because there is already agreement about its goals and objectives. Palumbo and Hallett found this view to be unrealistic. Their research of penal policy in Arizona revealed a clear plurality of, and sometimes conflicting, views about the value of the two Arizona programmes. For instance, the home arrest programme passed in 1988 by Arizona was surrounded by different goals and objectives. The Arizona State Legislature was Republican-controlled at the time of the Bill. To gain conservative support, the Bill had to be defined as a cost-cutting measure, which, at the same time, provided an intermediate form of punishment. Parole officers and members of the Parole Board perceived the economic aspects of the programme as less important. Instead, these stakeholders viewed home arrest as a way of instilling discipline and structure in the lives of dysfunctional inmates (Palumbo and Hallett, 1995: 19). Other parole members saw this as a rehabilitation exercise, enabling inmates to become integrated in society. These conflicting values and objectives meant that there were no shared criteria for evaluating the impact of the home arrest policy.

Dutch policy of drug control provides another vivid illustration of the fact that evaluation exercises are inherently tainted by politics, ideologies and sectional interests. Differences in opinion that inevitably exist about the impact of a policy, like the Dutch attempt to normalize soft drugs, in part follow James Q. Wilson's law on evaluating policy. This states that evaluation carried out by those implementing the policy is likely to be more favourable than external or independent assessments (see Parsons, 1995: 602). The Dutch in recent years have been especially defensive about their policy to normalize soft drugs. Critics argue that the Dutch policy encourages the drug market. The government has begged to differ – and has used evaluative research evidence in doing so. The Ministry of Health (1995a), for instance, recently published a document which has addressed some of the criticisms and misinterpretations of Dutch policy. The document provides a useful overview of policy trends. At the same time, there seemed to be an underlying political agenda: that of validating the policy position of the Dutch government through research evidence. Extensive evidence is presented, especially comparative data, to highlight the fact that there has not been a drug explosion in the Netherlands. And more importantly, the document uses comparative data on drug trends from other countries to make favourable claims about drug policy in the Netherlands. The document, in part, confirms Wilson's law, namely, that policy evaluation can never be truly objective or free from political values.

Clearly, there are notable defects in the positivist position of evaluation. To illustrate this point, the foregoing examined the application of quantitative techniques to the analysis of drug policy. These methods are bedevilled with theoretical and methodological deficiencies. In particular, quantitative methodologies may not offer the sort of reliable and objective evidence required by observers committed to a scientific epistemology. This does not discount entirely the significance or possible utility of statistical techniques. Such methods undoubtedly play a significant role when attempting to obtain a broad picture of a social phenomenon, and can be especially useful when used in conjunction with other methods. But, the argument being pursued here is this: that exclusive use of quantitative measures does not provide a sound basis for understanding the impact of policy. Scientific forms of evaluation rely on the mistaken assumption that it is possible to represent the way things actually exist. This assumption is made because reality is seen as a singular entity, external to observers.

The aspects of the social world attended to by impact studies, as shown by the issues of drug control programmes, do not easily lend themselves to being quantified. As shown, statistical evidence does not correspond entirely with reality. Moreover, the gathering and use of data for purposes of evaluation is inevitably influenced by the political context and the values of those carrying out the exercise (Guba and Lincoln, 1989: 44–5). A truly credible approach to evaluating the impact of policy has to free itself from a positivist straightjacket. It is important to realize that evaluating the impact of policy is a matter of interpretation. Often because of the political nature of policy-making, there are different constituents and stakeholders who hold distinct opinions about the effectiveness of government intervention. The seeming redundancy of an applied scientific approach is also confirmed in the way evaluation data is utilized. In theory, there is supposed to be a linear relationship between the production of evaluative data and its use to improve policy. Reality suggest matters are rather different. Such data, rather than producing concrete results, may 'influence the manner in which a policy maker generally conceptualizes a problem' (Rist, 1995a: p. xvi).

Hence alternative approaches to the positivist model of evaluation need to be pursued and developed. In fact, by the 1980s the policy field witnessed a rejection of the applied science model advocated by the likes of James Coleman. Parsons (1995: 563) observes:

> These doubts about the dominant (positivist, scientific, quantitative) paradigm were to grow, so that by the mid-1990s the field bears little resemblance to the textbooks of the 1960s and 1970s. It is more fragmented and more alive to the political, value-based nature of the activity. The analysis of a programme or a problem is seen by

many critics of the dominant paradigm as essentially a political process, full of values rather than some kind of scientific quest for truth or an objective answer.

Evaluating policy is not a matter of replicating the methods of science in order to produce objective data ready for application. The task is to explore the grey, ambiguous area of assessing the impact of a policy, while taking into account the influence of external forces and the varied interpretations of different stakeholders and participants. In the next section, we consider the style of approach congruent with these objectives.

9.3   A flexible process approach to evaluation

The analysis now turns to the specific issue of evaluating Dutch drug control policy. Estimates about the impact of this intervention cannot be made with absolute certainly. Hence, as argued above, an exclusively quantitative approach, underpinned by positivist paradigm, cannot do full justice to an area like drug policy; the reason being that evaluation analysis, as defined and applied to drug policy in this study, is a complex process. The objective of such evaluation is twofold. First, the task of analysts is to evaluate the extent to which policy intervention has impacted upon a given area like drug abuse. The aim of the analysis should be to distinguish between the impact of the policy and the possible influence of other extraneous factors on the target area. Rossi and Freeman (1993: 215) observe:

> The basic aim of an impact assessment is to produce an estimate of the 'net effects' of an intervention – that is, an estimate of the impact of the intervention uncontaminated by the influence of other processes and events that also may affect the behavior or conditions at which the social program being evaluated is directed.

Second, the evaluation process should assess the substantive achievements of the policy according to different criteria and viewpoints.

A positivist-based evaluation, as mentioned above, is deficient for this type of exercise. Alternative approaches are needed where evaluation is not wholly based on statistics; although there should be a place for such analysis in conjunction with other evaluative models. For some analysts, policy evaluation should retain an element of scientific rigour, while rejecting the ideological assumptions of positivism about causal relations (see Kelly, 1987: 286–7). Policy evaluation has to be multidimensional in focus, using historical as well as contemporary material and acknowledging the importance of values in the evaluation process. Altogether this has to be an iterative exercise, where evaluations are gradually developed while gathering information and data.

A variety of models displaying the characteristics iterated above emerged in the 1980s. These provided distinct methodological and theoretical positions to that of rational evaluation. One such alternative is Cook's multiplism approach. For Cook, analysis can never lead to a single, definitive evaluation of policy. The reason being that reality is multilayered and multifaceted. Evaluation is about producing interpretations that can be supported rather than about definitive conclusions. Hence, the mode of examination adopted to study the real world of concern to policy-makers should encompass several different sources of data, although Cook has a preference for qualitative modes of evaluation. Evidence in turn is triangulated to produce the most accurate explanations (Kelly, 1987: 287).

Another alternative to the applied science model is Guba and Lincoln's (1981, 1989) naturalistic inquiry approach. This shares many similarities with Cook's analysis, but provides, if anything, a more radical disavowal of positivist evaluation. The authors argue, like Cook argues, that reality, far from being composed of causal, law-like forces, is multiple and holistic. Truth does not correspond directly to reality. Evaluation involves constructors, informed by a value framework, reaching a consensus: 'Evaluation data derived from constructivist inquiry have neither special status nor legitimation; they represent simply another construction to be taken into account in the move toward consensus' (Guba and Lincoln, 1989: 45). This requires the meanings and perceptions of actors being incorporated into the evaluative analysis. For naturalistic inquiry, evaluations are specific to the contexts in which data were gathered and, therefore, cannot be generalized to other situations. In terms of research, Guba and Lincoln advocate qualitative as opposed to quantitative methodologies. Analysis of qualitative data takes a grounded approach, rejecting a priori assumptions.

The case study, according to Guba and Lincoln, provides the ideal methodological format for pursuing a naturalistic evaluation. Significantly, this technique generates the sort of detailed, qualitative data that naturalistic inquiry demands. This case approach is employed throughout this text in part for the reason stated by Guba and Lincoln (see Chapter 4 for a more detailed discussion). Moreover, the method tends to depend less on preconceived ideas about policy and builds evaluation during the process of investigation: 'In contrast to many other approaches to evaluation that depend on *a priori* instrumentation, design, or hypotheses, the case study is ideal for the presentation of the grounded data that emerges from the context itself' (Guba and Lincoln, 1981: 376).

The case study contrasts markedly with the positivist paradigm. This is because it can potentially encompass a variety of data to build an in-depth snapshot of a programme or make an intense study of a specific policy area. This methodological strategy is especially significant for an area like drug policy. A recent study by the European Commission evaluating the European Drug Prevention Week of 1994 included both quantitative and qualitative analysis. The data used included statistical estimates about the numbers reached through the campaign and percentage summaries of whether measures focused on national or local audiences. At a qualitative level, the report found that detailed analyses of different national programmes made it possible to assess the main factors within these awareness campaigns. This included a focus on health, education and local initiatives (Commission for European Communities, 1996: 4–9). Hence, if a multiple research strategy is required to evaluate an awareness campaign on drugs, it is equally important to adopt such procedures for examining a drug control policy.

These justifications for using the case study will similarly guide, inform and shape the strategy for evaluating Dutch policy below. This strategy, because it captures the ideas mentioned above, can be termed a flexible process model of evaluation. This is a flexible process because it is open to different sources of data and strategies in developing an evaluation of the policy and its overall impact. This means the evaluation will embrace a variety of different analytical inputs. In this respect, qualitative and quantitative forms of analysis are viewed as being in a complementary as opposed to conflicting relationship to one another; they are situated at different ends of the spectrum rather than on opposing axes. This openness to different sources of data provides the framework for a grounded style of evaluation. Here, existing theoretical models or paradigms do not necessarily dictate the direction and form of the evaluation. Rather, the evaluation emerges during the course of the empirical investigation.

Translated in practical terms, the flexible process approach has two main features. First, it examines the development of the Dutch drug control from a historical angle. Historical research as applied to the process of evaluation can add analytical depth to the proceedings. Such analysis can identify the impact that a policy makes over a period of time (Layder, 1993: 196). This is especially important because other forces often influence or shape the area that has been targeted by policy-makers. Guba and Lincoln (1989: 45) note: 'Interventions are not stable; when they are introduced into a particular context they will be at least as much affected (changed) by that context as they are likely to affect the context.'

Second, the flexible process approach to evaluation is open to different sources of data. Hence, official data statistical information is combined with more qualitative data. Data used from the qualitative end of the spectrum includes the views of those participants engaged in various aspects of Dutch policy. Such material has been obtained through semi-structured interviews with researchers, academics, practitioners and officials. Interview material is combined with secondary sources. This specifically includes analysis of secondary texts on Dutch policy and of research studies reported in books and articles.

These research materials will play an important part in complementing the historical survey. Surveying different analytical viewpoints means an evaluation can be made concerning the relative impact of Dutch drug policy, the aim being to assess the influence of government intervention in relation to other forces at work in this field. In addition, the analysis will switch from considering whether Dutch policy has been influential to what it has actually been achieved. The main issue is the extent to which the policy has succeeded in fulfilling its intended objectives. Documentary sources, secondary research and reported opinion will provide the empirical basis for examining these issues.

9.4 An historical analysis of a policy style

The main emphasis of this section is to decide whether Dutch policy has really made a difference to the drug scene. In many respects, this question appertains to a wider issue: that is, the extent to which political institutions and the policy process can effect change in any given sphere of society. Democratic societies are underpinned by the ideal that politics can deliver changes and make a difference in the real world. This belief can produce an overexpectancy among the citizenry.

Harrop (1992) notes that developments and changes in society might be due more to more fundamental forces than government intervention per se. Comparing France, Britain, the US and Japan, several areas are identified where external forces override the influence of government. For instance, states like France and Britain have increased spending on health care. However, improvements in the population's health is, according to Harrop (1992: 277), due more to changing lifestyles than government intervention. There are aspects of drug behaviour that may be beyond the reach of policy-makers and governments. Indeed, the Dutch policy is premised on the principle that not all drug-related behaviour can be controlled by government. Instead, a realistic option is taken by emphasizing the protection of those who decide to take part in illicit drug use.

Governments have undoubtedly shown themselves to be impotent in the face of large-scale forces, unexpected events and intractable social problems. But to impute from this that political processes are ultimately powerless and ineffectual would be a mistake. As Parsons (1995: 608) notes: 'Government may not be in as much control as it (and we) would or might like, but this does not mean that policy-making is of no importance.' There is a scholarly tradition which has asserted the significance of political processes and institutions as independent forces of social change (see section 3.3). For some writers in this tradition, the democratic state has a vital role to perform in social life, equal to that of civil society. It frequently acts upon its own preferences and is able to impose these over powerful groups in civil society. For some theoreticians, the influence of the state does not just extend towards civil society, but should also include the economy (Sharpe and Newton, 1984: 210).

This observation is significant because it embraces the idea that governments can make effective policy decisions which promote social well-being. Policy-making is potentially a highly significant mechanism for dealing with social problems and issues. To argue that governments are overwhelmed by external events and forces would be to deny the possibility of using this facility. As Parsons (1995: 608) argues, even when government operates at the margins, effective interventions can improve the quality of life. Effective government action can potentially lead to the creation of jobs, improve life expectancy, and regulate for a cleaner environment. At the same time, it should be acknowledged that policy may be one among a wide range of forces that contribute to social change or any social development.

The objective of impact studies is to assess the effects of intervention in areas of society already affected by a panoply of other forces. Sorting through the complex range of influences is a difficult task. Dutch drug policy illustrates this point. Drug abuse is just as likely to be influenced by trends in drug markets as it is by government intervention. The role of impact studies is to decipher the extent of influence enjoined by a policy programme. A number of analysts suggest that historical research is an analytical research tool that can potentially untangle this complex web of relationships. It is on similar grounds that Castles (1989) recommends the use of historical research for analysing public policy. He notes: 'History reveals the one sense in which it is meaningful to say that the sum is more than its parts: the sense in which human action is embedded in its particular context' (ibid. 12).

It is for such reasons that a historical summary of Dutch policy is viewed as necessary and imperative. Different phases in the development of Dutch drug control policy are distinguished by recourse to policy categories. The typology that will be adopted in this historical summary is that of a national policy style, as developed by Richardson *et al.* (1982). The concept alludes to the fact that there are distinct differences in the way policies are determined both within and between societies. In developing a typology of policy style, Richardson *et al.* note that there are two primary features of policy-making systems: '(a) *the government's approach to problem-solving and* (b) *the relationship between government and other actors in the policy process*' (ibid. 13; original italics). Within each primary feature there are two basic components. In terms of addressing specific issues and problems, governments either adopt an *anticipatory/active* stance, or a basic *reactive* approach. Regarding the relationship between policy-makers and public, Richardson *et al.* portray governments as either seeking to reach a consensus with organized groups, or looking to impose decisions. From this schema, various categories of policy style can be generated.

There is in the Netherlands a diverse range of policy styles. According to van Putten (1982), established departments of state, such as the Ministry of Justice, have tended to adopt a more formal approach to policy-making. The prevailing stance is for policy to be developed through formal legislation, involving cooperation between the executive and parliament. Contribution to policy is restricted to a small coterie of ministers and senior officials. The newer ministries, like Social Welfare and Culture, Recreation and Welfare, have demonstrated a different style of policy-making. There is a tendency for these ministries to adopt a more analytical approach in relation to social problems. In developing policy, they have also tended to form close collaborative alliances with relevant interests groups. Such inclusiveness contrasts with the formalized practices of established ministries (van Putten, 1982: 192).

Newer departments contrast with the policy style of older departments, although the postwar years have witnessed distinct changes in the way established departments operate (ibid. 184). Dutch policy-making has traditionally been the product of negotiation. In the past twenty years, the mode of negotiation has changed, increasingly going beyond the golden circle of officials and politicians to include advisory bodies and interest groups. Cabinet and parliament as a result are less prominent. One manifestation of this was the tendency to sectorize activity. By this is meant the tendency to create a large number of specialized permanent committees partaking in the policy-making process. Between 1948 and 1980 the number of specialized committees grew from 8 to 28.

9.4.1   The history of drug control style

It was against this changing style of policy-making that innovations in the actual content of policy was considered. One such area was that of drug control. Opiates have been a prevalent feature of Dutch society since the nineteenth century. However, the perception of drug-taking as a special problem grew dramatically after 1965. There were concerns that the illicit drug-taking associated with the popular counterculture of the period was appealing to 'normal' young people (Leuw, 1991: 241–2). Particularly disconcerting was the way in which middle-class youth and students, and other non-deviant groups, were being labelled as criminals for personal drug use (van Vliet, 1990: 722). The government authorities responded to the public debate by conducting a review of existing legislation and judicial procedures.

The policy review was not confined to an exclusive coterie of ministers and officials. Two specialist committees, with broad membership, were give the task of conducting the reassessment. The first of these committees was formed in 1969 by the state-sponsored Institution for Mental Health. This committee was named after its chair, the law professor, Loek Hulsman, who was known for his abolitionist views. The 14-strong member committee included scientists, sociologists, officials from the Ministries of Justice and Health, and heads of mental health bodies. Included in its analysis was an assessment of the risk potential of different types of drugs. This examination shaped the recommendations of the committee.

The second committee was formed a year later in 1970. The 15-member Working Group on Narcotic Substances, commonly known as the Baan Committee, was composed of senior administrative officials from the Ministries of Public Health and Justice. The working party also included a larger number of law officials than the Hulsman Committee. The original remit given to the working party by the health secretary was framed within a prohibitionist paradigm: that of using the criminal justice system to counteract drug abuse. The Baan Committee, however, adopted a distinct line of inquiry. Two main issues were considered: first, whether all drugs should be outlawed; and second, whether an integrated drug control policy could be developed, including welfare, health and educational measures.

The findings of both committees were very similar. The most significant recommendation from both inquiries was that cannabis should be distinguished from other illegal drugs. Cannabis, it was concluded, did not present the same unacceptable risks as opiates and amphetamines. Hence, the Baan Committee recommended that use and small-scale trade of cannabis should be made a misdemeanour, carrying a maximum sentence of one month's detention (Leuw, 1991: 242–4).

The recommendations contained in the 1972 Baan Committee report were accepted by the centre/conservative government. In 1973 a new centre-left government took office and proceeded to revise the prohibitionist Opium Act of 1928. However, the final Bill was not brought before parliament until 1975. During this hiatus, the authorities began to relax drug control procedures and to decriminalize the use and distribution of cannabis products. In 1975, the Conservatives were replaced by the more leftward leaning Social Democrats in the government coalition. Following this, the final Bill to replace the Opium Act of 1928 was presented before parliament (Leuw, 1991: 247). It was in 1976 that the Bill was subsequently debated and passed by a three to one majority. Although a penal reform, the Bill was sponsored and defended in parliament by the Minister of Public Health, the Social Democrat Irene Vorrink. This reflected the fact that the legislation was aimed at reducing the health risks of drug use.

The Opium Act of 1976 distinguished between those drugs presenting an unacceptable risk (heroin, cocaine, LSD and amphetamines) and cannabis products which contained less risk to individuals and society. The new legislation kept stiff penalties for dealing in drugs presenting 'unacceptable risks', and lesser penalties for the possession and retail of cannabis. The policy set by the Opium Act did not provide legal provision for decriminalization of cannabis as recommended by the Baan Committee. Such a provision would have contravened international agreements. However, more liberal guidelines were set for the possession of cannabis. It was established that possession of less than 30 grams was placed on the lowest priority level, which meant that no active criminal investigation or prosecution would be undertaken (van Vliet, 1990: 724–5). The Opium Act guidelines also made provision for special dealers that could provide cannabis products in youth centres and eventually in specific premises known as coffee shops.

The new Opium Act was finally adopted in June 1976. But how can it be classified in terms of policy style? It was shown above that in forming the new policy, the government encouraged input from a wide range of interest groups and experts. The other side of the policy-style coin concerns the way problem issues are addressed. The new legislation displayed the characteristic features of an anticipatory/active stance towards the issue of drug abuse. Here, policy-makers approach social problems by developing a systematic, methodical and carefully scrutinized plan of action. The point is to produce a realistic response to a particular issue. This was clearly evident with the new Opium Act of 1976. The central rationale of the Hulsman and Baan Committees, accepted by the government, was that of reducing the harm caused by drugs. The 1975 government White Paper on drug control observed that the main aim of Dutch drug policy would be: 'To contribute to the prevention of and to deal with the risks that the use of mind-altering drugs present to individuals themselves, their immediate environment, and society as a whole' (cited in Samsom, 1989: 26).

Underlying the rationale is a concern that people in society will indulge in drug abuse regardless of penalties that exist. The government has few instruments at its disposal to direct and guide individual choices in relation to illicit drugs. Nevertheless, the government argued that separating the markets would minimize the risk associated with illicit drug-taking. The government policy aimed to reduce the numbers that opt for consistent hard-drug use. Partial decriminalization of the use and supply of cannabis was seen as pivotal. The separation, it was envisaged, would ensure that those vulnerable to drug experimentation would be separated from the hard-drug market. Moreover, the increased transparency of cannabis use would allow authorities to survey the drug population and develop lines of communication. If certain drugs were given criminal punishments, this population would remain underground. This policy contrasts with the 'war on drugs' model propagated by the likes of Britain and the United States. In such a model, the criminal law system is the central instrument in drug control. This can be seen as a more *reactionary* policy style to drug issues, as it is often borne out of political expediency.

The anticipatory approach to drug problems, characterized by an emphasis on reducing risk, continued to influence the development of drug policy. The partial decriminalization introduced by the 1976 Act had not led to a huge increase in drug addicts. In fact, there is evidence to suggest that the legislation helped preclude vulnerable experimenting youngsters from developing hard-drug habits. However, the late 1970s and early 1980s saw heroin flooding into western Europe. In the Netherlands, this influx and availability of heroin led to a dramatic increase in the number of hard-drug addicts to an estimated 20,000. The groups taking up heroin included working-class youth, and Moroccan and Surinamese immigrants (van Vliet, 1990: 726–7).

As was typical of the proactive stance of the Dutch government towards drugs, a research project was established in 1983. The government sponsored a sociological study into the culture of drug abuse, the practice of drug-taking and the 'careers' followed by addicts. A report using the research, *Drug Policy in Motion*, was published by the Ministry of Welfare, Health and Cultural Affairs in 1985. The report introduced a new component to drug policy which complemented the idea of risk minimization. The new feature focused on the *normalization* of drug problems and drug users. The state secretary had argued before the report was published that treatment strategies had to be reappraised. The idea of eradicating drug use and achieving complete rehabilitation was unrealistic. Instead, it was felt that authorities should assist individuals to manage their drug habits, leading eventually to integration in society (Leuw, 1991: 258–9). The report indicated that assistance programmes should be less concerned with curing addiction than with improving the social and physical functioning of addicts.

Hence in the years following the publication of the report the government concentrated on developing low-threshold facilities. This included the provision of such services as free medical care, needle exchange programmes, housing projects and social guidance programmes. The normalization schemes tended to be concentrated in the larger cities. On a national level, the methadone programmes formed the mainstay of the normalization policy. This has involved easy access for addicts to the heroin substitute of methadone. These treatments have attempted to establish contact with drug users in order to provide forms of welfare assistance to those in need. For example, in Amsterdam the Municipal Health Service has organized and operated a network of sociomedical facilities for drug users. This network includes separate facilities for particular categories of drug users such as prostitutes.

The normalization programme, and harm reduction for that matter, expressed a high level of tolerance towards drug addicts. However, the reserves of tolerance were not limitless. By the mid to late 1980s, the *style* of Dutch drug policy began to shift. Whereas the previous decade had seen the authorities develop a health-orientated response to the drug policy, this period, in contrast, witnessed the emergence of a reactive attitude towards problem-solving and a propensity to impose legislation unilaterally. Much of this change in attitude was due to the criticisms levelled by other countries, particular those states sharing borders with the Netherlands – Germany, Belgium and France.

With the opening of European borders in the 1980s, governments began to complain that the liberal approach to drugs in the Netherlands was encouraging drug trafficking. Indeed with moves towards closer European integration, there have been pressures exerted on the Dutch government to realign its policy. The specific demand is that the Netherlands should embrace a prohibitionist approach. The pressures of integration and the criticisms levelled by European partners to a certain extent influenced those in government. There were accompanying policy changes, too. Symptomatic of this shift in policy style was the intensification of restrictions on coffee shops – the legitimate commercial outlets for the trade in cannabis.

In 1987, the municipal authorities of Amsterdam clamped down on a chain of coffee shops known as the Bulldog. The action was taken because of the size of the business, all of which attracted international attention. In fact, all coffee shops were given warnings about breaching advertising guidelines, and several raids were carried out on small premises. In response, coffee shops toned down explicit references to the commercial sale of cannabis products (van Vliet, 1990: 734–6). Similar restrictions were placed on coffee shops by other municipalities. Between 1994 and 1996, the municipality of the Hague reduced the number of coffee shops from 132 to 98. Over a one-year period from 1995 to 1996, Utrecht cut down the number of coffee shops to 21. This represented a 50 per cent reduction. The municipality of Maastricht had pursued a tougher policy on coffee shops from 1994 onwards, with their number being reduced from 30 to 19 (Ministry of Health, Welfare and Sport, 1996: 23). Also, the government, in response to criticism from neighbouring countries and border towns, in 1995 redefined the Public Prosecutions Department guidelines for the sale of cannabis. The statutory norm for many years for the quantity of soft drugs that could be possessed and commercially supplied stood at 30 grams. The revised guideline reduced this to 5 grams, although the government acknowledged that this would be difficult to enforce and police (Ministry of Health, Welfare and Sport, 1995a: 48–9).

Further indications of the tendency to react rather than plan, to impose programmes rather than negotiate with interest groups, was the policy that emerged in the early 1990s to reduce nuisance caused by addicts. Nuisance, according to one government document, refers to the antisocial behaviour caused not only by drug addicts, but also by those addicted to alcohol and gambling. Such behaviour includes disturbance to public order and theft. Nuisance is not only defined by objective measures like the penal code but includes 'types of conduct which are perceived as a nuisance by people in the vicinity, creating irritation and feelings of insecurity'

(Ministry of Justice and the Ministry of Health, Welfare and Sport, 1993: 3).

Concern about antisocial activities resulted partly from the prevalent involvement of drug addicts in certain reported crimes. The most common offences associated with addicts included domestic burglary, theft from cars, robbery and certain violent acts (Ministry of Health, Welfare and Sport, 1995a: 21). The pressures exerted on government to act on nuisance problems were also political in nature. Large municipalities took exception to the presence of groups of drug addicts congregating around public areas. As drug tourists have crossed the borders from Germany and Belgium to buy their goods, the drug market has spread from large population centres such as Amsterdam and Eindhoven to border towns like Arnhem. Local neighbourhood groups and small local parties opposed the influx of drug addicts and have campaigned vigorously against their presence.

A debate on drugs during March and April of 1993 focused on the nuisance caused by certain groups of addicts. Politicians demanded the implementation of certain measures to curb antisocial behaviour. The government reported back six months later with a policy note. The report summarised antinuisance measures being implemented and future plans of action to combat nuisance problems. The programmes to combat nuisance already in operation reveals extensive reliance by authorities on penal measures. In 1996, the government introduced a criminal law measure for the treatment of addicts (SOV) (Ministry of Health, Welfare and Sport, 1996: 29). The scheme involves a period of detention for addicts who create nuisance problems together with the provision of rehabilitation. A pilot project was established in Rotterdam late in 1996 and was enacted on the basis of existing criminal law provisions. To ensure the implementation of these measures the government formed a Task Force on Public Safety and the Care of Addicts. The Task Force has focused on the preparation of pilot projects for the treatment of addicted offenders, where the criminal law measures are used in conjunction with welfare provision.

The penal system has not entirely dominated the strategy to overcome nuisance problems. Outreach teams have been used in Amsterdam Zuidoost to establish initial contact with addicts who might potentially engage in nuisance behaviour. These teams cooperate with social workers and the police to help addicts adapt their lifestyles. General services like Social Housing and Housing for Young Runaways are involved in providing care for specific groups of addicts. The Job Services programme has attempted to integrate addicts into the world of work. Most significantly, a steering committee was appointed in 1994 to launch and evaluate projects that aimed to combat nuisance by combining care and criminal measures. The committee has adopted an open and inclusive approach, negotiating with a wide array of interest groups. This openness to negotiating and dealing with interest groups is a feature, as shown earlier, of the Dutch style of policy-making. Led by the Ministry of Health, the committee contained representatives from the Association of Dutch Municipalities, the National Association of Municipal Health Services, the Dutch Institute for Alcohol and Drugs, and the Bureau for Drug Advice (Ministry of Health, Welfare and Sport, 1995b: 2).

Undoubtedly, reactionary elements have crept into the Dutch policy on drugs since the mid-1980s. Nevertheless, as shown, the original risk-minimization philosophy has not been abrogated. This feature still remains a strong part of Dutch policy. A recent government policy document explained: 'The government has decided that in tackling the drugs problems it should maintain the course it embarked upon in the 1970s, albeit with a few adjustments' (Ministry of Health, Welfare and Sport, 1995a: 63).

Nowhere is this more evident than in the recent policy to combat the use of ecstasy. The government has acknowledged the alarming prevalence of ecstasy, particularly in the rave and clubbing circuit. The official response to ecstasy has been to develop a health-orientated risk-minimization approach. In so doing, the government seems to accept that illicit drug-taking of this sort will take place regardless of penal intervention. Integral to this anticipatory style of response is the national steering committee on drugs. The committee has drawn up and provided municipalities with guidelines for regulating house parties where ecstasy use will be prevalent. Included in the guidelines are a long list of requirements concerning health protection. It was recommended that first-aid workers should be available and that organizers should regulate air temperature, humidity and circulation. The most significant innovation was the suggestion that, if considered necessary by the municipal health service, the event organizer should provide a facility for expert testing of ecstasy and other drugs on the site (Ministry of Health, Welfare and Sports, 1995b: 16).

Historical analysis can make a significant contribution to the process of evaluating policy, particularly when adopting a grounded, qualitative paradigm. Our historical survey of Dutch drug policy contributes to the process of evaluation in two respects. First, it underlines the characteristic features of drug policy and the extent to which the government has endeavoured to address the issue at first hand. Second, it has provided an insight into those social and political forces that have influenced the priorities of policy-makers in this field. The following sections concentrate on the precise impact of Dutch policy, assessing the extent to which it has succeeded or been deflected from its aims. The next two sections use material garnered from interviews and secondary sources addressing these issues.

9.5 The view from the ground

The flexible process approach to evaluating policy shares many affinities with Guba and Lincoln's naturalistic or constructionist paradigm. Naturalistic evaluation draws upon Glaser and Strauss's grounded model of theory-building. This is done to develop an alternative model of evaluation to the applied science approach. Glaser and Strauss (1966) are highly critical of scientific investigation where the central preoccupation for inquiry is to verify hypotheses that are initially generated from a priori assumptions. Rather than judge the research data according to existing theoretical notions, Glaser and Strauss argue that theory should be discovered from the data. Grounded theory offers a more open-ended approach, as theories are generated from the information and observations that are gathered. Guba and Lincoln (1981: 71) maintain that similar notions should guide the process of evaluation.

Documentary materials and semi-structured interviews are appropriate research instruments for developing a qualitative form of evaluation. In this section, the views of individuals closely engaged in the drug field are used to develop a qualitative insight into Dutch drug policy. Such data were garnered from eight semi-structured interviews conducted with practitioners during two separate fieldwork trips to the Netherlands in October 1996 and April 1997 respectively (see Chapter 4). Those interviewed hail from various positions relevant to aspects of drug policy. They specifically include the following: a senior civil servant from the Division of Alcohol, Drug and Tobacco Policies in the Ministry of Health,

Welfare and Sport; a senior researcher of the drug field from the Criminological Institute in the Social Sciences Department at the University of Amsterdam; two senior officials from the TRIMBOS Institute (Netherlands Institute of Mental Health and Addiction), a research institute specializing in addiction; an Amsterdam-based consultant researcher in the drug field; the head nurse from the drug rehabilitation clinic in Zwolle; a lecturer with social work experience of the drug field; and an official from the European Monitoring Centre for Drugs and Addiction.

These interviews can provide qualitative data from which a detailed evaluation of Dutch drug policy can be developed. Looking at drug policy from the perspective of those actively engaged in the field allows researchers to record close details about the implementation of that policy. These interviews also offer perspectives which might be excluded from official documents.

As shown in the historical analysis above, the objectives of Dutch policy continue to be dominated by the original objective enshrined in the Opium Act of 1976: that of reducing risk and harm to individuals. This was confirmed by those respondents who were interviewed. The underlying point is that intervention by government authorities cannot eliminate drugs from society or convince individuals to cease using illegal substances. The head nurse of a drug rehabilitation clinic noted: 'We know that there are always people who will use drugs and sell them. It is better to control the situation. By allowing coffee shops to sell some drugs then you can have certain control of what they are selling there. You can watch and see what is happening' (*Fieldwork Interview*, Zwolle Clinic, 24 October 1996).

Hence, a more realistic aim for government authorities is to minimize the risk to those using drugs or to individuals vulnerable to experimentation with illicit substances. One senior civil servant from the Division of Alcohol, Drug and Tobacco Policies in the Ministry of Health observes: 'We think that if you approach people in a repressive way, put drug use underground, there is no access for prevention and health care. We like to consider people who are addicts as people who are ill. We like to consider their situation ... That in general is our philosophy' (*Fieldwork Interview*, Ministry of Health, 25 October 1996).

There is an admission that harm reduction has not had a significant impact on the number of hard-drug addicts in the Netherlands.

In fact, evidence seems to suggest that the number of hard-drug addicts has increased, although this figure has remained stable. One research consultant argues this may be due to the fact that harm reduction is helping to keep addicts alive:

> The drug users are not dying as fast, that is one reason why there is an increase ... We prolong addiction, or dependent drug use and keep them healthy. The health status, low number of overdose deaths, low number of drug-related AIDS cases etc have been used as criteria to say whether we have a successful drug policy in comparison to other neighbouring countries. At the same time it has the effect that we keep them alive but you keep them addicted. (*Fieldwork Interview*, 15 April 1997, METROPOLINK)

Other participants who were interviewed argued that certain drug-related activities have been shaped 'by the internal structures and dynamics in a particular drug scene' (*Fieldwork Interview*, University of Amsterdam, 16 April 1997). For instance, heroin addicts from ethnic minority groups were found in the late 1970s to be opting for non-intravenous modes of administering the drug. This was less due to government health campaigns than the fact that intravenous drug use is treated as a taboo among dealers and users in ethnic communities. But this is not to say that Dutch drug policy has been ineffectual. One interview pointed towards the unintended consequences of the policy:

> Another link with policy is that through the very flexible very easy accessible methadone programmes it makes the junkies very visible. It could put people off, that's not what you want to be ... Becoming a heroin addict or not becoming a user, it is possible that is related to Dutch policy; separating the markets, soft and hard, more clearly heroin has a big taboo, that is not what you want to be. You see those drugs are kept out of the coffee shops very clearly and addicts were visibly negative, not to be associated with people in your neighbourhood. I would define these as products of typical Dutch policy. It was not intended so strongly because the methadone is there to help them. But the effect is that you can see and perceive them and that you can associate that with hard drug use. (*Fieldwork Interview*, University of Amsterdam, 16 April 1997)

But those who support Dutch drug policy have argued that the government authorities became complacent about the policy: '[There is a view] that God created the world and the Dutch created alternative drug policy ... Ten years ago a sort of complacency set in' (*Fieldwork Interview*, TRIMBOS, 15 April 1997). A notable consequence of such complacency according to this practitioner is that repressive measures have become increasingly common: 'Although the basics of the policies have been unchanged – harm reduction is still a very important feature – but you see especially in the local policy a lot of repressive measures' (*Fieldwork Interview*, TRIMBOS, 15 April 1997).

Much of the pressure for the Dutch to get tough on drugs has stemmed from neighbouring European states such as France and Germany. The project of European integration has only increased demands for the Netherlands to realign its drug policy behind those of the other states: 'The constant process of working with European civil servants and European countries [is problematic]. It is the completely uncritical way that the war on drugs is accepted in those circles' (*Fieldwork Interview*, 15 April 1997, METROPOLINK). One senior official in the Ministry of Health is sceptical about whether the Dutch government in the future can retain autonomy over drug policy:

> I think there is a chance that we are going to lose the battle against these people who are so strongly in favour of a repressive drug policy. We can no longer avoid the strong intention from many countries to harmonize not only the policy but also the execution of the policy on a European level. Not every country is the same. It's ridiculous to harmonize. (*Fieldwork Interview*, Ministry of Health, 25 October 1996)

This view is confirmed by a representative from the European Monitoring Centre for Drugs and Drug Addiction, which is based in the Netherlands: 'I don't think there is any chance of changing policy in France within the next ten years, maybe that's a bit too long but you never know ... Cerac himself is trying to get the EU on his side and to decide on a law and order policy within the EU as far as drugs are concerned' (*Fieldwork Interview*, EMCDDA, 23 October 1996).

9.6 The role of secondary literature in evaluation

Analyzing relevant secondary literature can potentially complement the interview material reviewed above. Articles, official documents and texts clarify the extent to which Dutch policy has achieved its aims. The analysis below holds no pretence to be a definitive review of the available literature on Dutch drug policy. A select number of texts have been chosen because of their relevance to the question of evaluation.

The secondary literature reviewed acknowledges that assessing the impact of drug policies is highly problematic. Evaluating the impact of Dutch drug policy essentially involves a great deal of conjecture. Van de Wijngaart (1989: 991) notes: 'A problem in making any clear statement about the "success" or "Failure" of a certain [Dutch] policy is that such statements necessarily make assumptions about what would have happened if the policy had *not* been adopted.' Moreover, as shown in the historical analysis, factors other than policy can just as readily effect the use of controlled substances. Lenke and Olsson (1996: 107–9), reviewing the research literature, found that heroin use can be attributed to structural factors such as unemployment and the propinquity of a country in relation to major drug markets.

The literature nevertheless points to a number of aspects of Dutch policy which have made a difference to the drug problem in this society. In fact, the historical analysis presented above clearly showed that the Dutch policy amounted to a considered and anticipatory response to the problem of drug abuse. As one observer notes, the policy has been 'made on the basis of analysis, research, practical experience and an open public debate ...' (Grund, 1989: 993). There are three main areas where the Dutch policy has impacted upon the drug situation.

First, the separation of the drug markets has not led to substantial increases in drug addiction. Research has demonstrated that the level of cannabis consumption stabilized in the first few years after the Opium Act was amended in 1976 (see Ministry of Health, Welfare and Sport, 1995a: 41, for reference to work by Korf, Driessen, and others). However, nationwide surveys of school pupils between the ages of 12 and 18 have shown that cannabis use in this age group has increased (NIAD, 1995a). A government document on drug policy noted that similar increases were evident in other countries. The document observed: 'Use appears to be determined primarily by fashions in international youth culture and other autonomous developments, such as levels of long-term youth unemployment' (Ministry of Health, Welfare and Sport, 1995a: 41). A recent document from NIAD argues that much of the cannabis use in this age group is predominantly experimental.

Research also reveals the stepping-stone theory, that soft-drug use leads to hard drugs, as being redundant. The use of hard drugs among those from the 12 to 18 age band was very low. A national survey from 1992 found that 0.2 per cent of this group had recently used heroin. These figures must be treated with caution. Statistical evidence provides an indication of the social phenomenon under consideration and not an absolute measure. Yet, the number of studies completed and reviewed tend to confirm the pattern of behaviour outlined above.

A second, possibly more objective, measure of the impact of Dutch drug policy is the relatively low number of drug-related fatalities. All the available evidence seems to suggest that the Netherlands has one of the lowest incidences of fatalities resulting from overdoses in Europe. In addition, such deaths do not seem to be on the increase (see MacCoun, 1995: 218). Peter Cohen (1990), an experienced researcher in the drug field, attributes this, reasonably it seems, to Dutch policy: 'The Dutch drug control system is deeply enmeshed in a national health care system available to all Dutch citizens. And that drug control is also part of an extensive system of socio-economically based policies ... used to manage social conflicts and social inequality' (ibid. 23).

A third area where Dutch policy of normalization has proven influential is the easy access to, and availability of, treatment for addicts. The Dutch system of treatment is highly pragmatic and realistic: treatment and assistance is made available regardless of whether the addict wishes to pursue a drug-free existence. Methadone and needle-exchange schemes are also prevalent, especially in large metropolitan centres like Amsterdam. It is estimated that in Amsterdam the drug system manages to make contact with around 60–80 per cent of drug addicts in the city (Cohen, 1990: 23; Engelsman, 1989: 217). This is one of the most significant impacts of Dutch drug control policy. Drug addicts as a result are able to receive treatment and avoid fatalities.

More significantly, once it was established that HIV can be transmitted through needles, the authorities had ready a network of addicts to inform about prevention. Thus, the spread of AIDS amongst drug addicts is relatively contained in the Netherlands. Research done in the late 1980s showed that there was a fairly high awareness of HIV prevention among drug users and drug-using prostitutes (see Matthews, 1989: 17–18). This, according to research, has contained the spread of AIDS in these communities. In 1988, it was shown that 8 per cent of Dutch AIDS patients were drug users. The comparable figure for the rest of Europe in the same year stood at 23 per cent and for the United States at 26 per cent. More recent figures show only a slight increase in the number of AIDS patients among drug users. In 1994, the portion of injecting drug users that have contracted AIDS stood at 12.4 per cent, but this compared with 24 per cent in the United States and 38 per cent in Europe (NIAD, 1995b).

Detractors of Dutch policy have focused their criticisms on the separation of drug markets and the toleration of cannabis retail outlets. Heads of state and enforcement personnel maintain that the Netherlands provides a 'safe haven' for cannabis suppliers which disrupts the overall network of control (see Dorn, 1989: 96). The International Narcotics Control Board of the United Nations has been especially critical of the Dutch government on such grounds: 'The Board expresses its continued concern at the persistence of certain practices ... This includes ... permitting the operation of so-called coffee shops, many of which have fallen under the control of criminal elements, and continuing to stockpile narcotic drugs for non-medical purposes' (International Narcotics Control Board, 1995: 58).

These criticisms ignore the fact that the Netherlands' geographical location which makes it a prime target for drug trafficking. According to Interpol, it is one of the prime drug routes in Europe. The prevalence of drug trafficking in the Netherlands is just as much a product of its structural location as its liberal drug policy (Lenke and Olsson, 1996: 109).

Even so, the Dutch government and various municipalities have in recent years taken a more stringent line in response to criticisms. As documented above, this has included, *inter alia*, the following: tightening regulations against coffee shops; less tolerant treatment regimes; and tougher sentences for drug traffickers. This punitive turn in Dutch drug control policy has not been universally welcomed. The growing use of penal measures during the 1980s is regarded as counterproductive by many observers. The increased penalties on drug trafficking according to one commentator has done little to stem the drug market. Dorn (1989: 996) writes: 'The escalation of penalties has had a part in encouraging changes in the *organization* of the trade, its rapid *professionalism*, the *driving out* of amateurs, increasing *violence*' (original emphasis). To counteract and contain drug markets, argues Dorn, law enforcement should be more focused. This increases the chances of capture and thus acts as an effective deterrent.

The tougher policy against drug addicts to rid Dutch society of nuisance problems associated with drugs is seen as equally problematic. Commentators have been especially critical of persuasive treatment regimes and city centre banning orders for drug users who cause repeated offenses. Such measures go against the pragmatic approach of harm reduction that has characterized drug policy. Mol and Trautmann (1991: 19) make a significant observation: 'The fixation on the public order problem is interfering with the availability of clean syringes and other aid services.' Forced treatments are especially incompatible with AIDS prevention, for instance.

Despite the recent ideological and reactive turn in drug control, harm reduction continues to form a significant canon of Dutch policy, as demonstrated by the interview responses above. The pragmatic emphasis has prevailed because it has helped the authorities to anticipate and prevent some of the problems associated with drug use. This is the position of much secondary and documentary literature on Dutch policy. One recent government document observes: 'Health interests have always been at the forefront of Dutch policy on drugs over the last twenty years and in terms of these health objectives the policy can be considered to have been successful' (Ministry of Health, Welfare and Sport, 1995a: 61).

9.7   Conclusion

Evaluating policy is not a straightforward issue for either analysts or practitioners. The positivist paradigm advocates an applied science approach through the use of quantitative procedures. If this was truly possible, governments would find the task of governance a whole lot easier. For a start, it would take a great deal of the politics out of policy-making. A decision about whether to proceed with a programme of intervention would simply rest on the results obtained from scientific evaluation. However, the applied science argument is flawed. Quantitative analysis, which is orientated to finding definitive conclusions, overlooks the often ideological nature of evaluation. This form of evaluation is also poorly adept at dealing with questions about the impact of a policy. This is not to say that statistical analysis has no utility in policy evaluation. Such data add a degree of rigour, and can be used for the purpose of comparison. Instead, it was argued that a flexible model of evaluation should be utilized.

A case analysis of Dutch drug control served as a vehicle for developing a critique of, and providing an alternative to, the positive approach. The alternative framework of evaluation was a flexible process model. This was not dominated by quantitative methodology but sought to integrate statistical information with qualitative forms of analysis – historical information, secondary and official documentation and interview material. The objective was to adopt what Guba and Lincoln term an expansionist stance in relation to evaluating policy. The idea here is to evaluate a programme of intervention like Dutch drug policy in a way that understands the context of the phenomena and reflects the complexity of the issue.

STUDY GUIDE
Chronology of events surrounding the development of Dutch drug policy

1960s (late): Public concern was growing over the way the criminal justice system was dealing with the increase in illegal drug use, especially marijuana and amphetamines, among middle-class youth. Public debate grew about the criminalization of drug users and the health risks associated with drugs. These became key issues that helped to shape drug policy.

1969 and 1970: Two committees were formed to review Dutch drug policy. The first of these committees was formed in 1969 by the state-sponsored Institution for Mental Health. This committee was named after its chair, the law professor, Loek Hulsman, who was known for his abolitionist views. The 14-strong member committee included scientists and social scientists, officials from the Ministries of Justice and Health, and heads of mental health bodies. The committee looked at the risk potential of different types of drugs. This examination shaped the recommendations of the committee.

The second committee was formed a year later in 1970. The 15-member Working Group on Narcotic Substances, commonly known as the Baan Committee, was composed of senior administrative officials from the Ministries of Public Health and Justice. The working party also included a larger number of law officials than the Hulsman Committee. The original remit given to the working party by the health secretary was framed within a prohibitionist paradigm: that of using the criminal justice system to counteract drug abuse. The Baan Committee, however, adopted a distinct line of inquiry. Two main issues were considered: first, whether all drugs should be outlawed; and second, whether an integrated drug control policy could be developed including welfare, health and educational measures.

The Hulsman Committee published it findings in 1971, and in 1972 the Narcotics Working Party followed with its recommendations. The findings of both committees were very similar. Hulsman and Baan recommended that cannabis should be distinguished from other illegal drugs. Cannabis, it was concluded, did not present the same unacceptable risks as opiates and amphetamines. Hence the Hulsman Committee proposed that cannabis should be legalized and that trade in cannabis products should become a misdemeanour punishable only by a fine. The Baan Committee recommended that the use and small-scale trade of cannabis should be made a misdemeanour, carrying a maximum sentence of one month's detention.

1972: Heroin became widely available in this year, especially in urban locations. It was the spread of the new heroin problem which saw pressure exerted on the government to begin considering the Baan Report and the possibility of reforming Holland's drug laws.

1976: In this year, legislators began the task of reforming the Opium Act of 1928. Policy-makers took on board the Baan concept of 'risk criterion'. The aim of the new policy was to prevent the use of illegal drugs and to integrate drug control policy into the welfare system. Integral to this was the withdrawal of cannabis use from the criminal sphere. Hence, the Opium Act of 1976 distinguished between drugs presenting an unacceptable risk (heroin, cocaine, LSD and amphetamines) and cannabis products. The new legislation kept stiff penalties for dealing in drugs presenting 'unacceptable risks' and lesser penalties for the possession and retail of cannabis. The separation of the drug markets was implemented to prevent users of cannabis becoming involved in the illegal hard-drug scene. The Ministry of Welfare, Health and Cultural Affairs was made responsible for coordinating the government's drug policy.

1976: The policy set by the Opium Act did not provide legal provision for decriminalization of cannabis. However, the law made use of the expediency principle which prevails in the Dutch legal structure. To regulate the implementation of the 1976 Opium Act, the Minister for Justice issued guidelines for the investigation and prosecution of offences under the Opium Act to the Prosecutions Department. The guidelines set priorities for investigation and prosecution. It was established that possession of less than 30 grams was placed on the lowest priority level, which meant that no active criminal investigation or prosecution would be undertaken. The Opium Act guidelines also made provision for special dealers who could provide cannabis products in youth centres. These dealers would face prosecution if they openly projected themselves as such. Moreover, these dealers could only be prosecuted after consultation between the mayor, the chief of police and chief public prosecutor.

1978:   Following these guidelines, the dealing in cannabis products, especially in Amsterdam, became established in alcohol-free coffee shops. The coffee shops at this time faced few regulations, but various house rules prevailed. For instance, no hard drugs were allowed on the premises and dealing in stolen goods was prohibited. During these early years, the few coffee shops faced regular police raids. There was concern over the open commercial nature of these retail centres, and the amounts traded often exceeded the 30 gram limit.

Late 1970s: The MDHG (Medicosocial Care for Heroin Users) was formed in this year because of concerns over official drug policy. The group comprised doctors, social workers, the parents of heroin addicts, people living in close proximity to the drug scene and users, and former drug addicts. From being a platform for discussion and influencing policy, the MDHG developed into a body endeavouring to represent the interests of drug addicts. Hence the organization became increasingly involved in the daily problems faced by addicts, particularly in terms of their contacts with the police and legal authorities. As an interest group, it has stood for decriminalizing drugs and an adequate drug aid programme.

1979–1980:   During this period, there was a great influx of heroin into western Europe. The number of heroin addicts in the Netherlands grew to an estimated 20,000. Heroin addiction was found to be prevalent among working-class youth, and Surinamese and Moroccan immigrants. Those professionals involved in the drug scene concluded that prevention and treatment programmes were not sufficient. Emphasis was placed on the development of services that would help reduce the health risk of those addicts who were unable to give up drug abuse. Thus the government developed a 'harm reduction' approach as an integral part of its drug policy. This involved the setting up of outreach projects and the provision of treatment on demand for drug addicts. The aim was to provide treatment to those who would normally remain beyond the assistance of drug agencies, therefore, reducing the harm both to individuals and to society in general.

1980:   In the summer of 1980 further guidelines to the Opium Act were published by the Minister of Justice. These new guidelines prioritized action against the distribution of hard drugs and international drug trafficking. One consequence of this was that less priority was given to prosecuting the commercial distribution of cannabis products. However, coffee shops were prohibited from public advertisements and the selling of hard drugs. The coffee shops, after this policy shift, grew in number from around 20 in 1980 to around 300 in 1990. Moreover, the shops clearly revealed in their motifs and monikers the nature of their business and the products they were dealing in.

1985:   This was the year in which officials and politicians from the Ministry of Health, Welfare and Cultural Affairs introduced the 'normalization concept' into Dutch drug policy. This referred to the social and cultural integration of those involved in drug-taking. The policy of normalization was later formalized in the 1985 memorandum document, *Drug Policy in Motion*, produced by the Interministerial Steering Group on Alcohol and Drug Policy.

1985:   The then Secretary of State for Health, Joop van der Reyden confirmed the aims of the Dutch policy before parliament. He stated that the Dutch policy was not about the eradication of drug abuse – this was viewed as unrealistic – but was about the normalization and integration of drug users.

1985:   In the same period, the Ministry of Justice developed a variety of crime-breaking programmes. This was a response to increased levels of crime. There was a growth in burglary and drug trafficking. The government committed more financial resources to the police and extra prison capacity was created. A number of measures were introduced which made use of criminal enforcement as a means of drug control. Indeed, there was a distinct movement towards the use of law enforcement, rather than an emphasis on public health, in dealing with drug-related problems.

1985:   The Amsterdam Public Prosecution department announced that it was prepared to redefine the conditions for trading in cannabis products, especially clamping down on explicit advertising.

1985:   The European Parliament in this year created a commission to study drug problems in the European Community. In 1986 a report was drafted which was amended by right-wing members. This right-wing element sought the objective of ridding Europe of drugs. The left-wing minority on the commission argued for the normalization of the problem. By 1990 the majority that blocked the normalization approach no longer held sway.

1987 (November):   In this month, organized action was taken against a chain of coffee shops known as the Bulldog. The action was taken because of the size of the business, all of which attracted international attention. All the coffee shops were warned about their breaching of the guidelines, and several raids were carried out on small coffee shops. In response, coffee shops toned down explicit references to the commercial sale of cannabis products. Although there was a tightening of the guidelines, the Bulldog chain was not prosecuted.

1980s: There were significant moves towards a Single Market in Europe, which had important repercussions for Dutch drug policy. This project involved the removal by 1992 of border controls among the 12 members of the European Community. This resulted in the European Parliament becoming more influential in the area of European drug policy. Political developments witnessed the Schengen Agreement between the governments of Germany, France, the Netherlands, Luxembourg and Belgium. Representatives of these countries decided to open up borders by 1990. The agreement dealt with issues of border control, terrorism, drugs and immigration. The agreement was important because it brought together two countries – the Netherlands and Germany – with distinct policy models in relation to drug control. The Schengen Agreement and the move towards the Single Market placed a great deal of emphasis on law enforcement in dealing with internal and external threats to the security of participating countries. This to a certain extent did not provide a favourable climate for the Dutch government in which to pursue its public health-orientated drug policy. It is claimed that German officials placed consistent pressure on Dutch representatives from the Ministry of Justice to toughen up drug policy. The Germans were critical that the Dutch policy was having a detrimental effect on European citizens. The Ministry of Health was often excluded from these discussions. Accordingly, the pressure exerted by Germany has encouraged the wider use of law enforcement by Dutch policy-makers in dealing with drug problems, and, as shown above, has led to a tightening of soft-drug policy in Amsterdam.

1988: The synthetic drug ecstasy (MDMA) was added to the schedule of hard drugs. The related substance of MDEA was placed on the hard-drug schedule in 1993. The government made it clear that new variants of synthetic drugs would be swiftly brought within the remit of the Opium Act so that legal proceedings could be instituted.

1989 (June): The Dutch parliament failed to sanction final arrangements for the Schengen Agreement. This was due to a lack of information and the detrimental impact that the implementation of the agreement was likely to have. This delayed the Schengen process for part of the time.

1989 (September): The newly elected parliament in the Netherlands continued to make critical noises about the Schengen agreement. Parliamentarians argued that the agreement would interfere with privacy and the legal protection of individuals in general. Parliament concluded that it had the right to refuse ratification.

1990 (April): It was announced by the Dutch Prime Minister that a new Schengen Agreement would take place simultaneously with German unification, but a clear majority in the Dutch parliament opposed ratification.

1993 (March and April): A plenary debate on drugs took place in parliament, concentrating on the nuisance problems caused by drug addicts. The debate focused on measures to avoid nuisance problems and the possibility of intensifying the policy of *'drang en dwang'* or 'persuasion and compulsion' for rehabilitation treatment. The government was asked by parliament to present a plan of action in response to these perceived problems. These options were already outlined in a parliamentary paper entitled 'The use of persuasion and compulsion to help addicts'. After its publication, the policy was implemented on a modest scale in the municipalities most effected by nuisance problems caused by drug addicts.

1993: A document published by the Ministry of Health outlined further measures to reduce the nuisance problems caused by addicts. The various points outlined by the document were as follows. First, to develop a range of health care and treatment services. This might include Motivation Centres and facilities assisting addicts with psychiatric disorders. Second, to make more intense use of legal options offered by the justice system. Third, to improve coordination at local level.

1993: The European Council, acting on the authority of the Maastricht Treaty, seeks to harmonize the legal position of members states in relation to drug control. The EC was particularly keen to investigate ways of developing common action against the trafficking of drugs.

1994: In this year, the Steering Committee for the Reduction of Nuisance (SVO) was appointed to operate until the end of 1997. The main objective of the committee was to deal with the nuisance problem relating to drug addiction by combining care with criminal law measures. The SVO comprised representatives of the Ministry of Health, the Ministry of Justice and the Ministry of Interior. Regular meetings and consultations were held with the Union of Dutch Local Authorities. Through the SVO, the Ministry of Health has funded residential and outpatient facilities, and local authority projects for dealing with nuisance problems. The Ministry of Justice financed early intervention projects where addicts are given the stark choice between detention or treatment at a very early stage. The SVO coordinated its operations with those of the Task Force on Public Safety and the Care of Addicts, both of which had worked to produce a policy for nuisance which was published after 1997.

1995 (April):   The Minister of Health, Welfare and Sport provided all municipalities with a set of guidelines as a way of reducing the health risks of large-scale rave parties that might involve the use of ecstasy. The guidelines included recommendations on preventing drug dealing within the premises, the availability of chill-out rooms, cold drinking water, adequate climate control, first aid and emergency services, and on-site testing facilities for drugs. An important part of the policy towards ecstasy has been the operation of a monitoring system for new drug trends, like ecstasy, which are outside the orthodox care system. At national and local level, the extent to which ecstasy is used is measured by regular school surveys. The Drug Information and Monitoring System (DIMS) of NIAD collects information about new trends throughout the country – especially, ecstasy – through drug testing and data collected from users and dealers by the regional prevention agencies.

1995 (1 October):   The State Secretary for the Interior, acting on behalf of Health Minister and the Minister of Justice appointed a task force to deal with the problem of drug-related social nuisance. The task force included representatives from the Health and Justice departments, together with participants from three of the largest cities in Holland. The task force was given the task of overseeing the implementation of the priorities set out in the policy document of 1995. In addition, it would identify new trends and advise local authorities about the measures they could take in controlling the drug scene. The task force established pilot projects in cities like Rotterdam. These projects have attempted to use the criminal law in the treatment of addicts. It has also sought to expand criminal law instruments to deal with coffee shops and nuisance problems caused by drug addicts.

1995:   The Dutch government, through the Ministry of Foreign Affairs, Ministry of Health, Welfare and Sport, the Ministry of Justice and the Ministry of Interior, issued a major policy document on drugs. This was a review and evaluation of the Dutch policy and strategies were established for dealing with new developments such as ecstasy and the nuisance problem relating to drug use.

1996:   As revealed in a policy document published in this year, tighter controls were to be placed on the coffee shops through new administrative and legal instruments. For instance, legislation was drafted in 1996 that enabled burgomasters to close down coffee shops, even those not giving rise to nuisance problems.

1996:   A Bill amending the Municipalities Act was submitted in this year and if passed would empower burgomasters to close the dwellings in which drugs are sold and where nuisance problems are likely to arise. The Bill was submitted to the Lower House on 25 April 1996.

A reading schedule

Unfortunately, not all the usual policy texts cover the topic of evaluation. Parsons (1995: sections 4.5 and 4.7) provides a highly informative and comprehensive analysis of evaluation, and is well worth consulting. Hogwood and Gunn (1984: chapter 12) is useful, but less insightful than Parsons. There are numerous specialist texts, mainly American in origin, analyzing policy evaluation and impact studies. Rist (1995a) and Palumbo (1987), which contains a useful article by Rita Mae Kelly (1987), offer a contemporary analysis of the many positions and approaches to policy evaluation. For a similar approach to the one adopted in this text, reference should be made to Guba and Lincoln (1981, 1989). These authors provide a socially informed alternative to the positivist paradigm of evaluation. See Palfrey *et al.* (1992) for a British perspective on policy evaluation.

There is a growing corpus of literature on drug policy. For the Netherlands, articles by Leuw (1991) and van Vliet (1990) are indispensable. For a more general and contemporary overview of the situation in Europe, consult Dorn and Jepsen (1996), which contains some interesting articles about various aspects of drug control policy across the continent. Ruggiero and South (1995) provides a good sociological examination about the drugs market in Europe and is worth consulting for any project on drugs control. Estievenart (1995) provides a descriptive country-by-country breakdown of drug policies across Europe. Journals such as *The International Journal on Drug Policy*, the *British Journal of*

▶▶

▶▶

Addiction and the *Journal of Drug Issues* cover a wide range of drug-related areas, including matters relevant to policy.

Issues for revision and further consideration

Having studied this case study you should be familiar with several key concepts relevant to policy analysis. These are as follows: impact evaluation (sections 9.1, 9.2, 9.3); positivist evaluation (9.2); quantitative methodology (9.2); cost-benefit analysis (9.2); qualitative evaluation (9.3); policy style (9.4); harm reduction policy (9.4, 9.4.1, 9.6); normalization policy (9.4.1, 9.6); prohibitionist approach (9.4.1); multistrategy research/flexible process model (9.4, 9.5, 9.6, and also Chapter 4).

▶   To what extent can Dutch drug policy be described as an anticipatory/inclusive policy style?

▶   What are the relative merits of quantitative and qualitative methodologies in the evaluation of policy? What sort of thinking might be behind a multistrategy research design for evaluating policy? (See Chapter 4 for details.)

▶   To what extent does Dutch drug control policy show that policy-making and political institutions can influence social issues?

▶   Is it possible for qualitative-based or multistrategy evaluation studies to inform policy? To what extent can sociological evaluations of policy be used to help practitioners at the sharp end of things?

Chapter 10

Conclusion

10.1 Public policy: the process of government action

This book has attempted to examine public policy. Essentially, public policy refers to government action. The study of policy, as was shown, can potentially encompass a wide variety of areas and concerns. The most basic distinction is that between applied and analytical traditions of policy analysis, although undoubted links exist between the two spheres. The applied tradition attempts to provide knowledge of policy which is intended for use by policy practitioners – ministers, officials and service managers. The scope of such analysis may include the provision of data in order to assist policy-makers in their decisions. It could also entail attempts to install systems that improve the policy-making mechanisms in government. The second tradition is analytical in emphasis, seeking to generate in-depth analysis of policy often for the purposes of theoretical reflection.

One of the most prominent modes of investigation in this tradition concerns the study of the policy process. As indicated, this text has sought to focus in the main, but not exclusively, on this mode of analysis. Studies of the policy process focus 'on the stages through which issues pass and attempts are made to assess the influence of different factors on the development of the issue' (Ham and Hill, 1984: 8). This form of analysis delineates government action as a dynamic entity; it is a phenomenon that is ever changing and subject to a whole range of influences, as observed by Ham and Hill above.

Since the academic formalization of policy studies in the 1950s, numerous theoretical models have endeavoured to identify those factors responsible for driving policy. These theoretical models can be distinguished in terms of the relative emphasis attached to either agency or structure as the main influence over the policy process. This distinction is a perennial one in sociological thinking. The argument in this book is that a similar framework can be attached to theories about the policy process. On the one hand, there are those models which regard policy as being influenced in the main by structural forces which are the pre-existing conditions under which policy-makers operate. On the other hand, there is that theoretical tradition in policy studies which focuses on the role of individual policy agents.

As shown in Chapters 2 and 3, the different models that span each side of the agency–structure divide are far from being homogenous. For example, theories emphasizing the role of agency in policy-making have forwarded different arguments about the nature of individual action and its influence upon the policy process. Advocates of the rational decision-making model have portrayed the policy process as following a linear path from formation to implementation. Here the most significant actors are those occupying the higher echelons of government. Although Lipsky's analysis of street-level bureaucrats places a similar analytical emphasis on agency, the actual contribution of individuals to the policy process contrasts with that contended by rational thinkers. Engagement by individuals in the policy process according to this model is spread across policy institutions. Here, greater emphasis is placed on the ability of agents on the ground, responsible for delivering policy, being able to adjust and reshape policy. However, the analysis in this text did not stop at the examination of competing schools of thought and the relative weight attached by these models to structure and agency. Case studies were developed in the second part of the text to examine the nature of the policy process in real situations.

10.2   Case analysis: a view into the real world of policy-making

Case analysis was central to the examination of the policy process presented in this text. Case studies provided highly detailed accounts of some particular aspect of the policy process. These studies attempted to fulfil three main objectives.

First, to assess the extent to which policy concepts and theories are applicable to real policy situations. Although it was not possible to cover all the concepts and models described in Chapters 2 and 3, the case studies were organized in such a way that the theoretical mainstays of the policy process were given some form of coverage. For example, the case study on the Chelsea and Westminster

Hospital in Chapter 7 focused on the practical utility of top-down and bottom-up theories of policy-making. Chapter 8 on the Tomlinson review into London's health service, by contrast, used empirical material to consider theoretical models relating to the implementation of policy.

Second, the case studies were used to make an important point about the process of developing policy theory. The case approach was ideally suited to a gradual, inductive form of analysis and concept-building. Detailed analysis based on empirical case material was intended to show the utility of this type of theory-building and analysis.

Finally, the case studies were used to provide a methodological platform for examining the relative significance of agency and structure in the policy process. In this respect, the analytical themes of the studies were central. Moreover, the way in which the studies were organized in the text allowed the analysis to consider themes relevant to the agency–structure debate in policy-making. Hence the first three case studies in Chapters 5, 6 and 7 centred on different levels of the policy process – those of agency, of intermediate structures, and of external structures. In Chapter 6, the role of agency in the policy process was considered through a case analysis of compulsory competitive tendering. The following case study in Chapter 7 was more concerned with the way policy agents have to operate within institutional settings where policy is made and delivered. The last two case studies in Chapters 8 and 9 focused on different stages of the policy process. Here, a study of the Tomlinson inquiry into London's health service was the case subject used in Chapter 8, exploring how policy emerges and is eventually implemented. Chapter 9, by contrast, considered policy evaluation in the context of Dutch drug control policy. In a stagist model, this represents a reflective phase of the process, one that emerges after a policy has been implemented.

Each case study makes a particular contribution to the debate about the factors that influence the policy process. The aim of the following section is to explore the main conclusions provided by these case studies concerning the relative influence of agency and structure in the policy process. The main point is the extent to which policy is the outcome of interrelations between individual agents and the conditions in which they operate.

10.3   A sociological strategy for policy analysis

Discussions about micro and macro features of the policy process have been confined to particular analytical domains within the policy literature. Most notably, it is in debates about the significance of political processes and institutions that such discussions have been most conspicuous. The competing paradigms in this debate are normally separated into two distinct but heterogenous factions. On the one side, there is structural functionalism and Marxist theory, which give priority to the power of external structures over government. As shown in Chapter 3 (see section 3.2), both schools, while radically different, emphasize that political institutions have limited influence over society because they are constrained by wider structural forces – these are imputed to be either economic (Marxist theory) or social structural (functionalist theory) in nature. Contrary to this, there is a tradition of thought stretching back to the nineteenth century which asserts the independence of political institutions. The various theoretical schools of policy outlined in section 3.3 asserted that governments do make a difference and sometimes shape the development of wider structural forces. Hence this debate can boil down to the following point: the structural determinism of Marxist and functional schools that emphasize the potential of social and economic structures versus politically orientated models that emphasize the independence of agency.

This distinction between the two schools of thought is to a certain extent oversimplistic. Arguments concerning the autonomy and leverage of political processes in society should not be wholeheartedly equated with ideas about the influence of intentional human agents in policy. As demonstrated in Chapter 3, those thinkers in the political camp were just as much concerned with structural features as Marxist and functionalist theoreticians (see section 3.3 and 3.4). The main difference between them was that the latter tradition has emphasized the significance of political structures and the institutional context of government. Castles (1981: 121) makes a telling observation: 'The problem for the policy analyst is that ... macropolitical factors taken as proxies to signify the importance of politics are as much structural in character as the main features of the socioeconomic process'.

To illustrate the point being made, Castles compared the changes in socioeconomic and political factors in 18 Western democracies over a 20-year period, between 1950 and 1970. With respect to political factors, there were distinct fluctuations in Cabinet participation. But taken aggregately, Castles found that, like socio-economic factors, there was little variation found in the political sphere. Castles concludes from this comparative analysis that political institutions and functions display the characteristics of stable structural entities. He notes (Castles, 1981: 121) that such an observation may be 'somewhat anomalous for those who believe that the demonstration that political factors are associated with policy outcomes in some sense proves the importance of political agency and electoral choice'.

What should be garnered from the above discussion is that those structures that effect policy should not be confined to monolithic phenomena, such as the social system or the global economy. Those structures that impinge on the policy process should be regarded in broad terms as those objective conditions under which policy-makers have to operate. In this sense, they should include governmental and public sector institutions, as well as broader forces like the economy that are in certain respects independent of the polity.

Following on from this, agency should not be subsumed under, or be equated directly with, the operations of political processes. Analysts should specify more precisely the role of agency in the policy process. From the analysis carried out above, this concept is primarily concerned with the ability of intentional human beings to influence and shape the policy process. In policy terms, it means focusing on or giving methodological priority to the way individual policy agents operate in institutional contexts. For Castles (1981: 129) when it comes to agency 'it is frequently difficult to come to conceptual grips with its manifestation in individual choices, strategies and manoeuvres by means of the inherently generalizing methods of the social sciences'. However, the contention of this text is that the qualitative-based case study is well suited to examining individual involvement in policy. Chapters 6 and 7 endeavoured to examine closely through case analysis the role of agents in different policy contexts. Chapter 6 was concerned with the operation of individual agents in one local authority, Bath and North East Somerset. The study centred on the way officers responded to and attempted to establish a system of competitive tendering across a range of services. In Chapter 7, managers and officials in a district health authority came under the spotlight. The case study was particularly interested in how these agents attempted to balance the interests of various sectional groups in carrying out a programme of hospital closures.

As shown by these case studies, agents in the policy process are not mere puppets, and cannot be explained away in terms of social processes. However, the concentration on government action in policy studies means that it is all too easy to ignore the contribution of the individual purposeful actor. There are schools of thought in the policy field, especially from Marxist and functionalist perspectives, which seem to regard individual action as a secondary factor in the policy process. Agents and their decisions are seen as being submerged and determined by wider structural conditions – institutional networks, external forces and existing social conditions. This is not the position followed in this study. Individuals are not so much the prisoners of their own circumstances; policy agents are in the position to make a highly creative and influential contribution to policy. The respective studies of Lindblom, Barrett and Lipsky, among others, point to the ability of individual actors in developing, transforming and delivering public policies. Chapter 5 gave an insight into the contribution made by key officials and ministers to urban policy. Senior officials and minsters such as Peter Shore and Michael Heseltine helped shape the priorities and concerns of urban policy over time. But as Lipsky's work demonstrates, those agents that wield such influence need not be the ruling apparatchiks or high-ranking government ministers. Even those individuals operating on the ground have a crucial role in actually making policy. The case study of competitive tendering in Chapter 6 underlined how policy agents in local government endeavoured to redefine central policy prescriptions. This was done to ensure that relations between officers and departments were not completely undermined by the exigencies of competitive legislation.

At the same time, it would be foolhardy in the extreme to argue that the actions and decisions of policy agents are not affected by existing structural conditions. Policy-making, of all activities undertaken by human agents, is intimately tied to, and influenced by, social and economic conditions. Those agents involved in the policy process often have to address structural components and aspects of society, whether it be the asymmetrical distribution of power among social groups, the unequal distribution of wealth, or the complex range of interests found in institutional settings. The case studies in Part II clearly illustrate such a point. For example, the origins and priorities of urban policy are closely tied to the impact wrought by the international economy on areas and regions which have traditionally relied on heavy industry (see Chapter 5). In Chapter 7, it was demonstrated how key policy actors had to implement their programme of rationalization within an institutional context littered with powerful interest groups. As shown, these relations of power were central to the success or failure of the said policy. Policymakers in the Netherlands have had to face the fact that drug abuse is affected by certain structural factors – in particular, Holland's geographic position which places it close to drug-trafficking routes.

Thus policy agents cannot escape the social, economic and institutional context of the policy process. Within policy models, and social theory in general, there are 'very different ideas about the degree to which the enmeshment of people in social processes allows for levels of individual creativity and independence, particularly in instances of social transformation' (Layder, 1994, p. 207). For example, there is the neo-Marxist position as expressed by Gough (1979: 43–4):

> What distinguishes Marxist theory is not the view that a particular class dominates the institution of the state ... but that whoever occupies these positions is constrained by the imperatives of the capital accumulation process ... Within these constraints there is room for manoeuvre, for competing strategies and policies.

As shown above, this Marxist interpretation ultimately places agents in the position where they are dominated by the capital economy. In other words, while individual policy-makers retain some independence from the capitalist economy, the structural features of the capitalist economy are more crucial than individual action in explaining policy outputs.

Undoubtedly, Gough is right to assert that policy agents operate within specified structural conditions and that their policy decisions are intimately linked to institutional and external structures. But this emphasis leads to difficulties. Bottomore (1975: 160) gives expression to such problems in general sociological terms:

> As sociologists we want to say that every distinct society has a particular relational structure ...; and most of us would want to claim further that beyond or behind the unique structures of particular

societies there are more general structural 'types' ... The real problem is to formulate a conception of social structure which does justice to these elements of regularity and order in social life, while not neglecting the flow of historical action by individuals and social groups which sustains, recreates, revises, or disputes this order.

The following question thus becomes relevant: If structural conditions affect the policy process, what room for manoeuvre is there for agents and actors to make a creative input that significantly leads to social change? There are three points that should be made.

First, policy actors – ministers, officials, public officials and managers – as argued above, are not completely dominated and governed by the objective conditions which form an integral part of the policy process. To suggest that this is so would mean that pre-existing structural conditions in policy-making activities are immutable, with little or no possibility of being transformed and changed through intentional human action.

The second point is that structures not only constrain human behaviour, but also provide opportunities for actual social change. A range of key actors engaged in the policy process have access to certain governmental and institutional networks. These are independent entities; they are not entirely eclipsed and functionally subservient to existing structural conditions. As such, these institutional mechanisms of the state sector may be co-opted for the purpose of achieving policy or social change. For instance, the case study on the Chelsea and Westminster Hospital in Chapter 7 is an apposite example. It showed how central government intervention established certain financial and institutional conditions around which London health administrators and practitioners had to manoeuvre. Some health authorities were characterized by inertia. Key policy managers in others such as those at the Riverside District Health Authority used the institutional mechanisms at their disposal to achieve fundamental changes for the purpose of long-term survival.

Finally, structures, at the same time, undoubtedly pose severe constraints on the ability of policy agents to achieve progress and change. These structures, though, are not independent entities, completely devoid of human input. In fact, the structural conditions linked to the policy process are both affected by and comprise human involvement, and thus can be influenced by the countervailing action of actors. But, at the same time structures are not the aggregate products of individuals operating collectively, or phenomenon that are reducible to lone actors.

Following on from the above discussion, social structures and purposeful human action are dynamically linked in policy and other socio-political matters. There are, according to Mouzelis (1995), definite predicaments in store for those sociologists and social scientists who ignore the mutual links between individuals and the wider socio-political context. When such links are ignored it opens the door 'to all forms of crude, facile, reductionist explanations' (ibid. 155). Here, social analysts must seek not to ignore the differences between agency and structure but should endeavour 'to construct concepts that break down the barriers and strengthen the bridges between them' (ibid. 156). In other words, sociology should become sensitive not only to the multilayered nature of social life but also to the range of qualitative connections that pertain between various levels. These assertions are without doubt relevant to policy research and theoretical activity. Writings by the likes of Ham and Hill and Barrett and Fudge underline this assertion. Castles (1981: 129) makes the observation that such ideas might not be altogether welcomed by those wedded to narrow conceptual paradigms: 'It is perfectly possible for societies to be both structured and vary. Such a perspective may not be wholly welcome to the more committed protagonists of the battle of the paradigms, but it should be congenial to the practitioners of a comparative approach to politics and policy, for whom an understanding of structured variation is the very essence of their discipline'.

While intertwined, they have as Layder (1994: 88) notes, very distinct properties. These form different levels of the policy process. Each level is of equal analytical significance, each is intimately linked, and each one shares certain common features. Yet they are quite different entities. Policy analysis has to acknowledge the interdependencies that exist between individual dynamic agents and emergent properties of the policy process. It will often be necessary for analysts to focus on specific features or components of the policy process, while not imputing analytical priority to either individualistic or structural features. The case studies, particularly Chapters 5, 6 and 7, focused on specific levels of analysis or aspects of the policy process, while bracketing off other potentially relevant levels of the policy process. For analytical purposes such methodological bracketing is an important and convenient device, providing that there is no actual prioritizing overall of any particular level. However, the reality of policy-making is far more complex than is portrayed by such methodological procedures and analysts should be mindful of this. As suggested by one commentator with regard to social research:

> I suggested that in order to maintain a concentrated focus on one layer of social reality ... a feasible option would entail bracketing off the analysis of the other sectors while attention is fixed on the area of current interest. It is important to note that this is a purely expedient strategy to make relevant data more easily accessible and to stabilize one's focus. It must always be remembered that in reality the different sectors are bound together in an organic unity, and that a singular focus of interest is a matter of emphasis and strategic convenience. (Layder, 1993: 196)

To achieve this more open, flexible strategy, policy analysis should draw more readily on multiperspective social theories. These are in better position to understand the interconnections between the social structures, institutions, the economy, and individual agents in the policy process. In particular, the offerings of certain modern sociological thinkers provide such eclectic theoretical frameworks. For example, Habermas provides a careful synthesis between system properties and everyday interaction in the lifeworld. He carefully does not fall into the trap of submerging one area into the other, by insisting that these remain distinct social spheres. This theoretical model is useful for policy analysts as it integrates notions of power and conflict, while leaving room for purposeful human action. There is also Goffman's ideas about the interaction order and how this is loosely tied to the institutional networks. Less well known but equally important to the theorizing of structure–agency links in sociology is the recent work of Piotr Sztompka. He acknowledges the multidimensional nature of both structure and agency. For instance, social structure is seen as composed of different levels and is regarded as a dynamic entity, constantly in a state of flux. Agency, for Sztompka (1991: 124–9), can potentially transform structures, while noting the significance of power and hegemony in social situations.

For policy analysis to fully grapple with and reflect the perplexity of its subject matter, a greater willingness to draw upon these ideas would seem to be necessary. Significantly, it would ensure the intellectual vitality of the analysis *of* policy and, to some extent, help inform analysis *for* policy.

References

Aldrich, H. (1976), 'Resource dependence and interorganizational relations: local employment service offices and social services sector organizations', *Adminstration and Society*, vol. 7, no. 4, pp. 419–51.

Allison, G. T. (1971), *The Essence of Decision: Explaining the Cuban missile crisis*, Boston: Little, Brown.

Almond, G. A., and Powell, G. B. (1978), *Comparative Politics: System, process, and policy*, 2nd edn, Boston: Little, Brown.

Anderson, J. E. (1975), *Public Policy-Making*, London: Nelson.

Anderson, P. (1992), 'Ministers buy in evidence to back Tomlinson closures', *Health Service Journal*, 10 December, p. 3.

Aron, R. (1950), 'Social structure and the ruling class (an article in two parts: part one)', *British Journal of Sociology*, vol. 1, no. 1, pp. 1–16.

Ashford, D. E. (1981), *Policy and Politics in Britain: The limits of consensus*, Oxford: Blackwell).

AMA (1995), *Regionalism: the local government dimension*, an AMA discussion paper, London: Association of Metropolitan Authorities.

Atkinson, R., and Moon, G. (1994), 'The City Challenge initiative: an overview and preliminary assessment', *Regional Studies*, vol. 28, no. 1, pp. 94–7.

Aucoin, P. (1979), 'Public-policy theory and analysis', in G. B. Dearn and P. Aucoin (eds), *Public Policy in Canada: Organisation, process and management*, Toronto: Macmillan.

Audit Commission (1989), *Urban Regeneration and Economic Development: The local government dimension*, London: HMSO.

Audit Commission (1993), *Realising the Benefits of Competition: The client role for contracted services*, London: HMSO.

Bacharach, S. B., and Lawler, E. J. (1980), *Power and Politics in Organisations: The social psychology of conflict, coalitions and bargaining*, San Francisco: Jossey-Bass.

Baggott, R. (1994), *Health and Health Care in Britain*, Basingstoke/New York: Macmillan/St Martin's Press.

B&NES (1995a), *CCT Client-Side Work Programme*, Chief Executive Report to the Policy and Resources Committee, 20 November, Bath: Bath and North East Somerset Council.

B&NES (1995b), *Amalgamation of Direct Service Organisations: Key issues*, Policy Committee, 4 September, Bath: Bath and North East Somerset Council.

B&NES (1996), *A Strategy for Housing Management Compulsory Competitive Tendering (Housing Management CCT)*, Head of Housing Management Report to the Housing and Public Protection Committee, December, Bath: Bath and North East Somerset Council.

B&NES (1997a), *Corporate Criteria in Relation to Contract Packaging*, Principal

Policy Officer Report to the CCT Strategy Working Party, 30 January, Bath: Bath and North East Somerset Council.

B&NES (1997b), *Competition and the Decision Making Structure*, Principal Policy Officer Report to the Policy and Resources Committee, 13 March, Bath: Bath and North East Somerset Council.

Bardach, E. (1977), *The Implementation Game: What happens after a bill becomes law*, Cambridge, Mass.: MIT Press.

Barnekov, T., Boyle. R., and Rich, D. (1989), *Privatism and Urban Policy in Britain and the United States*, Oxford: Oxford University Press.

Barrett, S., and Fudge, C. (eds) (1981a), *Policy and Action: Essays on the implementation of public policy*, London: Methuen.

Barrett, S., and Fudge, C. (1981b), 'Examining the policy-action relationship', in S. Barrett and C. Fudge (eds), *Policy and Action: Essays on the implementation of public policy*, London: Methuen.

Barrett, S. and Hill, M. (1984), 'Policy, bargaining and structure in implementation theory: towards an integrated perspective', *Policy and Politics*, vol. 12, no. 3, pp. 219–40.

Battle, T. (1989), 'The role of management development strategies in managing organisational change', *Health Services Management*, August, pp. 169–72.

Benson, J. K. (1975), 'The interorganizational network as a political economy', *Administrative Science Quarterly*, vol. 20, no. 2, pp. 229–49.

Benson, J. K. (1977), 'Organizations: a dialectical view', *Administrative Science Quarterly*, vol. 22, no. 1, pp. 1–21.

Benson, J. K. (1983), 'Interorganizational networks and policy sectors', in D. Rogers and D. Whetten (eds), *Interorganizational Coordination*, Iowa: Iowa State University.

Berman, P. (1978), 'The study of macro- and micro-implementation', *Public Policy*, vol. 26, no. 2 (spring), pp. 157–86.

Bevins, A., and Boggan, S. (1997), 'It's a fight to the death', *Independent*, 23 April, p. 1.

Bobrow, D. S., and Dryzek, J. S. (1987), *Policy Analysis by Design*, Pittsburgh: University of Pittsburgh Press.

Bottomore, T. B. (1966), *Elites and Society*, Harmondsworth: Penguin.

Bottomore, T. (1975), 'Structure and history', in P. M. Blau (ed.), *Approaches to the Study of Social Structure*, London: Open Books.

Bottomore, T. (1993), *Political Sociology*, 2nd edn, London: Pluto Press.

Braybrooke, D., and Lindblom, C. E. (1963), *A Strategy of Decision: Policy evaluation as a social process*, New York: The Free Press.

Brindle, D. (1991), 'London hospital opt-outs halted', *Guardian*, 9 October, p. 1.

Brindle, D. (1994), 'Hospitals: under the knife', *Guardian*, 23 November, p. 26.

Brunsson, N. (1982), 'The irrationality of action and action rationality:

decisions, ideologies and organisational action', *Journal of Management Studies*, vol. 19, no. 1, pp. 29–44.

Buchanan, J. M. (1978), 'From private preferences to public philosophy: the development of public choice', in Institute of Economic Affairs, *The Economics of Politics*, Readings 18, London: IEA.

Bulmer, M. (1990), 'Successful applications of sociology', in C. G. A. Bryant and H. A. Becker (eds), *What has Sociology Achieved?*, Basingstoke: Macmillan.

Burch, M., and Wood, B. (1983), *Public Policy in Britain*, Oxford: Martin Robertson.

Burden, T., and Campbell, M. (1985), *Capitalism and Public Policy in the UK*, London: Croom Helm.

Burton, M. (1992), 'Framework for the future of CCT', *Municipal Journal*, 26 June–2 July, p. 13.

Butler, P. (1992), 'No gain without pain', *Health Service Journal*, 25 June, pp. 10–11.

Byrne, T. (1990), *Local Government in Britain: Everyone's guide to how it all works*, 5th edn, London: Penguin.

Castles, F. G. (1981), 'How does politics matter? Structure or agency in the determination of public policy outcomes', *European Journal of Political Research*, vol. 9, no. 2 (June), pp. 119–32.

Castles, F. G. (1989), 'Introduction: puzzles of political economy', in F. G. Castles (ed.), *The Comparative History of Public Policy*, Cambridge: Polity Press.

Cawson, A. (1982), *Corporatism and Welfare: Social policy and state intervention in Britain*, London: Heinemann.

Chinoy, E. (1964), 'Case study method', in J. Gould and W. L. Kolb (eds), *A Dictionary of the Social Sciences*, London: Tavistock.

Ciorra, T. (1993), 'Project-managing the commissioning of the Chelsea and Westminster Hospital', *World Hospitals*, vol. 29, no. 2, pp. 25–9.

Coatcs, D. (1984), *The Context of British Politics*, London: Hutchinson.

Cohen, P. (1990), 'Building upon the successes of Dutch drug policy', *International Journal on Drug Policy*, vol. 2, no. 2, pp. 22–4.

Colvin, P. (1985), *The Economic Ideal in British Government: Calculating costs and benefits in the 1970s*, Manchester: Manchester University Press.

Commission of the European Communities (1996), *On the Evaluation of the European Drug Prevention Week (EDPW) 1994 in Relation to the Commission's Activities in the Sector*, Luxembourg: CEC.

Committee of Public Accounts (1992), *The Westminster and Chelsea Hospital: Minutes of evidence*, 11 November , London: HMSO.

Committee of Public Accounts (1993), *The Chelsea and Westminster Hospital*, Twenty-Sixth Report, 22 February 1993, London: HMSO.

Conservative Central Office (1992), *The Best Future for Britain: the Conservative manifesto 1992*, London: Conservative Central Office.

Cooper, J. (1985), *The Creation of the British Social Services 1962–1974*, London: Heinemann.

Coventry CDP (1975), *CDP Final Report, Part 2, Background Working Papers*, Coventry: The Home Office and City of Coventry Community Development Project.

Davies, L., and Tym, R. (1993), *East Thames Corridor: a study of development capacity and potential prepared for the Department of the Environment*, London: HMSO.

Degeling, P., and Colebatch, H. K. (1984), 'Structure and action as constructs in the practice of public administration', *Australian Journal of Public Administration*, vol. 43, no. 4 (December), pp. 320–31.

De Groot, L. (1992), 'City Challenge: competing in the urban regeneration game', *Local Economy*, vol. 17, no. 3, pp. 196–209.

Denzin, N. (1989), *The Research Act: a theoretical introduction to sociological methods*, 3rd edn, Englewood Cliffs, NJ: Prentice Hall.

DoE (1994) *Bidding Guidance: A guide to funding from the Single Regeneration Budget*, Department of the Environment, London: HMSO.

DoE (1995), 'Guidance on the conduct of compulsory competitive tendering', draft circular to Chief Executives, 11 October, Department of the Environment, London.

DoH (1988), 'Secretary of State approves Westminster and Chelsea Project', Press Release, 88/474 22 December, Department of Health, London.

DoH (1993), *Making London Better*, Department of Health, Manchester: Health Publications Unit.

Derthick, M. (1972), *New Towns in-Town: Why a federal programme failed*, Washington, DC: Urban Institute.

Dietz, T., and Burns, T. R. (1992), 'Human agency and the evolutionary dynamics of culture', *Acta Sociologica*, vol. 35, no. 3, pp. 187–200.

Dillner, L. (1993), 'London's specialist centres cut by half', *British Medical Journal*, 26 June, pp. 1709–10.

Dilnot, A. (1995), *What Role for the State in the Economy?* The State of Britain Seminar III of a joint ESRC/RSA seminar series, Swindon: ESRC.

Dorn, N. (1989), 'Sideshow: an appreciation and critique of Dutch drug policies', *British Journal of Addiction*s, vol. 84, no. 9, pp. 995–7.

Dorn, N., and Jepsen, J. (eds) (1996), *European Drug Policies and Enforcement*, Basingstoke: Macmillan.

Dror, Y. (1964), 'Muddling through: "science" or inertia?', *Public Administration Review*, vol. 24, no. 3, pp. 153–7.

Dunleavy, P., and O'Leary, B. (1987), *Theories of the State: the politics of liberal democracy*, Basingstoke: Macmillan.

Dunsire, A. (1978), *Implementation in Bureaucracy: the execution process*, vol. 1, Oxford: Martin Robertson.

Dye, T. R. (1976), *What Governments do, Why they Do It, What Difference It Makes*, Tuscaloosa, Ala.: University of Alabama Press.

Easton, D. (1979), *A Systems Analysis of Political Life*, Chicago: University of Chicago Press.

Eaton, L. (1994), 'Hospital watchdog to get the chop early', *Independent*, 26 September, p. 4.

Edwards, J., and Batley, R. (1978), *The Politics of Positive Discrimination: An evaluation of the urban programme 1967–77*, London: Tavistock.

Edwards, J., and Deakin, N. (1992), 'Privatism and partnership in urban regeneration', *Public Administration*, vol. 70, pp. 359–68.

Elmore, R. F. (1978), 'Organizational models of social program implementation', *Public Policy*, vol. 26, no. 2, pp. 185–228.

Engelsman, E. L. (1989), 'Dutch policy on the management of drug-related problems', *British Journal of Addictions*, vol. 84, no. 2, pp. 211–18.

Estievenart, G. (ed.) (1995), *Policies and Strategies to Combat Drugs in Europe: The Treaty on European Union: Framework for a new European strategy to combat drugs?*, Dordrecht: Martinus-Nijhoff.

Etzioni, A. (1967), 'Mixed-scanning: a "third" approach to decision-making', *Public Administration Review*, vol. 27, no. 5, pp. 385–92.

Ferlie, E., Ashburner, L., Fitzgerald, L., and Pettigrew, A. (1996), *The New Public Management in Action*, Oxford: Oxford University Press.

Fothergill, S., and Gudgin, G. (1982), *Unequal Growth: Urban and regional employment change in the UK*, London: Heinemann.

Giddens, A. (1984), *The Constitution of Society*, Cambridge: Polity Press.

Glaser, B., and Strauss, A. (1966), *Awareness of Dying*, London: Weidenfeld and Nicolson.

Glasman, D., and Sheldon, T. (1991), 'Furious trust applicants protest over London snag', *Health Service Journal*, 17 October, p. 4.

Goffman, E. (1968), *Asylums: Essays on the social situation of mental patients and other inmates*, Harmondsworth: Penguin.

Goffman, E. (1971), *The Presentation of Self in Everyday Life*, Harmondsworth: Penguin.

Goldthorpe, J. H. (1979), 'Vilfredo Pareto', in T. Raison (ed.) (rev. edn P. Barker), *The Founding Fathers of Social Science*, rev. edn, London: Scolar Press.

Goodwin, M., and Duncan, S. (1986), 'The local state and local economic policy: political mobilisation or economic regeneration', *Capital and Class*, no. 27, pp. 14–36.

Gordon, I., Lewis, J., and Young, K. (1993), 'Perspectives on policy analysis', in M. Hill (ed.), *The Policy Process: a reader*, Hemel Hempstead: Harvester Wheatsheaf.

Gough, I. (1979), *The Political Economy of the Welfare State*, London: Macmillan.

Grant, W. (1993), *Business and Politics in Britain*, 2nd edn, Basingstoke: Macmillan.

Grindle, M. S. (1980), 'Policy content and context in implementation', in M.

S. Grindle (ed.), *Politics and Policy Implementation in the Third World*, New Jersey: Princeton University Press.

Grund, J. P. C. (1989), 'Where do we go from here? The Future of Dutch drug policy', *British Journal of Addictions*, vol. 84, no. 9, pp. 993–4.

Guardian (1992a), '300 health schemes hit as region runs out of money', 11 November.

Guardian (1992b), 'Extra £56m diverted to build hospital', 12 November.

Guardian (1993), 'Leading article: the trail of the wounded whales', 17 February, p. 18.

Guba, E. G., and Lincoln, Y. S. (1981), *Effective Evaluation: Improving the usefulness of evaluation results through responsive and naturalistic approaches*, San Francisco: Jossey-Bass.

Guba, E. G., and Lincoln, Y. S. (1989), *Fourth Generation Evaluation*, Newbury Park, Calif.: Sage.

Gyford, J., Leach, S., and Game, C. (1989), *The Changing Politics of Local Government*, London: Unwin Hyman.

Hakim, C. (1992), *Research Design: Strategies and choices in the design of social research*, 3rd edn, London: Routledge.

Hall, P., Land, H., Parker, R., and Webb, A. (1975), *Change, Choice and Conflict in Social Policy*, London: Heinemann.

Ham, C. (1981), *Policy-making in the National Health Service: a case study of the Leeds Regional Hospital Board*, Basingstoke: Macmillan.

Ham, C., and Hill, M. (1984), *The Policy Process in the Modern Capitalist State*, Brighton: Wheatsheaf Books.

Ham, C., and Hill, M. (1993), *The Policy Process in the Modern Capitalist State*, 2nd edn, Hemel Hempstead: Harvester Wheatsheaf.

Hambleton, R. (1981), 'Implementing inner city policy: reflections from experience', *Policy and Politics*, vol. 9, no. 1, pp. 51–71.

Hammersley, M. (1989), *The Dilemma of Qualitative Method: Herbert Blumer and the Chicago tradition*, London: Routledge.

Hammersley, M. (1992), *What's Wrong with Ethnography? Methodological Explorations*, London: Routledge.

Hanf, K. (1978), 'Introduction', in K. Hanf and F. W. Scharpf (eds), *Interorganizational Policy Making: Limits to coordination and central control*, London: Sage.

Harden, I. (1992), *The Contracting State*, Buckingham: Open University Press.

Harrison, P. (1985), *Inside the Inner City: Life under the cutting edge*, Harmondsworth: Penguin.

Harrop, M. (1992), 'Comparisons', in M. Harrop (ed.), *Power and Policy in Liberal Democracies*, Cambridge: Cambridge University Press.

Harvey, D., and Swyngedouw, E. (1993), 'Industrial restructuring, community disempowerment and grass-roots resistance', in T. Hayter and D. Harvey (eds), *The Factory and the City: the story of the Cowley automobile workers in Oxford*, London: Mansell.

Health Committee (1992), *London's Health Service*, Minutes of Evidence, Department of Health, 16 December, London: HMSO.

Health Committee (1993), *London's Health Service*, Minutes of Evidence, Department of Health, 2 March, London: HMSO.

Health Committee (1994), *London's Health Service*, Minutes of Evidence, Department of Health, 2 March, London: HMSO.

Heclo, H. H. (1972), 'Review article: policy analysis', *British Journal of Political Science*, vol. 2, pt. 1, pp. 83–108.

Heclo, H., and Wildavsky, A. (1981), *The Private Government of Public and Money: Community and policy inside British politics*, Basingstoke: Macmillan.

Held, D. (1989), *Political Theory and the Modern State: Essays on state, power and democracy*, Cambridge: Polity Press.

HM Treasury (1986), *Using Private Enterprise in Government: Report of a multi-departmental review of competitive tendering and contracting for services in government departments*, London: HMSO.

Higgins, J., Deakin, N., Edwards, J., and Wicks, M. (1983), *Government and Urban Poverty: Inside the policy-making process*, Oxford: Blackwell.

Hill, D. M. (1994), *Citizens and Cities: Urban policy in the 1990s*, New York: Harvester Wheatsheaf.

Hill, M. (ed.) (1993), *The Policy Process: A reader*, Hemel Hempstead: Harvester Wheatsheaf.

Hill, M. (1997), *The Policy Process in the Modern State*, 3rd edn, Hemel Hempstead: Harvester Wheatsheaf.

Hjern, B., and Porter, D. O. (1981), 'Implementation structures: a new unit of administrative analysis', *Organisational Studies*, vol. 2, no. 3, pp. 211–27.

Hofferbert, R. I. (1974), *The Study of Public Policy*, New York: Bobbs Merrill.

Hogwood, B. W., and Gunn, L. A. (1984), *Policy Analysis for the Real World*, Oxford: Oxford University Press.

Hogwood, B., and Gunn, L. (1993), 'Why "perfect implementation" is unattainable', in M. Hill (ed.), *The Policy Process: A reader*, Hemel Hempstead: Harvester Wheatsheaf.

Hughes, J. A., Martin, P. J., and Sharrock, W. W. (1995), *Understanding Classical Sociology: Marx, Weber, Durkheim*, London: Sage.

International Narcotics Control Board (1995), *Report of the International Narcotics Control Board for 1995*, New York: United Nations.

James, J. H. (1994), *Transforming the NHS: the view from inside*, Bath Social Policy Paper no. 18, Bath: Bath University Centre for the Analysis of Social Policy.

Jarman, B. (1994), 'Why Virginia Bottomley is wrong', *Observer*, 27 March, (Magazine), p. 22.

Jenkins, B. (1993), 'Policy analysis: models and approaches', in M. Hill (ed.), *The Policy Process: a reader*, Hemel Hempstead: Harvester Wheatsheaf.

Judge, D., and Dickson, T. (1987), 'The British state, governments and manufacturing decline', in D. Judge and T. Dickson (eds), *The Politics of Industrial Closure*, Basingstoke: Macmillan.

Keating, M., and Rhodes, M. (1982), 'The status of regional government: an analysis of the West Midlands', in B. W. Hogwood and M. Keating (eds), *Regional Government in England*, Oxford: Clarendon Press.

Kelly, R. M. (1987), 'The politics of meaning and policy inquiry', in D. J. Palumbo (ed.), *The Politics of Program Evaluation*, Newbury Park, Calif.: Sage.

King, D. S. (1987), *The New Right Politics, Markets and Citizenship*, Basingstoke: Macmillan.

King's Fund (1992), *London Health Care in 2010: Changing the future of services in the capital*, King's Fund Commission on the Future of London's Acute Health Services, London: King's Fund.

Laffin, M., and Young, K. (1990), 'The changing roles and responsibilities of local authority chief officers', *Public Administration*, vol. 63 (spring), pp. 41–59.

Lasswell, H. D. (1970), 'The emerging conception of the policy sciences', *Policy Sciences*, vol. 1, no. 1, pp. 3–14.

Lawless, P. (1986), 'Inner urban policy: rhetoric and reality', in P. Lawless and C. Raban (eds), *The Contemporary British City*, London: Harper & Row.

Lawless, P. (1988), 'British inner urban policy: a review', *Regional Studies*, vol. 22, no. 1, pp. 531–42.

Layder, D. (1993), *New Strategies in Social Research: an introduction and guide*, Cambridge: Polity Press.

Layder, D. (1994), *Understanding Social Theory*, London: Sage.

Leach, R. (1995), 'Political ideas', in M. Mullard (ed.), *Policy-Making in Britain*, London: Routledge.

Lenke, L., and Olsson, B. (1996), 'Sweden: zero tolerance wins the argument?', in N. Dorn and J. Jepsen (eds), *European Drug Policies and Enforcement*, Basingstoke: Macmillan.

Leuw, E. (1991), 'Drugs and drug policy in the Netherlands', in M. Tonry (ed.), *Crime and Justice: a review of research*, vol. 14, Chicago: University of Chicago Press.

Lewis, J., and Flynn, R. (1979), 'The implementation of urban and regional planning policies', *Policy and Politics*, vol. 7, no. 2, pp. 123–42.

Limb, M. (1991), 'Cash crisis threat to London RHA', *Health Service Journal*, 19 December, p. 6.

Lindblom, C. E. (1959), 'The science of "muddling through"', *Public Administration Review*, vol. 19, no. 2 (spring), pp. 79–88.

Lindblom, C. E. (1964), 'Contexts for change and strategy: a reply', *Public Administration Review*, vol. 24, no. 3, pp. 157–8.

Lindblom, C. E. (1965), *The Intelligence of Democracy: Decision making through mutual adjustment*, New York/London: The Free Press/Collier-Macmillan.

Lindblom, C. E. (1977), *Politics and Markets: the world's political–economic systems*, New York: Basic Books.

Lindblom, C. E. (1980), *The Policy-Making Process*, 2nd edn, New Jersey: Prentice-Hall.

Lindblom, C. E. (1988), *Democracy and Market System*, Oslo: Norwegian University Press.

Lipsky, M. (1980), *Street-Level Bureaucracy: Dilemmas of the individual in public services*, New York: Russell Sage Foundation.

MacCoun, R. (1995), 'Drug policies in America and Europe', in G. Estievenart (ed.), *Policies and Strategies to Combat Drugs in Europe: the Treaty on European Union: framework for a new European strategy to combat drugs?*, Dordrecht: Martinus.

Malpass, P., and Murie, A. (1994), *Housing Policy and Practice*, 4th edn, London: Macmillan.

Massey, D., and Meegan, R. (1982), *The Anatomy of Job Loss: the how, why and where of employment decline*, London: Methuen.

Matthews, A. (1989), 'Care and cure: a visit to the Jellinek Centre, Amsterdam', *International Journal on Drug Policy*, vol. 1, no. 3, pp. 16–18.

Mawson, J., Beazley, M., Burfitt, A., Collinge, C., Hall, S., Loftman, P., Nevin, B., Srbljanin, A., and Tilson, B. (1995), *The Single Regeneration Budget: the stocktake*, Centre for Urban and Regional Studies School of Public Policy, Birmingham: University of Birmingham.

Mawson, J., and Miller, D. (1986), 'Interventionist approaches in local employment and economic development: the experience of Labour local authorities', in V. A. Hausner (ed.), *Critical Issues in Urban Economic Development*, vol 1, Oxford: Clarendon Press.

Merrison Report (1979), *Royal Commission on the National Health Service*, Cmnd. 7615, London: HMSO.

Meyer, A. D. (1982), 'Adapting to environmental jolts', *Administrative Science Quarterly*, vol. 27, pp. 515–37.

Middlemas, K. (1979), *Politics and Industrial Society: the experience of the British system since 1911*, London: Andre Deutsch.

Middlemas, K. (1986), *Power, Competition and the State*, vol. 1: *Britain in Search of Balance, 1940–61*, Basingstoke: Macmillan.

Mihill, C., and Brindle, D. (1993), 'Tomlinson seeks rescue of hospitals', *Guardian*, 2 September, p. 5.

Miliband, R. (1973), *The State in Capitalist Society: the analysis of the Western system of power*, London: Quartet Books.

Mills, C. W. (1956), *The Power Elite*, London: Oxford University Press.

Milward, H. B., and Francisco, R. A. (1983), 'Subsystem politics and corporatism in the United States', *Policy and Politics*, vol. 11, no. 3, pp. 273–93.

Ministry of Health, Welfare and Sport (1995a), *Drugs Policy in the Netherlands:*

Continuity and change, Rijswijk: The Central Information, Documentation and Library Archives.

Ministry of Health, Welfare and Sport (1995b), *City Hall and House: Guidance for use by local authorities concerning large-scale manifestations and party drug use*, Rijswijk: Division of Alcohol, Drug and Tobacco Policies.

Ministry of Health, Welfare and Sport (1996), *Progress Report on Drugs Policy*, Rijswijk: Division of Alcohol, Drug and Tobacco Policies.

Ministry of Justice and the Ministry of Health, Welfare and Sport (1993), 'Note on the policy to reduce nuisance caused by addicts', manuscript.

Mintzberg, H. (1978), 'Patterns in strategy formation', *Management Science*, vol. 24, no. 9, pp. 934–48.

Misztal, B. A. (1996), *Trust in Modern Societies: the search for the bases of social order*, Cambridge: Polity Press.

Mol, R., and Trautmann, F. (1991), 'The liberal image of the Dutch drug policy', *International Journal on Drug Policy*, vol. 2, no. 5, pp. 16–21.

Moore, C., and Booth, S. (1986), 'Urban policy contradictions: the market versus redistributive approaches', *Policy and Politics*, vol. 14, no. 3, pp. 361–87.

Moore, W. (1988), 'RAWP revision – Robin Hood in reverse?', *Health Service Journal*, 28 July, pp. 846–7.

Mouzelis, N. (1995), *Sociological Theory: What went wrong? Diagnosis and remedies*, London: Routledge.

NIAD (1995a), *Netherlands Alcohol and Drug Report: Fact sheet cannabis policy*, no. 1, Utrecht: Netherlands Institute for Alcohol and Drugs.

NIAD (1995b), *Netherlands Alcohol and Drug Report: Fact sheet hard drugs policy, opiates*, no. 2, Utrecht: Netherlands Institute for Alcohol and Drugs.

Niskanen, W. A. (1973), *Bureaucracy: Servant or master? Lessons from America*, London: Institute of Economic Affairs.

Nordlinger, E. A. (1981), *On the Autonomy of the Democratic State*, Cambridge, Mass.: Harvard University Press.

North, D. C. (1990), *Institutions, Institutional Change and Economic Performance*, Cambridge: Cambridge University Press.

Oatley, N. (1995), 'Competitive urban policy and the regeneration game', *Town Planning Review*, vol. 66, no. 1, pp. 1–14.

Olson, M. (1982), *The Rise and Decline of Nations: Economic growth, stagflation, and social rigidities*, New Haven: Yale University Press.

Palfrey, C., Phillips, C., Thomas, P., and Edwards, D. (1992), *Policy Evaluation in the Public Sector: Approaches and methods*, Aldershot: Avebury.

Palumbo, D. J. (ed.) (1987), *The Politics of Program Evaluation*, Newbury Park, Calif.: Sage.

Palumbo, D. J., and Hallett, M. A. (1995), 'Conflict versus consensus models in policy evaluation and implementation', in R. C. Rist (ed.), *Policy Evaluation: Linking theory and practice*, Aldershot: Edward Elgar.

Parliamentary Debates (Hansard) (1992), 'Health Service (London)', *House of*

Commons – *Official Report*, Session 1992–3, vol. 212 (23 February), pp. 696–710, London: HMSO.

Parliamentary Debates (Hansard) (1994), 'Written answers: health, expenditure statistics', *House of Commons – Official Report*, Session 1992–3, vol. 241, 12 April, pp. 72–3, London: HMSO.

Parliamentary Debates (Hansard) (1995), 'Written answers: health service development, London', *House of Commons – Official Report*, Session 1994–5, vol. 257 (4 April), pp. 1043–5, London: HMSO.

Parsons, T. (1951), *The Social System*, London: Routledge and Kegan Paul.

Parsons, W. (1995), *Public Policy: an introduction to the theory and practice of policy analysis*, Aldershot: Edward Elgar.

Paton, C., and Bach, S. (1990), *Case Studies in Health Policy and Management*, London: Nuffield Provincial Hospitals Trust.

Patterson, A., and Pinch, P. L. (1995), ' "Hollowing out" the local state: compulsory competitive tendering and the restructuring of British public sector services', *Environment and Planning*, vol. 27, pp. 1437–61.

Peacock, A. (1984), *The Regulation Game: How British and West German companies bargain with government*, Oxford: Blackwell.

Perkins, G., Palmer, S., Roberts, B., Ward, S., and Woods, I. (1986), *Competitive Tendering in the Public Sector*, London: Institute of Personnel Management/IDS Public Sector Unit.

Pettigrew, A. (1985), *The Awakening Giant: Continuity and change in Imperial Chemical Industries*, Oxford: Blackwell.

Pettigrew, A., Ferlie, E., and McKee, L. (1992), *Shaping Strategic Change: Making change in large organisations: the case of the National Health Service*, London: Sage.

Pettigrew, A., and Whipp, R. (1991), *Managing Change for Competitive Success*, Oxford: ESRS/Blackwell.

Pettigrew, A., and Whipp, R. (1992), 'Managing change and corporate performance', in K. Cool, J. Neven, and I. Walter (eds), *European Industrial Restructuring in the 1990s*, Basingstoke: Macmillan.

Phillips, M. (1994), 'Losing their heads over hospital beds', *Observer*, 1 May, p. 27.

Poulantzas, N. (1973), *Political Power and Social Class*, London: New Left Books and Sheed & Ward.

Pressman, J. and Wildavsky, A. (1973), *Implementation*, Berkeley: University of California Press.

Pryce, K. (1986), *Endless Pressure: a study of West Indian life-Styles in Bristol*, 2nd edn, Bristol: Bristol Classical Press.

Quinn, J. B. (1980), *Strategies for Change: Logical incrementalism*, Homewood, Il.: Irwin.

Rhodes, R. A. W. (1992), 'Intergovernmental relations: unitary systems', in M. Hawkesworth and M. Kogan (eds), *Encyclopedia of Government and Politics*, Vol. 1, London: Routledge.

Richardson, J., Gustafsson, G., and Jordan, G. (1982), 'The concept of policy style', in J. Richardson (ed.), *Policy Styles in Western Europe*, London: George Allen & Unwin.

Ripley, R. B., and Franklin, G. A. (1982), *Bureaucracy and Policy Implementation*, Illinois: The Dorsey Press.

Rist, R. C. (ed.) (1995), *Policy Evaluation: Linking theory and practice*, Aldershot: Edward Elgar.

Rist, R. C. (1995), 'Introduction', in R. C. Rist (ed.), *Policy Evaluation: Linking theory and practice*, Aldershot: Edward Elgar.

Riverside CHC (1988), *The Westminster and Chelsea Project Consultation Document: Report of the Secretary*, 17 May, London: Riverside Community Health Council.

Riverside DHA (1988), *The Westminster and Chelsea Hospital: a consultation document*, London: Riverside District Health Authority.

Rivett, G. (1986), *The Development of the London Hospital System 1823–1982*, King's Fund Historical Series, no. 4, Oxford: Oxford University Press.

Robson, B., Bradford, M., Deas, I., Hall, E., Harrison, E., Parkinson, M., Evans, R., Garside, P., Harding, A., and Robinson, F. (1994), *Assessing the Impact of Urban Policy*, Department of the Environment, London: HMSO.

Rock, P. (1979), *The Making of Symbolic Interactionism*, Basingstoke: Macmillan.

Rossi, P. H. and Freeman, H. E. (1993), *Evaluation: a systematic approach*, 5th edn, Newbury Park, Calif.: Sage.

Ruggiero, V., and South, N. (1995), *Eurodrugs: Drug use, markets and trafficking in Europe*, London: UCL Press.

Sabatier, P. A. (1993), 'Top-down and bottom-up approaches to implementation research', in M. Hill (ed.), *The Policy Process: a reader*, Hemel Hempstead: Harvester Wheatsheaf.

Samsom, R. (1989), 'Perspectives for the development of drug misuse policies as seen from the Netherlands', in P. M. Fleming (ed.), *The Years Ahead*, Proceedings of a Conference, 19 October, Wessex Regional Drug Problems Team, Wessex: Wessex Regional Health Authority.

Satyamurti, C. (1981), *Occupational Survival: the case of the local authority social worker*, Oxford: Blackwell.

Scharpf, F. W. (1978), 'Interorganizational policy studies: issues, concepts and perspectives', in K. Hanf and F. W. Scharpf (eds), *Interorganizational Policy Making: Limits to coordination and central control*, London: Sage.

Schumpeter, J. A. (1976), *Capitalism, Socialism and Democracy*, 5th edn, London: George Allen & Unwin.

Scott, J. (1979), *Corporations, Classes and Capitalism*, London: Huchinson.

Scott, J. (1995), *Sociological Theory: Contemporary debates*, Aldershot: Edward Elgar.

Sharpe, L. J., and Newton, K. (1984), *Does Politics Matter? The Determinants of Public Policy*, Oxford: Clarendon Press.

Shaw, K., Fenwick, J., and Foreman, A. (1994), 'Compulsory competitive tendering for local government services: the experiences of local authorities in the north of England, 1988–1992, *Public Administration*, vol. 72 (summer), pp. 201–17.

Sheldon, T. (1991), 'Cash reforms held back "to avert hospital closures"', *Health Service Journal*, 12 December, p. 3.

Sheldon, T. (1992), 'Managers divided over future of London hospitals', *Health Service Journal*, 20 February, p. 7.

Silverman, D. (1984), 'Going private: ceremonial forms in a private oncology clinic', *Sociology*, vol. 18, no. 2 (May), pp. 191–204.

Silverman, D. (1985), *Qualitative Methodology and Sociology*, Aldershot: Gower.

Simon, H. A. (1957), *Models of Man: Mathematical essays on rational human behavior in a social setting*, New York: Wiley .

Simon, H. A. (1976), *Administrative Behavior: a study of decision-making processes in administrative organization*, 3rd edn, New York: The Free Press.

Simon, H. A. (1977), *The New Science of Management Decision*, rev. edn, Englewood Cliffs, NJ.: Prentice Hall.

Smith, B. (1976), *Policy-Making in British Government: an analysis of power and rationality,* London: Martin Robertson.

Smith, J. (1993), 'Improving London's health service', *British Medical Journal*, vol. 306, 27 February, pp. 535–6.

Snell, J. (1995), 'Three years after Tomlinson: why millions are still unspent', *Health Service Journal*, 12 October, pp. 22–4.

Spruit, I. P., and de Zwart, W. M. (1994), 'Use of substances and gambling behaviour in our society', in I. P. Spruit (ed.), *Dutch Annals of Addiction 1994: Trends and perspectives*, Utrecht: Netherlands Institute of Alcohol and Drugs.

Stein, H. (1952), 'Case method and the analysis of public administration', in H. Stein (ed.), *Public Administration and Policy Development: a case book*, New York: Harcourt Brace Jovanovich.

Stewart, J. (1989), 'The changing organisation and management of local authorities', in J. Stewart and G. Stoker (eds), *The Future of Local Government*, Basingstoke: Macmillan.

Stinchcombe, A. L. (1990), *Information and Organizations*, Berkeley: University of California Press.

Stoker, G. (1991), *The Politics of Local Government*, Basingstoke: Macmillan.

Strong, P., and Robinson, J. (1990), *The NHS – Under New Management*, Milton Keynes: Open University Press.

Swingewood, A. (1991), *A Short History of Sociological Thought*, 2nd edn, Basingstoke: Macmillan.

Sztompka, P. (1991), *Society in Action: the theory of social becoming,* Cambridge: Polity Press.

Tilson, B., Mawson, J., Beazley, M., Burfitt, A., Collinge, C., Hall, S., Loftman, P., Nevin, B., and Srbljanin, A. (1997), 'Partnerships for regeneration: the Single Regeneration Budget challenge fund round one', *Local Government Studies*, vol. 23, no. 1 (spring), pp. 1–15.

Tomlinson, B. (1992), *Report of the Inquiry into London's Health Service, Medical Education and Research*, London: HMSO.

van de Wijngaart, G. F. (1989), 'What lessons from the Dutch experience can be applied?', *British Journal of Addictions*, vol. 84, no. 9, pp. 990–2.

van Putten, J. (1982), 'Policy styles in the Netherlands: negotiation and conflict', in J. Richardson (ed.), *Policy Styles in Western Europe*, London: George Allen & Unwin.

van Vliet, H. J. (1990), 'The uneasy decriminalization: a perspective on Dutch drug policy', *Hofstra Law Review*, vol. 18, no. 3 (spring), pp. 717–50.

Vincent-Jones, P., and Harries, A. (1996), 'Conflict and co-operation in local authority quasi-markets: the hybrid organisation of internal contracting under CCT', *Local Government Studies*, vol. 22, no. 4 (winter), pp. 187–209.

Walker, B. (1993), *Competing for Building Maintenance: Direct labour organisations and compulsory competitive tendering*, London: HMSO.

Walsh, K. (1991), *Competitive Tendering for Local Authority Services: Initial experiences*, Department of Environment, London: HMSO.

Walsh, K. (1993), 'Local government', in A. Harrison (ed.) *From Hierarchy to Contract*, New Brunswick: Transaction Books.

Walsh, K. (1995a), 'Competition and public service delivery', in J. Stewart and G. Stoker (eds), *Local Government in the 1990s*, Basingstoke: Macmillan.

Walsh, K. (1995b), *Public Services and Market Mechanisms: Competition, contracting and the new public management*, Basingstoke: Macmillan.

Weatherley, R. A. (1979), *Reforming Special Education: Policy implementation from state level to street level*, Cambridge, Mass.: MIT Press.

Widdicombe, D. (Chairman) (1986), *The Conduct of Local Authority Business: Report of the Committee of Inquiry into the conduct of local authority business*, Cmnd. 9797, London: HMSO.

Wildavsky, A. (1979), *The Art and Craft of Policy Analysis*, Basingstoke: Macmillan.

Willmott, P., and Hutchison, R. (eds) (1992), *Urban Trends 1: a report on Britain's deprived urban areas*, London: PSI.

Winkler, J. T. (1976), 'Corporatism', *European Journal of Sociology*, vol. 17, no. 1, pp. 100–136.

Yin, R. K. (1994), *Case Study Research: Design and methods*, 2nd edn, London: Sage.

Author Index

Subject Index